Acclaim for Mary Gordon's

The Shadow Man

"Passionate and extravagant. . . . The reader . . . must testify . . . to the dominance of such absolute literary power."
—*The New York Times Book Review*

"The rich and painful memoir of a daughter's loss, and of the myriad ways in which a vacuum can shape a life. . . . It possesses a candor that is neither self-conscious nor artful."
—*Boston Globe*

"She is a splendid writer, first, last, and foremost, and a brave one. . . . One feels no small amount of admiration for the author who could make this difficult emotional journey."
—*Chicago Tribune*

"This knotty, deeply personal book is irradiated by flashes of lyric brilliance."
—*The New Yorker*

"A compelling, disturbing story. At its best, it echoes all of our attempts to 'really know' our parents."
—*Dallas Morning News*

"Incredibly brave . . . brilliantly intense, dazzling. A masterpiece."
—Alice Adams

"Elegantly and luminously written."
—Margaret Drabble

"A searing memoir. . . . Beautiful, painful, shocking, a profound exploration of love, memory, shame—a remarkable book."
—*Kirkus Reviews*

50¢

Mary Gordon

The Shadow Man

Mary Gordon is the author of four bestselling novels—*Final Payments, The Company of Women, Men and Angels*, and *The Other Side*. She has published a book of novellas, *The Rest of Life*; a collection of stories, *Temporary Shelter*; and a book of essays, *Good Boys and Dead Girls*. She has received the Lila Acheson Wallace–Reader's Digest Writer's Award and a Guggenheim Fellowship and is a professor of English at Barnard College.

Also by Mary Gordon

The Shadow Man

The
SHADOW
MAN

◆

Mary Gordon

VINTAGE BOOKS

A Division of Random House, Inc.

New York

TO AUNT HATTIE

AND AUNT ROSE

ACKNOWLEDGMENTS

First I must thank my husband and my children, who lived through this book with me. I couldn't have endured some of the more painful truths I uncovered without their love and support.

Thanks go to many, many people.

To my cousin "Peppy," Joseph Barquinero, for yet another instance of years of love.

To Father Gary Siebert, who made the last chapter possible, and whose friendship and example sustain me daily.

To my three constant readers (and re-readers), Richard Gilman, David Plante, and Jan Zlotnik Schmidt.

To Arlene Rich, whose detective work was nothing short of heroic, and to Rabbi Sheila Russian, who led me to her.

To Chester, Stephanie, and David Gordon, A. B. Glickman, and Mr. and Mrs. Ron Gordon, for all their help in untying the complicated knots of kinship.

To Josh Freeman and Sean Willetz for pointing me to the archives.

To William Joyce of the Princeton University Library; Rosemary Cullen of the Hay Library, Brown University; David Sloane, University of New Haven; and Father Pat Samway at *America* magazine.

To Eddie Jaffe, who helped bring my father alive by his stories and memories.

To Walter Lister, whose loving memories of my father made me feel less alone.

To Tom Downey and the Honorable Sherrad Brown for helping me untie bureaucratic red tape.

To Nola Tully, whose patience, intelligence, and organization keep me from drowning.

And, long overdue, to Sandra Gildersleeve, whose secretarial and editorial skills—as well as her child-caring ones—have helped me more than I can say for fifteen years.

CONTENTS

TO THE READER

It is a winter afternoon. March 25, 1994. I am in a dark room, a windowless room in lower Manhattan. Varick and Houston streets, the National Archives and Records Administration—Northeast Region. I am looking at the census for the years 1900 and 1910, looking for facts about my father and his family. I'm doing it out of some impulse of studiousness, or thoroughness, an impulse whose source is not desire, even the desire to know, but a rote habit. The habit of doing things as they should be done. In this case it is an unfriendly habit, because in this dark room, illumined by the silver light of the screens of the microfilm readers, at the age of forty-four, I discover I am not the person I thought I was.

This was only the last and perhaps most obvious stop on a journey of discovery and loss, of loss and re-creation, of the shedding of illusion and the taking on of what might be another illusion, but one of my own. I was looking for my father. I always understood that in looking for him, I might find things that I wished I hadn't, but I didn't know the extent to which this would be the case. And I didn't know that some of the things I'd thought most essential to my idea of who I was would have to be given up.

My father died when I was seven years old. I've always thought that was the most important thing anyone could know about me. I've told his story hundreds of times, because I thought his life was extraordinarily interesting, extraordinarily complex, and in telling his story, I took on the luster of having an interesting and complex father. No one could know me very well without knowing some of the high points of his history: His riotous youth at Harvard, then in Paris and Oxford in the twenties. His career as the king of Cleveland soft porn, the editor of a "humor" magazine called *Hot Dog*. His conversion, in the thirties, from Judaism to Catholicism, his turn at that time to the political right; his becoming a Francoist, a Coughlinite.

I am primarily a writer of fiction, but I knew I couldn't present him as a fictional character because the details of his life, presented as fiction, would be too bizarre to be believed. I did use some elements of his life in some of my characters: the father in *Final Payments* has his politics; the artist in *Men and Angels* meets someone like him in France. But why did it take me so long to get around to writing his life as biography, or memoir, or some nonfiction genre whose proper name hasn't yet been found? I've been a writer for as long as I have conscious memory, or perhaps it is better to say I have no conscious memory of myself as not a writer. Now I am forty-six. Why did I wait so long to write this book?

This isn't the first book I've written about my father. When I was ten, and he'd been dead only three years, I attempted his biography. It began, "My father is the greatest man I have ever known."

For many years I believed it. Well into my adulthood, he was the untouched figure of romance. He was so much more compelling than other people's fathers. He was a writer, and a convert. While he was still alive, I'd watch him walking to the station on his way to work in the city, wearing a hat and hard brown shoes, holding a thin leather briefcase. Unlike other children's fathers, who wore caps and carried lunchpails. On his way home from the train station, he would fill his pockets with candy and walk down the street giving sweets to all the children on the block. "Thanks, Mr. Gordon," they would say, the children who didn't speak to me and to whom I had no wish to speak. No wish and no need. Why should I talk to children? I had him.

But the whole enterprise was a charade, a costume drama. He wasn't going to work. His "work" was a series of schemes to get rich men to bankroll him and his magazines. Occasionally he was successful, but not for long. Never long enough for him to support us. It was my mother's money that bought the candy for the children; he was the Pied Piper on her salary. And his gifts didn't make the children stop taunting me with the information their parents had given them: "We know your father doesn't have a job."

I was ashamed that he didn't have that thing that seemed so meaningful to them, a job, but I was proud of his going off, wherever it was he went off to. I watched him walking up the street, urbane, elegant, his long strides eating up the sidewalk, eating my heart because all day we would be separated. He was the handsomest man in the world, as handsome as the movie stars I loved: Jimmy Stewart, Fred Astaire.

But when I look now at pictures of him, he doesn't look at all handsome. In the photo on my desk, he's slumped on the couch. He looks awful: old, sick, and miserable. In another picture, in which I must be only a few days old, he's holding me, enraged. A new father should be smiling, not enraged. I don't remember an enraged father. In almost all the pictures, he's toothless. How can the glamorous father of my memory be a man who doesn't put his teeth in when he knows he's being photographed?

How can my Fred Astaire, my Jimmy Stewart, have a pot belly that sticks out over his belt? Looking at the pictures, I remember the slit he made in the waistband of his pants so he could fit into them, and my mother telling him he couldn't go out on the street like that. I remember her saying he couldn't wear the shoes he did, shoes whose toes curled up like Persian slippers because they were too big (he said he liked them big; his feet sweat in the summer). These are not the accoutrements of a glamorous man.

My adult life with my father has been marked by reversals and undoings, moments of frozen incomprehension, shutting my eyes, turning away. Finding and then hiding the evidence that says my childhood image is not one I can live by now. When I suggested naming my son after him, my husband said, "That would be fine, but you'd be naming him after a madman." I told him I thought that was rather strong. My father was unusual, eccentric, but mad? Not my father. Not *mine*.

My husband reminded me of a manuscript I'd shown him before we were married. I'd shown it to him because I was ashamed of it and I felt he needed to know about it, as I would have felt I had to tell him about a murder in the family, or a tendency to albinism or club feet.

The manuscript was a biography my father wrote about the conservative French Catholic poet Paul Claudel. Or, rather, my father called it a biography; there are almost no details of Claudel's life. It's really a diatribe against André Gide, against Modernism, against the infection of the Jews. "The Jew Proust. The Jew Bergson. The Jew Masoch, the Jew Léon Blum," my father wrote.

My father, born a Jew in the last year of the nineteenth century, wrote this ten years after six million of his blood were murdered. I remember the look on my husband's face when he read it. Sorrow clouded the blue of his Protestant eyes, furrowed his midwestern forehead. "But this is mad," he said. I refused to absorb his interpretation. I said it was not mad but evil.

This is not a happy position for a loving daughter to be in: to be forced to choose between seeing something her father wrote as mad and seeing it as evil. I chose the second. I chose as my father's daughter. He would have considered it a cowardly evasion to call something mad that was quite possibly evil. So I called his manuscript evil, then forgot about it. I named my son for him, adding the middle name—Dess—of my husband's mother, a happy woman whose fulfilled life ended at the age of ninety-six. I thought her goodness and normalcy could cleanse my father's curse, and what would be left to my son was his grandfather's brilliance, his inventiveness, his passionate heart.

For I have always known that I lived at the center of the heart of a passionate man. My desire not to move from that place led to a kind of memorializing that amounted to entombment. The construction of a mausoleum made up of desire and need, snippets of events or reports of events, lyrics of songs, lines from stories. Made up, too, of forgetfulness, refusal of evidence, misplacing of crucial things or precious information, denial of facts.

I needed this mausoleum in order to be myself. His death was a great shock, an early death for me, the death of my childhood and the death of a way of life that included pleasure and play. My father was a man who loved children. Before I happened to him, he adopted families. He became a magic uncle to his friends' children, people now in their fifties or sixties, who remember him as indulgent and imaginative, rescuing them from ordinary life. He liked large families. But I was born when my mother was forty-one and he fifty-five. She, a polio victim, gave birth in an aura of miracle. So there were no more children, and that was too bad. He would have been wonderful with a lot of money, a lot of children. He should have been able to open the door of a large, untidy house and make his way over children sprawling all over the floor, his own children and the friends of his own. But for me, his only child, he distilled all his abstract love for children into the hard diamond of adoration and devotion. "I love you more than God," he once told me. This was serious; he was a religious man. I didn't know, and still don't, if he meant he loved me more than he loved God or more than God loved me. It almost doesn't matter. It was a serious thing to say and it scared me. Whichever he meant, he was right.

He was a jumpy, almost hysterical man, but with me he was unfailingly patient. Only now that I have children of my own do I realize the extent of his patience. But no child realizes an adult is being patient with her: even if she did, the idea would be meaningless to her, one of the arcana of adulthood, like the fear of aging or the desire for money in the bank.

He understood how much children love the ordinary domestic life that adults have access to and from which they are barred. Marriage, cocktails, are to children as exotic as dragons. So every night, when he told me a story before I went to sleep, he gave me a choice of four situations: I could hear a story about a mean old woman and a nice old man, a nice old woman and a mean old man, a mean young woman and a nice young man, or a nice young woman and a mean young man. In these stories, someone was always degraded and always in conflict. But it seemed to me that these couples simply went about the business of their simple lives, and their lives enthralled me.

When he died, my mother and I moved in with my grandmother and my aunt. My aunt was a polio victim like my mother; my grandmother was seventy-eight. I was the only

able-bodied person in the house. A house of pious and se-
verely law-abiding laborers who thought that life was difficult and that my dreamy ways were something it was their
responsibility to "knock out of me." I think they believed
they were doing it for my own good, but it was a joyless experience, and I grieved for my father all the more because
not only he, but joy, had been lost from my life.

I turned to religion, to reading and writing. I did what he
wanted me to do: I prayed. I read and wrote. What was he
bringing me up to be? What could he have imagined, insisting I grow up in a working-class neighborhood but teaching
me to read at three, having me memorize, at five, the Latin
of the Mass?

He was bringing me up to be his partner: someone who
would get his jokes and help him with his work.

For a large part of my life I believed that such a life would
have been the best of all possible lives. It would have been,
I thought, a life without dullness, without bourgeois responsibility, without excess and slowness. We would spend
our time in the great cities of Europe; I would always wear
classic, beyond-the-fashion clothes. I would be known as my
father's daughter.

I have not become that woman. Just as there is much
about my father's life that horrifies me, there is much about
me he would have hated. He didn't want a daughter who
was a feminist, a leftist, divorced and remarried, the media's
usual suspect when they need the insiders' rap sheet on the
Catholic hierarchy or the pope.

I did, though, become a writer. Would he have liked it if
he'd known I'd be writing about him? What would he think
of my writing this book?

People ask me, "Why are you able to write it now?" I
think they're looking for some answer appropriate for a TV
talk show. They expect me to say, "I can do it now because

I am a mother. Because I have a solid body of work." The answer is more mysterious. In a way, it happened by accident.

In 1984, Sara Bershtell, then of Pantheon, asked me to
contribute to a volume called *Fathers*. Rather easily and
quickly, I wrote a piece called "David." It lays out the facts
of my father's biography, of the difficulties of it, but it ends
with a promise of "love that passes understanding." In a way,
I now see, it was a refusal to go further. A desire to be not
the writer exploring my father but his loving child.

At that time, I was finishing my novel *Men and Angels*,
after which I began another novel, *The Other Side*. I didn't
write any more about my father for a while. Then, in 1991,
I was seized by the image of the lawn outside my aunt's
house, and then by memories of my grandmother's furniture. This led to a meditation on my father's death, called
"The Important Houses," which was published in *The New
Yorker*. My childhood, as a subject, was beginning to seep
into my bones. I wrote another meditation on the strong
presence of death in my childhood, called "The Other
Deaths," published in *Salmagundi*.

I had a lot of pages about my father. It seemed I was writing a book. It seemed that it was time to go on a journey to
try to find—something. My father was with me all the time.
I began writing him a long letter. I had scores of folders, la-
beled "Fathers," "Daughters," "Memory," "Loss," "Fascism,"
"Kafka," "Proust," "Anti-Semitism," and so on. I wanted to
tell him everything I thought.

I entered the cave of memory, which nowadays seems like
a tourist trap in high season. Everyone's talking about memory: French intellectuals, historians of the Holocaust, victims of child abuse, alleged abusers. It's a subject of
conversation in the academy and on morning chat shows—
even on AM radio. As I began to explore my memories, I
was caught up in the impossibility of memory as a reliable

source. What I had trusted as a text to live by began to seem as malleable as last week's gossip, and as undependable. This loss of faith in memory was the first of the losses that came to me as a result of writing this book.

My memories weren't my only way of knowing my father. He was a writer, a published writer. I could learn about him by reading what he wrote. I had a box full of his articles and poems, which I had read from time to time, sometimes appalled, sometimes refusing to take in the content and concentrating on what I called his felicity of style. But I'd never studied his writing, using the training I have as a literary critic. I never read what he wrote as a text. I'd never used the resources at my disposal to try to find if there was anything he had published that I hadn't already found. I know that I read him so cursorily because I was afraid that some things he'd written might be distressing to me. But it was only when I read him carefully, over and over, in the way that one must when one is writing about something, that I experienced the anguish I'd tried to forestall. Reading him as a professional reader and writer, I tried to understand him not as a father but as someone who had written the words I had to interpret. I saw not only the horror of his ideas, but the weakness of his style. I lost another father: the father of the brilliant sentence, the brilliantly shaped phrase.

After I felt satisfied that I'd read everything of his that I could find, and had read it thoroughly, I went to public records. I asked the help of historian friends of mine, and they pointed me in the direction of government offices, archives, and libraries. I contacted genealogists, Jewish historians, the Mormons, passport offices, military records, death certificates, and wills. I traveled to my father's hometown, Lorain, Ohio, where I had never been before. I spoke to people in the community and possible relatives. I learned less than what I'd hoped, but enough so that I understood that his life had been made up of lies, some tragic, some pathetic, all of them leaving me with the feeling that I'd been stolen from. I had lost him as the figure in history I thought he was; I had lost my place in America.

I couldn't even try to verify any of what I'd learned with my mother. At the very time that I was engaging in this project of memory and discovery, my mother, in her late eighties, was losing her memory, and losing her grip on her present life. I was losing both the father and the mother of my childhood at the same time. I had to come to terms with this both in my life and in my writing about my life. I had to learn that with some things it is impossible to come to terms.

Or that I had to come to terms using methods I never would have dreamed of. I became a storyteller to my father, and then a detective in the department of magic realism. Finally, it was only by turning my father into a fictional character after all, by understanding that I could never know him except as an invention of my own mind and heart, that I could make a place for him in my life.

But perhaps this is true of all of us. Perhaps that is what it is to grow up: to understand that the parent of your childhood is your invention, that if such a person ever lived, he or she is no longer living. That the living parent of your adulthood is not the reconstituted giant of the child's mind and heart.

The psychoanalyst Hans Loewald says that an analysis is successful if it succeeds in transforming ghosts into ancestors. Perhaps if we substitute "maturation" for "analysis," the statement remains true. My father was a beloved and a looming ghost. If the process of transforming ghosts into ancestors is a grueling one for everybody, I believe it was especially intense in the case of my father and me. His love for me was so extravagant; he was more than ordinarily engag-

ing to my imagination; his contradictions are more than ordinarily extreme. Nevertheless, in the process of transforming him from the looming ghost determining my every
breath into the benevolent ancestor at my shoulder, I have
done what everyone who wishes to make peace with his or
her parents must do. Or, at least, I have begun to do it. I
even had his remains moved from the grave of my mother's
family to a new grave, where he can be a patriarch, the head
of a family he never saw.

This book is a chronicle of my attempts to transform myself and my father. It's also a book about America. My father's family came to America in the great wave of
immigration at the end of the nineteenth and the beginning
of the twentieth century. He lived the dark side of the
American immigrant's story, the one that isn't usually told:
He was a Jew in a time of pervasive anti-Semitism. He was
a young man at a time when it seemed endlessly possible for
young men to make and remake themselves. When the fire
that fed the melting pot burned at a very high flame. When
the pressure to pick up the dominant tone of the American
tuning fork was both great and unquestioned. I have always
liked to think of my father as absolutely unique, but this is
another idea I've had to give up. He was a man of his place
and time.

Ideally, the writer should follow the example of Saint Au-
gustine, who begins his *Confessions* with only the lightest of
directions to the reader: *"Tolle, lege."* Take and read.

I haven't been able to do that. I don't know whether it's
a fault of character or a fault of the age, this need to explain
myself, to be a visible partner in the reader's enterprise. Perhaps anyone writing about herself at such length must fight
the impulse to apologize. The terror that no one will care.
So I approach you, the reader, in a way I wouldn't ordinar-

ily, asking indulgence and attention. But is it you, really, whose indulgence I ask? Or is it my father, whom I lost, and found again, whom I both metaphorically and literally un-buried and reburied in the course of writing this book.

When I ask myself if I'm glad I've pursued this project or wish I'd never begun it, I feel as if I'm in a scene from one of those science-fiction movies in which one scientist tries to discourage another from going forward. The mustachioed man in the impeccable suit says to his wild-haired colleague, "There are some things, Dr. Poliakoff, which are better not known."

Certainly, much of what I learned involved pain and loss. But I haven't lost my father. He's still *there;* occasionally he still overwhelms me. He's like a wave that breaks over me, involves me, overturns me, exhilarates me, carries me, then disappears, leaving only a trace of itself in the sand, the print of a tongue, a lip. I have freed him to live among the dead, in a place I will no longer join him. Now he must come to me. We are together in a new place now, among the living. Each year at Rosh Hashanah, Jews pray, "May you be in-scribed in the book of life." This is what I've tried to do. To place or re-place both my father and myself in the book of life. The book of the living.

Now I know that whether I am in silence or listening to music, in a dark room or walking through New York streets, swimming in the ocean, about to fall asleep in a strange bed in a foreign city, talking about Flaubert or Joyce to students, beating eggs or stirring soup, feeding my children or listen-ing to their stories, making love beneath the body of a man he could not even have imagined, I am always my father's daughter. Having lost him, once, twice, I will have him for-ever. He is always with me, always mine.

I

—

KNOWING MY

FATHER

*T*he night of my father's heart attack, January 14, 1957, my mother and I went to my aunt's house to watch television, as we always did on Friday nights. We watched shows about silly crackbrained girls: *My Little Margie*, *My Friend Irma*. Then the prizefights started. The women and the children disappeared. We played or talked somewhere else: we could hear the bell signaling a knockout or the end of a round, but it seemed terribly far away, in some country that had nothing to do with us.

My uncles drank beer out of glasses that I believed had come from Germany. They frightened me; the war hadn't been over many years, and I had visions of women with their heads shaved, made to stand naked in town squares, shot by Nazis. Or children starving, heroic, with one chocolate coin between them, which they ran a wet finger over each day, licking their finger, making the chocolate last for a month. I got the idea of women with shaved heads from television: *Playhouse 90*, a show my aunt and my mother were watching one night while the uncles were out at a basketball game. It was a show I wasn't supposed to watch. All the children were meant to be asleep, and my cousins were, but

I crept down and watched the television from a stairwell, where the women didn't see me. I'd stolen a box of chocolate stars and shoved them hypnotically into my mouth as the television spoke about the woman with her shaved head.

I was sick with guilt and sugar. But I always was when I went to my aunt's house. We were always allowed to eat too much, too many things that were bad for us. We ate potato chips and cheap sweets and drank all the Cokes in the refrigerator; we laughed too much and were warned that that kind of laughing would always end up in tears. Sometimes it did, but not always, and it made us distrust our mothers because we knew they believed it always would. My cousins and I fought because we all wanted to be the mother—except occasionally one cousin would agree to be the child if she could be spanked on her bare bottom, hard. Afterward, I'd lie in my bed, feeling I'd just escaped something modern and dangerous.

That night, after I'd fallen asleep, the phone rang. It was Bellevue Hospital: my father had had a heart attack in the Forty-second Street library.

There is a sound of disaster, and a quiet after it, when the universe becomes still from shock, the wind stops, the light is colorless, and humans have no words because no words fit the enormity. Then a hum enters the air, and normal activity begins again, but slowly, as if everyone were underwater. People move, pick things up in their hands, walk from place to place, but the hum supports each action. You can mark the time when the disaster is complete and something else—the rest of life—begins. You know this because the hum no longer supports each act. I have never been in an earthquake, or the aftermath of battle, but I know their sound: the shocked sound of proximity to death. I heard it when my mother hung up the phone and said, "Your father's had a heart attack."

For thirty days, my mother drove to the hospital each evening to see my father. I wasn't allowed to go. I stayed with my grandmother. I slept in her dark room with the frightening pictures: the brown replica of the Shroud of Turin, a picture of Christ with long, smooth, girlish hair, pointing to his Sacred Heart, the size and shape of a pimento or a tongue. Most mysterious: a picture made of slats. You turned your head one way: it was the Scourging at the Pillar. Another turn of the head produced Jesus Crowned with Thorns. If you looked absolutely straight ahead, you saw the Agony in the Garden. I was kept awake by these pictures and by the room's bitter smells: lavender, ammonia, hair oil, liniment. Pine Sol always at the bottom of the commode: a green pool reminding you inevitably of the corruption that you, as a human, had no right pretending you could rise above.

One Monday night, I woke for nothing. It was nearly midnight. I went into the living room. My mother let me sit on the couch beside her and watch television. We watched Jack Paar. Ten minutes later, the phone rang. It was the hospital. My father had just died.

It was then that my life split in two, into the part when my father was alive and the part when he was not. Since the first part lasted only seven years, my life has always felt unbalanced. The part of my life after his death kept growing; there was no way to stop it, except by my own death. There was no way to lengthen the other, to have more time with my father as a living man.

I understood what had come to an end. My mother and I moved out of our apartment into my grandmother's house. I never saw the apartment again, and I never saw most of the things I'd had there.

I don't know what happened to it all. The furniture, the lamps, the cheerful dishes. And my toys: my windup Cinderella, my tin dollhouse, the Alice in Wonderland rug.

They were banished. Were they burned, sold, put upstairs in the attic? I was afraid to ask. My aunt who lived with my grandmother, with whom I would now live, said I had to remember there was very little room in the house. I understood. But nobody said anything to me about what had happened to my things. Everything was simply gone, no longer on earth. It had disappeared, as my father's body, for no better reason, had disappeared.

My mother bought twin beds and flowered cardboard dressers. We moved into an empty room in my grandmother's house. My mother impressed upon me that my aunt and grandmother were doing us a big favor in letting us live with them, that we mustn't seem to be in the way. I saw that she was happy. She had come back home. She wouldn't have to work so hard; she wouldn't have to come home from the office and cook the supper and do the washing and the ironing.

But she seemed to have forgotten what we'd had. She didn't miss our apartment, which was clearly much more like the movies than my grandmother's house. She didn't miss the Pyrex dishes in Technicolor shades, her wedding china with its playful patterning of unnaturally colored fruits. She didn't miss our trips to the movies, or listening to the radio (we'd had no television; my father wouldn't allow it). She didn't miss the songs we sang from musicals, our imitations of Irish priests and Italian barbers. She didn't miss going out to eat. She seemed to prefer my grandmother's dark living room, the lamps with golden handles and maroon bases and pictures of men and women with flowing hair and hats with feathers. The bust of Christ crowned with thorns, the tears flowing down his cheeks, which I enjoyed touching, feeling I'd stolen grace. And beside the head of Christ, a thin black stork riding on a turtle's back. It was said to be bronze, but no one believed that. Next to the stork there was a clump of peat, wedge-shaped and porous, that my grandmother had brought from Ireland. She wasn't frightened, as I was, of the bathroom upstairs with its blue-black linoleum and its pitcher full of overripe philodendron, whose stems I could imagine rotting in the yellowish water in which they stood.

She didn't seem to miss my father. There was no trace of him in my grandmother's house, and he was talked about only if I brought him up. I understood that if he was to be remembered, it would be up to me.

For a while, I thought he would come back. At night, I'd climb the dark stairs, certain that when I lit the light in the bedroom, he'd be there waiting.

Sometimes I wasn't sure whether or not I too had died. Often when I was near the edge of sleep, or ill, or cold, or when I became hypnotized by a repetitive physical event— the water going down the bathtub drain, a record spinning on the turntable—I would be caught up in a frightening spiral of language. I would hear a voice, my own, but speaking from so far away that it was barely recognizable. The voice was saying, "What does it mean to be alive?" And the words had no meaning. Particularly the two important ones: "mean" and "alive." I was looking down at myself like a spirit peering at a corpse. And yet neither the spirit nor the corpse had any connection with each other or with me, the thing once comprehensibly known as "I" but now something else, something I couldn't name.

I had to allow for the possibility that I might be only an idea—but in the mind of whom? Or what? Not God, certainly. I knew it wasn't God; at that moment God was only one more instance of failed language. I longed for someone to rescue me, but I didn't know what would be rescued or what rescue would entail. The past was blotted out and memory obliterated. I inhabited a sickening present without words. Without, therefore, a future. If I was dead, I must always have been, and I would always be. The region I inhabited wasn't one where I would be reunited with my father. What was my father? Only another word I didn't understand. A figure in a mist, stirring no impulse of recognition or recall.

After a few minutes, a few hours, a few days (time had become unmeasurable), I would return to a place where I could use words without terror, that is to say, use them without questioning their meaning as I spoke. I could understand, be understood. I still felt unrooted, but at least I knew what I was about. I had a task. I was looking for the place where my father and I once were and where we could be once again. I peered through fog for a glimpse of a man who could not be touched or joined. I knew I wouldn't see my father's face again, or feel his breath, or hear his voice, but if I was journeying back in memory to places we had been together, I was engaged in a quest that was not only admirable but, most important, meaningful.

But this search wasn't my only job. I had another one, only partially connected with my father: I was trying to obey the law. A law that was not monochrome and flat but complex, full of color and gradation and interlocking design. Law like a peacock's tail that spread and spread and could repay endless attention. At the center of the fan, in the densest, most vivid place, were the Ten Commandments; then lighter, less crucial, the Six Commandments of the Church, related to the rules of worship. There were the Seven Deadly Sins; and then, farther out, more remote, and opposite them, their reverse, the Virtues, Theological, Cardinal, Moral; and the Works of Mercy, Corporal and Spiritual. But the law I continually broke was one of the most basic. My specialized knowledge did me no good. Every few days found me in a state of mortal sin. Impurity was its name.

My experience of mortal sin wasn't like the ones I've read about in semicomic memoirs. I wasn't afraid of going to hell. Knowing the law so well, I knew that even if I were hit by a car, there would be one moment of consciousness that would allow me to say the word "sorry," even the syllable "sor," and that would be enough. Perhaps I would have years and years of Purgatory, but Purgatory was, in its way, desirable. Yes, the agonies would be real, but all the fine people, the interesting sinners, would be there, undergoing a process of chastening or burnishing that in its communal aspects seemed noble. So it wasn't eternal damnation that I feared; it wasn't even fear that moved me. It was shame, a sense of my defilement in relation to the infinite purity of God's love. A filthiness that seemed as if it should be public, made worse because in the public eye, in fact, I was perceived to be exceptionally good. The nuns in school who chose me as class monitor, the slow or unruly children who were made to sit next to me and look up to me as an example of probity and industry—what would they think if they knew the degradation that was the truth of my inner life? I went to confession every three or four days, always confessing the same sin in the same words: "I was impure with myself." The worst moments occurred before I spoke, when I could see the priest's shadow on the screen that separated us, and imagine his chastisement, which mostly never came. The priests wanted me out quickly; they were probably more embarrassed than I. But the words of self-accusation, once spoken, were the gate that led to my exaltation. Only by saying them could I earn absolution and the most perfect sentence I have ever yet heard spoken: "Go in peace."

Since I came to life, or a kind of incorporeal life, in these moments of exaltation, it was natural that I should try to do my job—remembering my father—by enclosing my understanding of his life and death in one of the shining vessels that the Church provided. Ecclesiastical language is full of names for vessels: chalice, ciborium, monstrance, pyx; there must be containers to enclose, keep safe, keep intact, keep protected from the world's contamination the sacred matter—the Body and Blood of Christ—in the form of the natural and the ordinary—bread and wine. This transformation of the ordinary into the sacred is called transubstantiation, and that was what I needed for my father's history.

I needed to think of it as only appearing to be ordinary—like the host and the wine—so I could bring myself to life, or back to life, so I could save myself or resurrect myself. His history was my lifeblood, as the Eucharist was the lifeblood of the Church. And so I contained my father's life and death in one of the forms the Church provided, as it provided the containers of precious metals for the Host, the wine. The mysteries of the faith were held in sacred stories. And I wrote my father's history as one of the Lives of the Saints.

By doing this, I could see my father's death not as something that could have happened to anybody, an expected consequence of living, and therefore without meaning. Loss, absence, the half-life of my life, weren't ordinary or purposeless. My father's life and death became part of something grand, enormous. And so mine did, too.

But what I am saying is an understanding come to in 1992 by a woman in her forties, whose father had been dead thirty-five years. When he died, I was a child of seven. I didn't know what I was doing. What I was doing was telling myself stories. They were richer, more colorful, and more enjoyable than the texture of my daily life, which was marked by wrongness and loss. Everything about me was wrong, and I had lost the part of my life that, like a false, colorful beam illuminating some minor theatrical tableau, had transformed it from pathetic to heroic.

It is very easy for me to call back the atmosphere of that earlier time, even the quality of the light in which I lived.

When I think of it, I think of the light in the Holland Tunnel. It was a yellowish, acidic light, like the breath of a lethal chemical. Even with my father, I'd always been afraid in the Holland Tunnel. It wasn't being underground that disturbed me. When we took the Lincoln Tunnel I was quite relaxed; it seemed well-tended, clean, its light was violet-blue, the color of the neon letters of familiar signs: PHARMACY, FLORIST, BAR AND GRILL.

When we drove through the Holland Tunnel, saturated in that yellow light, I knew we were driving into and through death. And I knew I couldn't say anything about it, even to my father. I had only one consolation. I saw that in our danger we weren't quite alone. There was a policeman in the tunnel, walking its length on a narrow ledge six feet or so above the cars, tapping his nightstick on the palm of his free hand. He looked down at the travelers, the workers, the puzzled foreigners, the families on their way to pleasant destinations. I trusted him, and I worried for him, breathing the bad air and kept all day from sunlight. I was immensely proud of him for enduring those conditions for our sakes. I thought of him often, even if I hadn't gone into the tunnel for months.

After my father's death, I became the policeman. On patrol, vigilant and apart, in the yellow light of the dead. I was alert, looking out, in case my father would appear; maybe he was not really dead but was missing or banished, a political exile, and I, by the right word or signal, would be able to recall him.

Thirty-five years later, in 1992, I can begin again to bring myself into that tunnel. I can bathe myself in that light; I can see or become the policeman. I begin not to fear the half-light. Then I realize I can't answer certain questions: How did I know what I say I know? Who was my father, really?

How as a child, a grieving child, did I construct the story that I have lived by? The story by which I named and knew myself, and in which I cloaked myself; the envelope in which I saw myself and presented myself to the world.

I have so habitually thought of myself as alone with my father that it's only recently that I've understood that my project of biography was collaborative. First, there was my father, who told me things about himself. And there was my mother, who had lived beside him, the wife of the saint, in the place of privilege I could never step into.

I remember only one story she told about him. I could not ask her to tell it often; I hoarded my opportunities, asking her rarely, and when I did, she always told the story the same way.

This story happened during one of my dance recitals. It is a performance by the students of Miss Lottie Atherton's School of the Dance. The school is located upstairs from a bar and grill, beside a railroad station.

Miss Atherton is English, highly rouged and yet respectable in spite of all the rouge. Her husband's name is Lorne. She has a daughter who married an American soldier; this is why they are all in America.

Miss Atherton must be in her sixties when she teaches me, and I don't remember ever seeing her dance. She has an assistant, an eighteen-year-old named Marlene. They both wear black tights, topped by plain men's shirts. I don't enjoy the class much.

But the recital is a great event. Held in the auditorium of the public high school. Watched by a packed house. On the night of the recital, my first public performance on this earth, my father comes down with a violent stomach flu. Everyone says he won't be able to go. I am crushed, but silent about my disappointment. Bravely, I hold back tears.

But he declares that he will go. He won't sit down, he'll

stand in the back of the auditorium, where he can rush out to the bathroom if he has to.

My father is standing at the back of the theater. He sees me on the stage. The music starts up. I begin to dance. He rushes up the aisle, shouting as he travels, "That's my little girl." And he stands slap up in front of the stage, staring rapt.

My mother told this story as the daughter of her mother's house, so she told it disapprovingly, as proof of my father's habitual excess. But I had another mother, who took me places away from my grandmother's house, who brought me to people who were touched by my father, as if he'd appeared to them in a dream and, disappearing, left their lives impoverished and flat.

Each summer my mother and I went on vacation with her two best friends to visit the priest who'd been their confessor in the thirties and forties, before he'd moved away. He was also my father's confessor, and he'd married my parents, although he thought the marriage was a mistake. He said my father was a man of the spirit; he should not be shackled by the concerns of the flesh.

I now think that my mother was in love with Father D. and Father D. was in love with my father, though I have no evidence for either supposition.

But I do have some pictures of my mother, looking amorously ecstatic, sitting before a fireplace next to Father D., a dashing black Irishman in a Roman collar, with the rather hawkish looks of the young Lionel Barrymore. And I have a letter he sent to my mother on my father's death, including the words, "Say nothing to me of your grief. You at least have a child of his loins. I have nothing."

I didn't meet Father D. until two years after my father was dead. The year that I was born, Father D. had fought with his superiors about the increasing liberalism in his order. He walked out of the monastery one night and, from

a pay phone in Springfield, Massachusetts, called the bishop
of Albuquerque, volunteering to work among the Indians.
He sent us beaded necklaces and headbands from New
Mexico. Then he quarreled with the bishop. The next thing
we knew he was in Sudbury, Ontario, ministering to the Indians who worked in the sulfur mines. The similarity of the
words—"Sudbury," "sulfur"—confused me. I knew that sulfur was yellow; I imagined Indians disappearing down a
golden shaft, coming up covered in gold dust, like pollen,
walking, incandescent, through the freezing dark to Father
D.'s chapel, which they had helped him build.

The summer of 1959, when I was nine, I was the only girl
at a boy's camp run unsuccessfully—ruinously, in fact—by
my aunts and uncles. They had bought a derelict estate in
the Adirondacks, with five houses on a series of hills, close
to a lake. I was miserable and isolated there. I was no good
at sports, and I had no interest in playing with boys. I helped
my grandmother, who was the camp cook; I read the books
in the camp library—*Oliver Twist* and *The Last of the Mohi-
cans*—sitting on the floor of an abandoned bathroom that
smelled like wet earth. I helped the two high school girls
who were responsible for the dishes. Whenever I thought of
my father, I burst into tears. My aunt told me I had to get
hold of myself. She bought me a postcard with the face of
Mad magazine's Alfred E. Newman. Alfred was smiling his
idiotic gap-toothed smile and above his head were the
words "Keep Smiling." Whenever she caught me teary-eyed,
my aunt said, "Keep smiling," pointing to the place in her
own mouth where Alfred E. Newman would be missing a
tooth.

One day my mother called the camp to say Father D. was
coming, driving up from Miami, where he was now, myste-
riously, assisting in a parish. She and her two friends would

come up to the camp, and he would meet us there. They hadn't seen him for nine years.

My aunt installed them in a house on the top of a hill where the campers never went. I was sent down to the property gate on the highway. I was to steer him away from the houses used for the camp and direct him up the hill to the place where the women were waiting for him, as the Jacobites waited for Bonnie Prince Charlie.

He drove up in the first foreign car I had ever seen driven by someone I knew. It was as though he'd driven straight from Europe, over the ocean to the place where I stood. He stopped as soon as he saw me. He leaned over and opened the door. For a moment, neither of us said anything. We looked at each other in silence. Then he spoke. "So you are Mary Catherine," he said.

No one ever called me by my full baptismal name. I knew he was doing it because I was my father's daughter, and it seemed thrillingly correct. I nodded, yes, I was. He made a sweeping gesture in the direction of the passenger's seat, I got into the car. Silently we drove up the hill. The women were standing in the doorway. He and I walked up the path to the house together.

Recently, I was telling this story to my husband. I said, "I think it was the happiest moment of my life." He said, "That's not something a man who loves you wants to hear." I told him I was sorry, but I couldn't take it back.

After that summer, my mother and her two friends rented rooms in a motel on Route 17 near Elmira, New York, and we sat, in my case literally, at Father D.'s feet for two weeks every summer. We began the day with Mass. The rest of the time, we talked about my father.

Sometimes, Father D. would cry. It was a shocking but exciting moment. He was so masculine, so stoic, so devoted to a Greek or American Indian model of the hiding of emotion, that his weeping seemed almost sacred in itself, like the tears of the women in the Grünewald paintings of the dead Christ.

He let me talk about my father as much as I wanted. I would bring what I'd been given, what my father had told me, mostly stories about his early childhood that painted the picture of a mischievous, intelligent boy, the skinny darling of his doting mother. His mother is so worried about the thinness of his legs that she makes him eat goose grease on bread, which he hates. His father owns a saloon: I imagine a bearded patriarch sliding shot glasses down a polished bar to cowboys. But it is happening in Ohio; my father is a product of the Middle West. His ancestors were French Jews, wealthy people, cultivated, who nevertheless shut their ears to the truth. He is an only child. His parents are religious; his grandfather is a rabbi.

Father D. and my mother and the other women would pick up the narrative after his childhood. It must be from them that I learned what I then knew about his education, his early professional life. I don't think my father would have told me about going to Harvard—Harvard wouldn't have meant anything to a seven-year-old. I know he told me he'd lived in France, because he sometimes spoke French to me. But at what point did I place him in Paris in the twenties with Hemingway and Gertrude Stein? And how old was I when I learned that he'd been the editor of a successful girlie magazine called *Hot Dog*, learned that he'd had to give up "worldly success" (how easily the phrase came to our lips) in order to save his soul. It is at this point that the story of my father's life conforms most closely to the pattern of the saint's life: the colorful, sinful past, the proud defier knocked off his horse by the breath of God, by the whispered sentence, heard from nowhere: "What does it profit a man if he gain the whole world and suffer the loss of his immortal soul?"

From here on, my father's life becomes not just a saint's life but a martyr's. His persecutors are the Jews, who can't forgive him for leaving the faith of his people. Father D. told me that my father told him that he'd been blacklisted by the Anti-Defamation League of B'nai B'rith. We all accepted this as the explanation for my father's inability to get a job, or to keep the two he eventually lost, bartender and cab driver. Father D. said I had to understand that my father was number one on the B'nai B'rith list. I never asked what the list was.

While my father was still alive, we included his martyrdom in our prayer life. We began every day praying for him to find a job. We made a pilgrimage so that he'd find one. It was our only vacation; we went to Quebec to the shrines of St. Anne de Beaupré and Cap de la Madeleine. Nearly forty years later, my husband and I go to Montreal, and sitting at the Ritz Bar, I remember I've been in the Province of Quebec before. And I realize I can't say to my husband, "When I was four years old I made a pilgrimage. We were praying for a miracle."

The details of my life with my father require a language for which there is often no place in what has become my present life.

The next summer, of 1960, when I was ten, I asked Father D. if he thought it was possible that my father was the prophet Elijah. I'd been thinking about it a lot because I'd learned that Elijah had to come back to earth to die a human death, since he hadn't died, merely been carried up in a fiery chariot. I said that it made sense, because my father had been born Jewish. Father D. said that anything was possible with God.

My father's Jewishness presented no problem for the form of the saint's life; conversion was a staple of the genre. But my Jewishness was a problem for me.

Because of my father, I was a Jew. But he'd placed me in an Irish Catholic world, where I was visibly an outsider, a stranger. I looked like him, not like the people we lived among. I often cried because I wasn't pretty. He said I was beautiful, but I knew better than to believe him. He wasn't one of them; he wasn't right either. How could he know their standards or their rules? One night when I cried because I didn't have blue eyes, he said, "But you have eyes like mine, you have my eyes." I told him those were not the eyes I wanted. "They're the color of steak," I told him. "Light brown. Like when you cut into a steak." My mother, like many of the Irish, served our meat well-done.

I walked the streets of the neighborhood marked by my dark hair, my large nose, my full lips. During any lull, at any quiet point in a game, when the neighborhood children were bored or lustful for a cruelty, the words they always had a right to say came readily to them. "We know your father's a Jew. So you must be one too."

What did that mean to me? Except for my father, the only Jews I thought of had been exterminated by the millions only a few years before I was born. I thought of them, as I thought of the devastation of the war, as part of myself, something that would catch up with me one day, but in a way I couldn't see. The starving children, the separated children, the skeletal children, would take their place in my life sometime, but not yet, not yet. I knew I wasn't one of them, although my father blessed me every night in Hebrew. But my father seemed to think we were connected with them in some way. He said to me once, "If Hitler is still alive somewhere, in South America, and the Nazis come back into power, you and I will have to go to a concentration camp, but Mommy won't." I remember knowing he was right, and I knew that when the moment came, I would go with him happily, and that our departure would have the grandeur of all inevitable acts.

But how could I know what it was to be a Jew? I had Jewish blood, but no knowledge of those whose blood I shared. We had one picture of my father's mother—not a beauty, with an almost grotesquely wide nose in the middle of a wide, benign face, and eyes that could charitably be called quizzical, though it might have been a cast. There was no picture of his father.

My father kept the details of his Jewish childhood a darkness to me. But he did tell me the family had sat shiva for him when he converted. He didn't use the word "shiva"; he said that he'd been declared dead.

They had buried a living man, a son. They had sat in a circle and mourned his passing from this life. Yet not far from them, in Cleveland, in Chicago, in Los Angeles, and then in New York, someone with the name they mourned was living a life. I wasn't yet born, so in consigning him to non-aliveness, they were consigning me, prematurely, to nonbeing. Somewhere in his body, dry, encoded, was the story of my future life, which they insisted could not be told. Yet when my father and I spoke about this, neither of us was angry. We both understood that in his passing from Judaism to Catholicism, one man had, indeed, to die. We felt the justice of the Old World's acknowledgment of this, the rightness all around.

And so it seemed right that my father's family didn't inquire about me. And how could I think about them? I had no picture of what a Jewish family might be. In fact, most of the references to Jews I heard were a product of the anti-Semitism of some members of my mother's family. Jewish dialects. Jewish jokes. A song they made up, communally, one Christmas, called "Finkle Bells," sung to the tune of "Jingle Bells." I remember three lines: "We don't believe, you know / But still we take their dough / Oh, what fun to sit and watch the lovely sheckels grow." I remember feeling sick and frightened, knowing I ought to speak, but fearing their scorn.

Mostly, they referred to Jews as "Hebes," but they also had a family code. They referred to Jews as "the Persians," a habit that puzzled not only me but also my uncle's wife, whose father had been born in Iran. The explanation was that a character in the musical *Oklahoma!*, a peddler, clearly Jewish, tries to pass himself off as "Persian." They also spoke the sentence that was most horrible to me, one I would hear from time to time, the tone of which gave me the only clue I have ever needed to the timbre of real hate. "That's the *Jew* in you," they would say whenever I did something they didn't like. Even now the memory of their emphasis on the word "Jew" frightens me like the reports of the noise of Kristallnacht.

I would have had to be braver and more imaginative than I was to want to identify myself with, to think of belonging to, the Jews, my father's people. I couldn't really think of them as my father's people, since he didn't want to be a Jew, and if he didn't want it for himself, had worked so hard to separate himself, surely he wouldn't have wanted Jewishness for me.

Also, my only moments of certainty emanated from the Church. My identity was too unsure for me to risk those moments for a setting I would have had to invent. And like most people in a weak position, I needed to feel that I was allied with the party of the winners. Catholics did seem to be winning in those years: John XXIII was in the Vatican and JFK was in the White House. Why wouldn't I want to be part of that triumph?

Most of the time, though, I didn't feel triumphant. Most of the time I was alone. And it was in those hours that I created another way of knowing my father. I was no longer part of the lively chronicle of the saint's life, in the center of a pageant inscribed on the pages of an illuminated manuscript. I was in a theater; I was in the world of silent film.

I see myself in a windowless room, with no light but the light of the projector, fed by me. I am simultaneously running the projector, feeding the film, creating the images that make the scenes, and starring in the scenes themselves.

It was a long process, and a demanding one. There was a great deal of waste footage: I had to replay and replay scenes until I had distilled the right image, which would have the simultaneous dimness and distinctness of a dream. What was finally projected was the essential thing, an unfolding event that was not only itself but the emblem of my father's life with me, entirely our own, and yet suggesting something that had always been, and had always been true.

The films are silent because one of the first things I lost was the sound of my father's voice. Even now, if I heard my father's voice on a tape recorder, it's likely I wouldn't recognize it. I've always believed that if I heard my father's voice again, and knew it to be his, it would change everything, or make up for everything I'd lost.

But I'll never hear my father's voice. Instead, again and again, from childhood until now, I enter and leave the theater. I play and replay silent films. I am watching my father and myself. I am feeding the machine. I am standing in the darkness, seeing a living man, a living child. I'm trying to know them.

In the first film, I'm five years old. I'm standing in the driveway, in the landlord's driveway. We are tenants. We don't own the place where we live; we live above the people whom we pay. But we're very quiet. We never have to worry about making noise or displeasing them, and anyway they are very kind people, Italians. The mother has dark rings under her eyes, and when we children misbehave, she tells us to "make nice." The youngest daughter is supposed to be my friend, but we don't really like each other, don't move to play together of our own accord. We have to be pushed together by the grown-ups.

Once the older girl asked my father to buy her a dictionary, and he did. My mother was furious. I heard her shouting, "Where do you think the money's going to come from? You think money grows on trees? It comes out of my skin. You let people make a fool of you." She uses too many images: I have to see money on trees, then as a kind of eruption, a boil on the surface of her body. I don't know what to think. I don't like the older girl, who often torments me and, assuming I know more about sex than she does, asks me a lot of questions I don't know the answers to. Some, which I do know the answers to, are about my father's body, but I pretend I don't know. He doesn't know that I don't like her. But even if he did, he might still buy her a dictionary, because he has told me a million times that being generous is the most important thing. I don't want to think of what he's done, but I know it's a daring act, a pure act, to buy a dictionary—what could be more important than a dictionary?—for someone outside your family, someone your daughter might not even like.

The night I'm in the driveway, I'm not with the landlord's daughters or with my father or my mother. I'm alone; it's a summer night and the air is a sheet of agate; it falls straight from the cooling sun down to the earth without curve or undulation. It surrounds me like an airy house: my own. I spin in the clear air. I am trying to make myself dizzy. My arms are straight out at my sides, and I have lost myself completely in movement. I am lost and yet I know where I belong, exactly where I am, in the blur, in the whirl, in the heat and breeze created by my body.

But I haven't been careful; I've gone too far. I fall backward; my head hits the gray concrete of the driveway. My legs, my arms, are splayed as if I've just been shot. I hear myself cry out, but it is a cry without knowledge. I don't know who I am. Then my father is beside me. My head spins and pounds, but I feel only delight and transport. Nothing is required of me but to lie and surrender to the blur of images: *x*s and oblongs, a darker blue against the blue slate of the air.

My father lifts me up. He carries me. He can take me wherever he wants. I will go wherever he wants to take me. Wherever he takes me will be a place of luxury and joy. Also of health and safety. Of prosperity.

He sits me on the kitchen table. He and my mother bathe my forehead. I am still not with him, but he is in charge of the place where I am.

This is the second time I have badly hurt my head. Once I fell against the side of a step and gashed my forehead. My father carried me into the doctor's office, down a dark corridor with rooms on either side that I knew were inhabited by corpses. The doctor came to me from shadow. He stitched my forehead: we were alone. He'd made my father leave. I screamed in pain. Later, he told my father I didn't scream. My father mustn't have heard me, or he pretended to believe the doctor and praised me for being brave. But I knew I wasn't brave. I'd heard myself scream.

My father carried me into the car and held me on his lap while my mother drove. My head was bandaged. He put me to bed. I sat up, a good little soldier, more in love with my face in the mirror than I had ever been.

He must have remembered how I liked my bandaged head. The night I fall in the driveway, he makes a pretend bandage of dishtowels and wraps my head. We pretend I am more wounded than I am, and this makes us all happy.

My head is hurting, but only enough so that my parents

will both stay with me. There is no question of my having to do anything. With my throbbing head, I can be nothing but good. I am smiling; my parents are smiling at me.

My father says, "What would you like?"

I say, "An ice pop."

In a second, he is back from the store. He's bought me a grape Popsicle. He peels off the white paper. The ice is purple, serious: a color I would never have had the nerve to select for myself. Little girls are supposed to want pink ice pops, cherry or raspberry. His bringing me a grape pop is a proof of how well he knows me. Because of him I can have things I long for and would never dare request. My head is throbbing and the throbbing spreads, deep into the soft organs of my stomach, in the strong bones of my back. Deep, too, is the taste of purple. I can drop down to this taste; it will support me. More: it will exalt me. Now I am exalted, wounded, sitting on the kitchen table. My parents are smiling, telling me how good I am, how good I have always been.

In the second film, I am on a merry-go-round, and I'm frightened. I am afraid of so many things: heights, bad smells, men with thick eyebrows, loud voices, fat or gristle on meat. The worst part is that I'm afraid of many things that are supposed to be treats for children: bicycles, seesaws, merry-go-rounds—symbols of indulgent, innocent, and opulent play. My frequent sense of fear is the dark lighting for this film.

My eyes are open too wide; I'm gripping my father's hand. I'm afraid of falling off the horse, into the visible mechanism, with its gears and teeth. And I'm afraid of the mortification that will reach me if I refuse, and people see me huddled with my father in the seats, the thick, upholstered leather couches in the center, while around me happy children yearn, lean, reach for the brass rings, for which, it seems to me, they foolishly and yet beautifully risk their lives.

I'm less afraid of riding on the stationary horses, the ones that don't go up and down, a less shameful position than sitting on the seats. With desperation, I search the painted expression on the horses' faces, reject the wild eye, the flared, adventurous nostril, at last convince myself that I have found an older horse, a compassionate animal whose goal is to save mankind and not to outsmart us.

The merry-go-round is indoors, in a kind of terminal. I hear the noise of subways screeching to a halt, the buzz and rush of purposeful passengers stopping for hot dogs on their way from one place to someplace else. The neon signs spell out HOT DOGS, LEMONADE. They shine in the busy darkness. The air around the carousel is fetid. No one seems to be waiting for the riding children. They are all commuters, they are on their way somewhere; the carousel is of no interest to them. No one is paying attention to us. And my father isn't paying good enough attention. The air, the rush, the darkness, suggest to me that no one can pay proper attention here, the attention I need to keep me from danger.

My father seems to be looking for a stationary horse, but the machine is starting up. The bell clangs, warning us. Any minute we will be swept up in the moving circle. The bell is urgent, threatening. No one, without great courage, could ignore it. My father feels the necessity in the sound, and he lifts me and straps me onto a horse. My skirts ride up; I'm afraid that everyone can see my underwear.

In the first seconds of movement, I can see that it is not a stationary horse. It starts moving up and down. My father sees it too. There is fear in his eyes. He understands the danger, and this makes me more desperate. When the horse pumps down, I reach for him, he reaches for me, but there is no time. I am lifted up, and away from him. It is hopeless;

I can never touch him, or I can touch him for a second and then I am pulled away. His face is mortified. I can see his mouth moving in the shape of "I'm sorry. I'm sorry?"

The machine will never stop. I will go on forever. My father will never be able to reach me. I will not reach him. I am leaning dangerously out of my harness to try to be nearer to him, but I can't get near enough. If I fall he won't catch me; the circle moves too fast.

When it stops, I drop down into my father's arms. But I don't forgive him, and he knows it, and we both know there is nothing to be done.

Now, when I replay this film, I ask myself if this can be a real memory. Where, in what possible place can there have been a merry-go-round in a subway terminal? Could I have seen him, as I circled, mouthing, "I'm sorry. I'm sorry"?

Asking these questions, I come up against the silence of the grave. The impossibility of knowing what happened to or with the dead. This is the curse the dead lay on the living. It is their punitive, their cynical, hold over us: they will tell us nothing. They ensure that we will be, in relation to their lives, incapable of distinguishing fact from invention. They guarantee the falsity, the partiality, of our witness.

But when I was a child, playing these films to keep myself alive, I didn't ask questions. I watched.

I am still watching. And now, when I feel my spinning head, taste the grape ice, see the horse's flaring nostrils, I am certain that these memories are in fact memories and not invention, that they are real, they really happened. But then I tell myself that it is impossible for me to remember what it's like to have a father. What it's like not to live without a father. Not to live as fatherless. To live as not fatherless. To live as one fathered.

As I repeat the word "father" in all these forms, the word becomes unreal, meaningless, and infinitely precious, and I lose his face, or what I believe to be his face. I am spinning again and lost in the spiral, the darkness, or becalmed in the still ocean of oblivion.

Sometimes now, watching the films, I become afraid. I try to slow them down, focus the camera on some objects I know without doubt to have existed. I'm much more secure if, on the screen, but fixed, unmoving, I can project objects that I know once touched his body:

a pink shirt
a silver ring with the imprint of a miraculous medal
a reproduction of Holbein's *Sir Thomas More*
a black typewriter with the word "Underwood" written
 across its carriage
a hairbrush with a light wooden handle and soft bristles
a black comb

None of these objects are pathetic. A disconnected object is always noble, unless it seems ripped out of human context: a single shoe, a photograph on the pavement, a sofa left for the trash. It is only our connection to objects that weakens them. Left alone, they can only give us hope. The ring, the hairbrush, and the shirt root themselves, durable and stoic, in the solid world. But set them afloat in a sea of stories and their certainty melts. Narrative corrodes objects' inherent truthfulness. It distorts; it beautifies or perverts. It thins the texture, clouds the air. Objects afloat in narrative give me no certainty. They are no proof against my great fear, that I have invented everything. The whole world. Including my father. That I am, and have always been, entirely alone, and will be until my death.

But objects will not stay fixed. They are swept away by a sea of story, which carries me up with it, although I know I mustn't trust it. I try to hold on to objects in the narrative flood. Now I am clutching in my hands a peppermint heart. I feed its image into the machine and project it, but it won't stay. It won't resist entering a story, becoming a series of moving pictures.

In the film of the peppermint heart, I am playing in the driveway, the same place where I hurt my head. The driveway is a long slab of concrete beside a shady lawn that scares me and where I never go. Farther back, behind the stone-colored garage, there is a wild, unkempt space where weeds flourish and where, for the few months they had him, our landlords kept chained to a post a small, black, snappish mongrel dog.

I am singing loudly, pretending the concrete driveway is a stage. I am alone and completely absorbed. And suddenly, as happens with children (the dip and disappearance of the sun beyond the horizon), I am bored with what I'm doing, completely finished with it. I can't bear to be doing it one more second. I have to go into the house.

But the house is locked. I knock and knock and no one answers. I know my father is upstairs. Why isn't he coming for me? The sun is too sharp. It strikes the white front of the house like a blade. I sit on the brick steps. The stone is evil against the bare backs of my legs. I am wearing a plaid cotton dress and brown sandals, dark blue socks. No one is coming for me.

Then the landlord's wife walks up the sidewalk. I tell her I'm locked out, but that I know my father's up there. She suggests he's in the bathroom, but neither of us believes it. We don't know what to think. Perhaps he's disappeared.

When I get upstairs, I find him in the living room, reading. My courage is at an end. I had to be brave sitting on the step, but now there's no reason for bravery, no reason not to weep at the extent of my bravery, the extent of his failure. He offers no explanation for not answering the door. But now he doesn't fail me. He comforts me. He says he has a present for me. He goes to the linen closet, with its thin smell of new wood. He takes out a flat silver-colored box and gives it to me. I open it. Resting in tissue paper is a large heart-shaped wafer, no thicker than a Host. I can tell by its smell that it's peppermint, a flavor I don't like but assume I will like when I grow up. I adore the faint sugary whiteness, the granular plane. Most of all I adore the lettering. Down the right side of the heart, in faint pink, like the trace of blood on the chest of the crucified Christ, the words "I love you." My teeth and tongue ache to bite the crisp wafer and then have part of it dissolve in my mouth. I pick up the whole heart and, in a gesture at once brutal and delicate, take a large bite but spare the letters.

I am thrilled by the harsh taste, but most of all by the shocking crack when the perfect shape is destroyed. It will never be what it was. I feel that I've done something dreadful, but I'm elated. The sad remnant with its message is nothing to look at now; without honor, a failure, a lapse, a minor devastation. I put it back into its box, but we both know I'll never look at it again. There's nothing desirable about it anymore, marred by my tongue, my teeth, the bite mark with its traces of saliva; the letters mean nothing now or less than nothing: supplicating, pitifully detached from the form that gave them meaning, power, place.

It is 1992. I turn on the lights in the theater. I ask aloud, "Was there ever a peppermint heart?" But no one answers. I shout out louder, "What about the little model of the shoe?" Silence. I play the film.

It's Christmas, 1956. My mother has gone, in my place, to the Thom McAn shoe store to buy a present for me to give him. A gift certificate for a pair of shoes. This isn't a pure gift, or it is a gift not entirely for him, perhaps primarily for her. The way he neglected his shoes drove her wild. She was a cripple; she had to wear high shoes, cruel-looking boots. It infuriates her that he could wear nice shoes but makes his nice shoes dreadful. Down at the heels. At night she slips his shoes into a paper bag and drops them at the shoemaker's. When they're repaired, he doesn't notice the difference.

The gift certificate from Thom McAn isn't a piece of paper. It's a little miracle: a four-inch model of a shoe molded in bronze-colored plastic. I convince myself it must be precious. It sits in a small green box with the name Thom McAn in a distinctive script, printed in white.

He is pleased with this present, but he understands immediately how in love I am with the model of the shoe and asks if I would keep it for him. I take it to my room and put it on the shelf beside the statue of my guardian angel.

Now I am no longer the child in the film. The machine whirs; the film flaps in gray air. It is 1992. It is the end of what I know.

I don't know if my father went to Thom McAn, tried on a real shoe, left with a pair of them. I think he did, and they excited me by being loafers, not shoes that tied but loafers, which seemed to me modern, youthful. But I may be confusing a pair of real shoes with the model of the shoe, which was in the shape of a loafer.

He had his first heart attack on January 14. It would have been like him to let three weeks pass without cashing in a gift certificate. On the other hand, since it was a present from me, he might have done it immediately.

Since either of these is possible, since his nature contains both possibilities (also the possibility of furiously refusing to buy shoes on principle, and many others which I cannot even think of), how will I ever know?

I'm sure, though, that there was a model of a shoe. Even after we moved, it was on my shelf. But I don't know what's become of it.

As I don't know what became of the lock of his hair, which I asked my mother to request the undertaker to snip off as he lay in his coffin.

She gave it to me in an envelope. I could see the shape through the paper: a crescent. I would look at it, holding it to the light, but only sparingly, once or twice a year. Once when I was twelve, perhaps thirteen, I opened the envelope to see the color of his hair. It was gray, with a light wash of brown. I kept it in my mother's bureau drawer.

I've lost it. I don't know where. I have no idea how I would even begin to look for it.

Is the loss my fault? Most objects don't last thirty-seven years in one person's possession. Or do they? Isn't it true that most people keep track of the things that are important to them?

Of course it's true. Another kind of person would have kept track of the last remnant of her father's body.

My father was not that kind of person.

In being caught up in the enterprise not only of loss but of losing, I am about my father's business.

It's strange, and undoubtedly due to him, that something I can only call lostness is such an important feature of my life. Perhaps because I had to be complicit in the loss of all my things after my father died. I lose many, many important things. When I discover I have lost things, I am covered with a cold bath of shame. No moisture in fact sluices my skin, but the sensation of damp cold oozing from inside my body,

like the disgusting eructation of a mollusk, is no less real for
not being physically actual. My throat fills with nausea. The
unlost objects of my daily life become my murderous enemies. Shape shifters, they are maleficently engaged in the
enterprise of disguising themselves, also hiding the sought-
after, the treasured lost thing. "There is more rejoicing over
the lost one that is found than over the ninety-nine that
never went astray." They know this, these relentless siblings
of my lost one, and are pledged to thwart me.

Time, too, becomes my enemy, the beast with red eyes
breathing down my back. I will be jailed quite soon; everything I have worked for will be lost. "What kind of person
are you?" I hear the voice of my enemy thrumming inside
my bloody skull. "You deserve nothing. You should have no
possessions."

I don't only lose objects; I often lose my way. Walking,
driving, I am overcome, smothered in confusion. I don't
know where I am. I have no faith in my fellow walkers, drivers. I may go so far as to ask them for directions, but I don't
listen to what they say. Or that's not it: I do listen, but the
words make no sense. I could be listening to a German, a
Pole, speaking with his smiling mouth, words in a language
I have never heard. Turn right, turn left. Straight ahead at
the third stoplight. I nod, wave gratefully, then proceed in
the opposite direction. The buzz of the furies is in my ears.
"No one will ever find you. No one knows where you are.
No one recognizes you. If people give you information, it
will be no help. You will wander aimlessly, aimlessly. Night
will fall. You will be unable to find shelter. Eventually you
will die of exposure, and no one will take pity on you. What
kind of person *are* you? The ones in your life who need and
love you will be enraged by your stupidity. But no one loves
you enough to look for you. No one would know where to
look."

My father could find me. He would take me by the hand. My terror would be over. I could follow him in the darkness. We could sail together, in our rudderless boat, past responsibility, justice, fact. If he wanted, he could find me. But he is wandering himself, among the dead. And if I don't find him, accompany him someplace, he is lost forever.

It's a less hopeless prospect for me to imagine that I can find him than to imagine that he can find me. I am, after all, the one who lost him. "She lost her father," I've often heard people say. "She lost her father when she was very young." As if his death were the result of my carelessness, my inattention, my failure to keep him in sight. And now he is gone from my sight. I have lost sight of him. I will never have the sight of him again. And if I see him again, how will I recognize him? How will I know it is my father?

How then, could lostness not be my most true, most fixed, most natural home.

But I must have lost the lock of his hair relatively early in my career of lostness. What does it mean that in the years when my love for him was unquestioned, I was careless about the last remnant of his body?

Does it mean I wanted to be free of his body?

I can no longer deny that aspects of his body did make me uneasy. Especially his teeth.

His teeth, like his shoes, were something we talked about, argued about. A source of shame and anxiety for me, outrage for my mother, a superior sense of aggrievement for him. What kind of father was he, to have his shoes, his teeth, spoken about at the family table? A father should at the very least be in charge of his shoes, his teeth.

But were the teeth his? Yes, of course, since he had bought them. Did he pay for them, or did my mother, or some anonymous benefactor with a taste for Orthodox Catholicism, literature with a fascist bite? But the teeth weren't his in that they didn't emanate from his body. They weren't flesh of his flesh, as I was. So it is possible to say that I was his daughter but they were not his teeth. Then whose teeth were they? They were made to fit his mouth. He couldn't have lent them to anyone else, although perhaps this is done among the very poor. But he was not one of the very poor. We were not.

They didn't fit him well. My mother always said he didn't give them a chance. She pointed out that her mother kept her teeth in all the time. The way she said this made it sound unusual. It was only in adulthood that I understood that people with false teeth wore them continuously, without thinking about it, without thinking they had a choice. It was only then that I found it odd, even inexplicable, that my father had walked around the world with a toothless mouth. Only then did I see it as a sign of something crucial, madness or despair, taking himself out of the loop, the loop a man should take care to inhabit if he is the father of a child, particularly a girl.

I didn't like his toothless mouth. I was repulsed and shamed by it. But I kept this quiet, except to complain about wet kisses. I thought that if I loved my father, I couldn't be ashamed of a ruined mouth. But once I asked for the favor of his putting in his teeth.

I have a film of that night, but it's not one I like viewing. But now, in 1992, I feel I have to run it.

It's my grandmother's seventy-fifth birthday. All nine of her children are giving her a party at the VFW Hall. Everyone I've ever known is there.

My father agrees to put in his teeth. In the buzz and hum of the party, amid the noise of the clinking glasses, loud shafts of laughter piercing the air like dangerous rays of sun, he comes in front of me. He squats down until he's my height. He snaps his teeth open and shut. He makes extravagant biting gestures. He looks delighted. But I'm mortified, doubly so for having to pretend that I'm pleased when in fact I'm frightened of this biting father.

I rip the film from the projector. It's not a movie I want to see. There are others, more cheerful, faster-moving. I've replayed them many times; they let me know the kind of life it's right for me to want.

The films of my father and me in the city seem more recent than the others, in sharper focus. And there is sound. My father is speaking. But I know it's not his voice. I don't know whose it is, but it's not his.

We take the subway to the city, getting the IND at 169th Street, Jamaica, Queens. We ride the train forty-five minutes and get off at a stop called Fifth Avenue, right across from the Museum of Modern Art. We would never think of stopping there. He tells me modern art is bad and dangerous, and ugly, too.

Of course he's wearing his teeth, along with his suit, his hard brown shoes, his gray felt hat. He is my handsome father, my elegant father. Younger fathers seem provisional and second-rate. We are the envy of everyone, the handsome father and his calm, proud daughter.

Everyone we pass is charming, gifted. There's no need for them to acknowledge us: we all know we're peers. The men in their hats and hard shoes, the women whose heels clip-clip on their way to some delightful errand or romance—we belong among them, my father and I, walking hand in hand to start our day in the observance of the Lord's way and his word.

When we go into St. Patrick's Cathedral, I look up at the ceiling first, to see the dead cardinals' rotting hats. I imagine that the dust from those hats permeates all the air in the cathedral, and that we take in fragments with our every breath.

In the darkness, the red and blue of the windows shines like the promise of eternal life. My father dips his index finger in the holy water stoup. I know this is wrong, a sign of his not being born to the Church. Cradle Catholics use their middle fingers for holy water, sometimes only the third finger, sometimes the second, third, and fourth. We do it automatically, as we automatically hold our forks in our right hands. But I never tell my father this: his lapse is endearing, like a foreign accent or spats. I hug my superiority to myself—a weapon even against him. At the same time I adore the fact that this sign—his using his index finger—distinguishes my father from every other Catholic in the Universal Church.

We leave the cathedral and head for Radio City. The huge openness of the lobby, the vastness of the staircase, inspires the same devotional cast of mind as the cathedral did. I climb the stairs next to my father as if we were about to attend the coronation of a bishop. Thomas à Becket, perhaps, or Richelieu. We look down at the Art Deco goddesses, nude, but from the same higher world as the Virgin and saints we've just been praying to. Even the things we see onstage seem to have a sacramental tinge. The Easter show, in which the Rockettes are dressed as angels or nuns, the Christmas pageant, in which the bright star hovers and then descends, showing, as the Wurlitzer plays, the place of the infant Christ. I wonder if the Magi were Rockettes, but I don't think there is any way of my finding out.

We're watching *The Swan*, starring Alec Guinness and Grace Kelly. Alec and Grace have been elevated by the Catholic press to sacred status. They seem entirely out of the immigrant fray we Catholics were inevitably caught in, she because of her beauty, he on account of his Englishness. And yet these perfect ones are ours, kneel as we kneel, cross themselves as we do, say the same words to confess their sins (but we can't imagine them sinning), open their perfect mouths to take in, like us, the Sacred Host.

In Schrafft's, we talk about Grace Kelly's marriage to the prince. My father isn't pleased, but I'm thrilled. I tell him they were introduced by a priest. "A cheap publicity stunt," he says. "Don't fall for those phonies."

We are served by Irish waitresses in black uniforms with white collars. My father is the only man in the room, and this gives me a kind of unease. But everything is colored by unease: the conversation is a little above my head, and I feel honored by my own confusion. I ask him about Marilyn Monroe: "How can you like her when the priest on Sunday said we shouldn't?" "I like a woman who knows how to make a joke of herself," he says.

I don't know what this can possibly mean. Womanhood seems so desirable to me, so fragile, so elusive. I am very far from it and fear it might never be bestowed on me at all. To make a joke of it seems to court degradation. Yet when my father seizes the phantom of degradation and stares it in the eye, I feel safe from it, and this safety makes me feel free to be argumentative, even rude. I can tell him I hate Marilyn Monroe. My self-righteousness amuses him. "My daughter will be either a nun or a lady of the night," he says, taking my face in his hands. I imagine myself running through dark air, veils flowing behind me—only they are held down by diamonds rather than by the bands of linen that would be part of my habit as a nun.

We are having a conversation. He wants to know what I really think, what's important to me. He's giving me crucial information—a kind of information I can't get from my mother—about being an adult, and the sort of woman I have never met but long to be. I ask him the meanings of certain words that might pertain to me someday: "Sophisticated." "Don't let me hear them calling you that," he says. I want to be sophisticated because I've seen a hair spray ad that says, under the picture of a brunette with a French twist, "The sophisticated look," and under the picture of a blonde with loose long hair, "The casual look." The fact that there is an alternative to blondness gives me a new hope, and my father dashes it by saying I mustn't aspire to being called sophisticated. We use the word "contemplative." He says, "Perhaps that will be your vocation." When I was very little, we had a parlor trick. He would say, "What do you want to be when you grow up?" and I would say, "A contemplative." But I meant it. I'd seen a nun in a sky-blue habit kneeling in a circle of light, and I thought there was nothing more beautiful, more desirable in this world. He says that, whatever else, I'll be an intellectual. "Certainly that," he says. "Certainly that."

Now, in 1992, I have become a woman who no longer believes in these conversations. I no longer have faith in my films. I don't know why this has happened. For the past several years, I've been living with my father in a new way: the way of a writer trying to make him visible and comprehensible to strangers. This has made me feel an urgent need to certify some memories as real. I keep wanting to rid myself of the false, knowing all the time there is no such thing as truth.

It is September 1992. My father died thirty-five years ago. I was a child of seven when he died. I always said his death was the most important thing that could be known about me. I placed what I called my memories of him at the center of what I called myself.

I know that memory is composed of invention and interpretation. But invention and interpretation of *what*? Surely some things I remember really happened. But even if I can say what happened, how do I know which of all the things that happened will give me a true picture of my father? Of myself?

I begin not to trust my own memories. I can't trust the stories the others told me either. How did *they* get *their* information? Why should I believe them? They, too, needed my father, or their idea of him, to help them live their lives.

How can I tell which images tell the truth? Is the handsome father in the city the same as the toothless one, the one I am ashamed of, and the one I need to protect from the knowledge of my shame? The one who can do nothing for me, nothing for himself? Is he the same as the man who bought me a grape Popsicle and a peppermint heart? Is my father the reborn prophet Elijah, or the man who locked me out of the house? Is the girl walking with him, holding his hand, always the same girl? Which is the real father, the real daughter? The ones that can't be changed or lost?

My father is dead. I won't see him again. But who is this person I will never see?

The only thing I can say about him that I know is true is that my father is a dead man. How would I have had to live if knowing a dead man was the most important thing in my life?

Like a convicted robber, sitting in my prison cell, repeating, over and over, the numbers of the combination of the safe in which I've hidden my treasure.

Like a captured spy, keeping the code in my brain alive by constant repetition, making it more pressing than the torturer's accusations or his blows.

Like a customs official, vigilant for contraband.

I didn't do it. As the years went by, life interfered more and more with my sense of my vocation as a mourner, a rememberer, a chronicler, at once the projectionist and the screen for the scenes of the past. New impressions drowned the originals; they were covered over by relentless and obliterating seas of new experience, new sights and sounds.

People got old. Now, almost everyone who knew my father is also among the dead. Now, there is no one to repeat the stories to me.

I waited too long. I lived my life.

In living my life, I allowed my father's image to blur or crumble. I insisted that my contributions to this image would be at least as important as his. I allowed him to be vulnerable to my history.

Now, if I saw him, and if he were to say, like the voice in the burning bush, "I am who I am," perhaps the only way I could respond would be to ask this flaming or illuminated stranger: "Who are *you*?"

I have set myself the task of certifying the credentials of the dead.

I have installed myself as a bureaucrat of ghosts.

The task's impossibility doesn't mean I'm spared the obligation to accept it.

II

READING MY
FATHER

I t is the end of January, 1993. I have just got in the mail my author's copy of the new issue of *The Nation*, in which I am one of the writers selected to compose an open letter of advice to the newly elected President Clinton. Broadway, as I walk down it, is a soupy river of unlovely slush, but I pass through the wet gray streets with a high heart. I'm going to a newsstand to buy a magazine that has something of mine. It isn't enough for me that the magazine came to me in the mail. I have to go out into the world to buy a copy, so I can know the whole thing isn't a trick, or something I've made up. I'm really a writer! Nobody can deny the claim.

Pretending I'm making an innocent, a disinterested, purchase, pretending I'm just anybody, I put down my money. I walk down the street, cloaked in a penumbra of false modesty, hoping some stranger will pass and, pointing to the magazine, cry out, "I just read what you've written in there. It's brilliant, absolutely brilliant."

As I walk, reading my own words, something begins to reverberate. I remember that my father published in *The Nation* as well. I even remember the year: 1918. Seventy-five years before me, his words appeared in the magazine that has just published mine.

I know this because over twenty years ago, when I was living in Poughkeepsie, I spent a day in the Vassar library, looking up his name in *The Reader's Guide to Periodical Literature*. I found things he had written in *The Nation*, *The New Republic*, *Harper's*.

But what caused me to look? I can't remember. I remember I was studying for my doctoral exams. I remember it was a summer day, that the campus, for all its generous trees, was steamy and hot. I remember the tan metal of the bookshelves. I remember my trembling hands when I found my father's publications. But was I led to them by a clue he left somewhere? What did I do with these articles and poems that I xeroxed in the Vassar library? What did I do with these words of my father's? I am supposed to be a daughter who loves her father. Is a loving daughter someone who loses things, who can't remember?

Twenty years later, thirty-six years after my father's death, I know, with a sense of elation, that it's time to begin to look for my father, the writer. Some substance, released from who knows where, allows me to move in ways that were formerly impossible. I am going to write about my father, and if I'm going to do it, I have to do it right. I have to try to know not only the man who was my father but a man who had a life before me. And there's more than that: He was a writer, and he published. "Published" has the same root as "public." I want to know my father as a public man.

I have no memory of my father that doesn't include my knowing that he is a writer. And that this is important to me. I used to think he wrote only for me, because among the first things I read were the two issues of his magazine *The Children's Hour*. I know that I have copies of *The Children's Hour* in a box in the closet, along with another magazine of his, *Catholic International*, and some essays and poems from the Jesuit magazine *America*. But I don't want to go home, open the closet door, and look through a dusty box. I don't want to be alone with my father. I want to be with him in a public place, our favorite kind of public place. I want to be with my father in the library.

As I walk the two blocks from my home to the Columbia library, I remember going to the public library with my father. It was just one room, a large room on the second floor, above a paint store. The librarian was portly, rigidly corseted, except for the doughy flesh of her arms, which was visible when she wore a short-sleeved dress. She was uniformly, constantly displeased. She never looked happy when we took out books. We could tell she would have preferred that the books be left on the shelves, untouched, unopened, only thought about.

My father and I went to the library every Saturday. We climbed the stairs and separated; he went to the adult section, I to the children's. I always felt an anxiety about choosing: I didn't know what the criteria were, and suppose I made the wrong choice? His policy was to let me wander, let me alone, but that wasn't what I wanted. I wanted him to tell me what to want. I wanted guidance, from him, from the librarian, even though at that time I had never had the experience of reading a book I didn't like.

The reason my choices were crucial was that I was allowed to take out only five books at a time. I always finished all the books the same day I got them, and then I had the rest of the week to get through, absorbed in the highly unsatisfactory task of rereading. Why would I want to reread a book? I was interested only in books that would tell me something I didn't know.

I don't know what I read on those dry days. Nor do I remember any of the books I took out of the library. Except one. It was called *Minty's Magic Garden*. It was about a girl called Araminta. She had a garden full of magical plants. She wished for a brother and slept with a few sprigs of baby's breath under her pillow. Quite soon, the brother she desired was born.

The only reason I remember *Minty's Magic Garden* is that it was one of the few things that traveled with me when we moved from our apartment to my grandmother's house after my father died. I hoped no one would find it. It was a souvenir, a talisman, a proof of a life lived with him that I was already beginning to doubt. But I knew I couldn't keep the book. It didn't belong to me. It belonged to the library.

My mother told the librarian the story of my father's death, explaining the lateness of returning the book. She would never, she wanted to make the librarian understand, have allowed this to happen in ordinary circumstances. She'd never had an overdue book in her life. The librarian waived the fee.

So I had to suffer doubly. Once, as a careless person, a delinquent, and again, as an object of pity. Three times, because I also suffered the loss of the book. But if I'd kept it, I would have been guilty of two sins: lying and theft. Loss, I knew, was preferable to that.

My father taught me to read very early. I was only three. So I have no memory of a nonreading self, no memory of print being an obstacle, of black type on white pages being anything but a smooth canal down which he and I can sail, well embarked, contented, with all the time in the world.

When my father and I are reading, we lounge and sprawl. He is on his green chair and I am on the floor near his feet. Or we are on the rose-colored couch with its upholstered flowers, or sitting up together on my bed. We are in a place where the people we live among don't go. They aren't readers. *We* are almost nothing else.

Reading with my father, I am always safe and he is always handsome. Not someone I have to worry about or be ashamed of. Not someone with missing teeth or ripped trousers or shoes that are too big. Reading, we're removed from anything that can accuse or harm us. If there's anything in a book I don't like, he makes it go away. Because I'm scared when we read *Peter Pan*, he takes a scissors and cuts out every reference to Captain Hook. He reads to me from a book full of holes, full of spaces, spaces he fills in with something he invents, something that will bring me joy.

I am in love with books, but not the books that other children have. I don't like the Little Golden Books, available in every drugstore and most supermarkets, stories about animals or trains or characters other children (but not me, my father won't allow it) see on television. He brings me books from the city, books like no one else's. Books that tell me things I need to know about my future life. A French coloring book called *Le Jour de Jeanne*. He writes the translations over the words I cannot understand: comprehensible English ink above the locked French print. From this I learn something quite exciting: There are other languages, other ways to live. Not only ours, which seems so difficult. Words can be unpacked to reveal meaning, therefore worlds, in ways I hadn't suspected.

And my father has the key. *Le Jour de Jeanne*. He translates the title for me: "Jane's Day." Jane has a day very different from mine. She wears *sabots* and a kerchief. I can't remember anything else about her except the energetic steps she took in her *sabots*. And the wonderful tilt of her nose (not like my father's and mine; our noses hook, point down, indicate not good cheer and forward-lookingness but heaviness, seriousness, perhaps inevitably, wrong choices made too late, things taken only because they are what's left).

I don't color in Jeanne's kerchief or her little dog, to say nothing of her marvelous clothing. I wouldn't dream of spoiling the adorable openness of the black lines enclosing nothing. What is important for me is that my father has unlocked the words under the outlined shapes. His voice, unlocking. His writing, opening up.

I remember the first book I read, because its form was unusual. In the center of the cardboard cover was an oval hole. I believe the succeeding pages were meant to fill in the hole with different faces wearing different hats signifying different jobs, but I can't remember how it worked.

But both my father and I knew no ordinary job was in my future. The book we both took seriously in this regard was called *The Nuns Who Hurried*. In the lower right-hand cover was the modest attribution "By one of them."

It wasn't really a book, it was a kind of pamphlet, a series of pages stapled together. But not glossy, like most pamphlets in the pamphlet rack in church. Plain matte paper. Witty pen-and-ink drawings. From it, I learned to read words that were hard for me, but only for a little while: "missionary," "catechetical." But soon I was as at ease with those words as with the words of the lush *Grimm's Fairy-Tales* he brought home one day. Or the English edition of *A Child's Garden of Verses* with his inscription in the front. "My darling Mary Catherine, you have asked me to write you love letters in other languages, so here they are."

In German, French, Greek, and Latin my father was writing that he loved me. Now forty years later, my vanity, my sense of superiority over all living women, makes me pat my hair, stroke my cheeks, as if I've just been complimented on my beauty. Was there ever a little girl who was given anything like this? A girl who asked her father for love letters in different languages and got them?

This is the world of reading and writing into which my father leads me. But he doesn't stop there; he doesn't stop even with our love for each other. Books will also lead me to my salvation. He gives me *Six O'Clock Saints*, from which I learn, besides the story of Saint Nicholas reassembling some little boys who'd been dismembered and then pickled, that "color" can be spelled with a *u*, "colour," a way I know to be superior. And he gives me Father Lascelles's *A First Prayerbook for Young Catholics*. It has a blue leatherette cover with letters stamped in gold, pages edged in gold, and, on the frontispiece, a lamb, his paws folded, his body run through with a cross that somehow does not cause him to shed blood.

As if he knew he would die prematurely, not live to see me reach adulthood, my father left books for me that he inscribed in his handwriting. I have always loved my father's handwriting. I never feel so courted and so prized as when I see my name in his handwriting. He has inscribed me in the world. He has never ceased to think of me.

His wonderful handwriting, like no one else's, half printing, half script. For me it is the New World. Skyscrapers. Tabloids. Snap-brim hats. His handwriting is walking down Fifth Avenue saluted by everyone, greeted by everyone. The sun sparkles on the windows of the buildings his handwriting passes. Doormen greet his handwriting. His handwriting is ushered into the highest places. Because of his handwriting, I need have no fear of being unaccompanied. Anywhere. Until my death. I am assured of my value for all eternity. Because he has written my name, it is mine. Also his. Therefore inviolable, invaluable. The pearl of great price. His body and his mind, his hands and his tongue. The love of my father. Imprinted. Changeless. Unless of course, there is a cataclysm. Fire. Flood. Or in case I lose it.

But I've managed not to lose a few of the books he left behind. I haven't lost them, but I haven't read them either. What I've read, over and over, are the marginal notes he made. What's in his handwriting.

· · ·

When I say I've never read the books, what I mean is I haven't finished them. I've never been able to—they're too tedious; it's too depressing that they are what my father thought was the best he had to offer me. One is called *With Love, Peter*, by Christopher Hollis. It's an epistolary novel, a cakewalk of literary Toryism. My father has underlined a lot of sentences about the importance of being a good Latinist. He's written, "Never lose your Catholicity, my daughter. It's the one thing no one can ever take from you." He's translated a line of Virgil: "Among the dead, there are so many thousands of the beautiful."

The father who translates Virgil is the one who gives me everything. Who makes everything possible. Who opened the door of reading and writing for me, ensuring there would be a place where I could always be at home. My father, one of the beautiful dead. I wrote the line on a slip of paper. I keep it in my wallet; it's with me all the time.

Another book he inscribed for me, *The Life and Letters of Janet Erskine Stuart*, is by a superior of the Religious of the Sacred Heart. Its copyright is 1923. It's a heavy book with a faded blue cover. Her picture is on the frontispiece, forbidding and severe. The margins of its pages are full of his notes to me.

Mother Stuart was one of those intellectual English women converts my father loved, whom I think he must have wanted me to model myself on. It's certainly possible that he wanted me to be a nun, but he didn't bring me up for it. He made it inevitable, because he loved me with so much passion, so much vocal passion, that I would want a passionate life with a man.

If he wanted me to be a nun, he should have been quieter about his love for me. He shouldn't have looked at me the way he did, as if I were the center of the world. He shouldn't have said to me, "I love you more than God." Because he said that, I wasn't surprised when, later, a man told me he loved me more than his life. I wasn't even, perhaps, properly grateful.

Believing he might want it, I thought until I was a teenager that I might become a nun. Just this summer, I had a chance to see myself in the image of what I might have been if he hadn't died, if I'd become what he wanted. I was in Provincetown with my daughter, who was thirteen, six years older than I was when my father died. This alone makes her very different from me. I was with her and a friend, her best friend from babyhood, and his parents, who have been my dear friends for twenty-five years.

We passed a place called Photo Fantasies. Through computer graphics, your head can be placed on top of another body. Reed was photographed as Arnold Schwarzenegger. Anna was the Mona Lisa. The choices for women were limited: Cindy Crawford; topless goddesses; Glinda, the good witch. I was drawn to only one: the nun's veil and wimple with the empty darkness where a face should be.

The woman photographer seated me, moved me around, took pictures, fooled with a computer. In seconds, there was a photograph of me as a nun.

I thought I looked beautiful. I pretended to think it was funny but I liked it very much.

I did it for my father. So I could be the thing he would have liked to look at.

The Life and Letters of Janet Erskine Stuart isn't, for me, a book by or about Janet Erskine Stuart. It might as well be a series of blank sheets for my father's check marks, parentheses, underlinings, and marginal notes, which I take as secret messages to me. He wants me to know from them that he feels overwhelmed and a failure, that he both fears and longs for death. In spite of the few places in the book in which he speaks of his joy in me, I have to understand that he wanted to die. Was he in love with death, with the idea of death, was it a desirable place he imagined going to, or did he just want to be out of his misery, like an old dog tormented by his sores? Whatever it was, his love for me, which he might have looked to for comfort, wasn't enough.

There's only one note addressed directly to me. It's a bracketed passage in which Mother Stuart sympathizes with the storms of adolescence. The note says: "Mary, read at 18."

When I was eighteen, I was losing my virginity, marching in demonstrations, participating in the takeover of university buildings, smoking pot, and sleeping anywhere in the name of justice and peace. I wasn't reading *The Life and Letters of Janet Erskine Stuart* in 1967. I was reading *The Wretched of the Earth.*

I could have been reading Fanon in the place I'm going to now, in 1993. I'm going there not to find my father but to research David Gordon, who was writing thirty years before I was born.

I walk into Butler Library, Columbia University.

Nothing in this building is closed to me, because I flash an ID card at the gate. I am what is called an Officer of the University. I even have tenure. Would my father have guessed that one day I would be given a place at the most distinguished university in New York, our city, the city where we walked, where he placed me and taught me to be at home. Around the top of the building are engraved the names of great thinkers, some of whom I haven't read. I know that my father wouldn't admit to having failed to read any of them. But he wouldn't have been allowed into this library. When I think of this, I want to say to the guard, "If you won't let him in, don't let me in either." At the same time I want to tell my father, "It's only because of you that I'm here."

I am at home in this building, temple to high Protestantism. I've been coming here for twenty-seven years. I came here for the first time during my first week of college, when my father had been dead only ten years.

If he'd lived, he wouldn't have allowed me to come here, to study at this secular institution. He would have seen to it that I went to college in Quebec, in Belgium, in Ireland, one of the Catholic countries, where dangerous ideas wouldn't permeate. I believe that if my father had lived, I wouldn't have rebelled against him. Even my mother once said, "You went against me, but you wouldn't have been able to go against your father."

I am here in this place of marble, silence, high windows, chandeliers, this place where I am happy, where I have always been happy, where I always think I will be learning something of great value that will bring enlightenment and joy. A place my father would have kept me from, and yet a place he enabled me, by his love, to inhabit.

I'm not the only one who could be doing this research. Anyone in the world could be looking up David Gordon in *The Reader's Guide to Periodical Literature* for 1918. It doesn't have to be a daughter. But would that faceless researcher, dedicated only to straightforward discovery, experience such a beating of the heart, such a sickish delight, at seeing "David Gordon, 'Francis Ledwidge, War Poet,' October 18, *Nation*." Would anyone else take the elevator to the grim, alarming stacks with such a sense of rendezvous? Surely, no other would expect to see the face of a man thirty-six years dead when she turned the dial for the timed interval of light—a minute and a half—before the darkness became once again fully sepulchral?

· · ·

The Nation of October 1918 is in a bound volume, large and liver-colored. The pages crumble when I touch them. But there is my father, there is an article, which I've already read, copied, and lost. It is 1918. World War I is on. He's writing these words in Cleveland: "The skeptical lover of poetry has been unusually cautious in approaching the literary celebrities of the War."

The war. It's Ford Madox Ford's war, Hemingway's war, Fitzgerald's war. The war that changed everything. The war Virginia Woolf wrote about, the war of the period I studied when I worked on the Ph.D. I never got. Was it my father I was looking for in that literature? What is the intersection of literature and my father, a boy sitting in Cleveland, dreaming of the Golden Dead in Flanders Fields. Dreaming of those he was spared from joining. A Jew, a midwesterner, writing for *The Nation* a critical article on a World War I poet, Francis Ledwidge? Who is Francis Ledwidge? Why was my father writing about him, using phrases picked whole out of literature: "The seneschal of the untaught muse." Writing some sentences I would be proud to have written: "The poet must have, from long study and from continual preoccupation with the language, a knowledge of the chemical or herbal quality of words."

I find a poem of his published in *The New Republic* of that same year, 1918. My father isn't speaking about the war; he's decrying the corruption of the times.

> Henceforth by casuistry must we live
> (Each system dying with each casuist)
> Our instincts to the Social Thinkers give
> Our Passions to the Psychoanalyst
> By "earnest minded men" shall we be led
> Who show elaborately the Host is bread.

I'm trying to place this voice. It's not original, I know that, but I can't locate it. It doesn't seem to be my father's, my playful, loving father's. It doesn't sound American. Certainly, it doesn't sound like a young Ohio Jew. Why is he talking about the Host? Why is he trying to sound like a smart-alecky British clubman, the young duffer on guard against the pseudolearned arriviste. Lord Peter Wimsey and his secret confabs with archangels.

Would anyone not the daughter of the writer have any interest in this poem? Anyone who didn't secretly hope that her father would appear if she said the words he wrote often enough, hitting the right tone, the tone that would enable him to rise from the dead.

Nineteen eighteen. Nineteen ninety-three. Outside the library window, I can see the statue of Alma Mater, where I demonstrated more than twenty-five years ago against the war in Vietnam—a war my father would have supported. He would have said we were fighting Communists, the enemies of the Church. I stood on the steps of Low Library, nineteen and not a virgin. I was shouting, "Ho, Ho, Ho Chi Minh, N.L.F. is gonna win." I didn't allow myself to think of my father.

But I am not nineteen, I am forty-four, and I am doing research. I travel on the subway to Forty-second Street for the second leg of the pilgrimage to my father, the writer.

I am always with him in the Forty-second Street library, a building that has always made me believe that anything is possible, where I have lectured and received awards, the building where he suffered his fatal heart attack, the last place he inhabited in the outside world, the world outside a hospital, outside an oxygen tent. Outside the world of the dying.

I request the journals in which his work appears: journals

from the 1920s. I do this near the end of a century that was-n't the century of his birth. He was born in the nineteenth century. So I have a foot there as I stand, staring at the board where a number will light up (as at a butcher's or a train sta-tion) to indicate I can get my books. I am among people who seem to be standing only in the present, only in this century, this decade: high school girls writing term papers on AIDS, Asian men studying engineering, frantic, scholarly women and men copying microfilms of God knows what. All of them are more alone than I. I am with my father.

Did he slump over on one of these tables? Did he fall out of his chair? Did he think he was dying? Was he thinking of me, that dying meant he wouldn't see my face again? If only I could be with him, in the ambulance, comforting him, or beside him here, not dead, but dying, so I could protect him from his death.

But I'm not here to protect him, I'm not even his daugh-ter. I'm the hunter, the detective. I'm here to find informa-tion.

In *With Love, Peter*, my father has written a note telling me about an article he wrote for *The Hibbert Journal*, pub-lished in Oxford, 1920.

I find *The Hibbert Journal* for that date in the catalogue of the library's holdings. I try to imagine Oxford, 1920. The Waugh years. The *Brideshead Revisited* years, when men wore yellow socks and ate plovers' eggs or pigeons' eggs or whatever those expensive speckled eggs were that came packed in straw. Wasn't that the time when young men, spared the war or returned from it, were drinking out of women's slippers? Is that what my father was dreaming of in Cleveland, writing in the voice of a midwestern Protes-tant, comparing two parsons, one following the other as the spiritual leader of his congregation.

It's an astonishing performance: the attempt at nothing

less than a virtuoso style. My father invents two clerics, one whom he calls Mr. Francis because he reminds him of Saint Francis of Assisi.

Where did he get this taste for Christian metaphysics? This idealized, generous-hearted version of Europe? His Mr. Francis is

> versed in the ways of the world and moves in a homelike manner through its avenues, but with a sort of sense of displacement, an aspect of dreamy acquaintance with more Elysian territories, like one of Heine's gods in exile making an excellent wood chopper, or some truly *spiritual* Jesuit, participating effectively in thumb screwings, knowing them to be for ultimate benefit of the victim and the world.

I try to imagine what he read to give him those ideas. I imagine him dreaming of Europe, dreaming of Oxford. My beautiful, young father, in love with the smell of books. But he gets some things quite wrong. Francis of Assisi was an ascetic who didn't include in his religious vision the idea of ordinary pleasure, like Mr. Francis, who "loves a good game of golf, a glass of champagne, and married the most beautiful girl in the neighborhood." Is it up to me to tell my father this? That I know more than he does? Know better? If I do, it's because, unlike him, I was brought up with these things. I learned about Saint Francis from a book he gave me, one that we read together. My dreams of Europe came from my father. His came from air, from no one. So of course he made mistakes.

He does in the *Hibbert Journal* piece what he does in everything of his I read: he tries to get too much in. Is he showing off, or simply bursting with a young man's exuberance? In six pages he mentions all these names: Dante, Saint Simeon, Saint Francis, Savanarola, Meleager, Wordsworth,

Heine, Plato, Donne, Herbert, Vaughan, Herrick, Ovid, John Addington Symonds, Theocritus. And a minor Victorian sonneteer, Edward Cracraft Lefroy: "I have always had my own, individual darling in literature and this curate-poet is one of them." Always? Since when? My father was a boy when he wrote this. A boy with an undeniably Jewish face, a provincial haircut, parted down the middle.

It startles me to see that my father and I share stylistic tics. He couldn't have taught me to write, and I was well formed as a stylist before I read any of his prose. Why is it, then, that we both love the colon and the semicolon: in one sentence of his I count four colons and a semicolon and two long clauses separated by commas. Why do we both go in for the long, argumentative paragraph that ends in a punchy accusation? Why do we both have a taste for parallelisms? Did I hear them in his speech? Or is style something imprinted, like the color of our eyes? It thrills me to think I am echoing my father, the one who came before me. And I am proud, reading his article, of his love of the physical world, even as I'm jealous because he includes a reference to a mythological Greek girl, "Bombica, the honey pale." I want to say, "Would you have preferred me to be a blonde? Did you like the way I looked best, as you said you did? Were you capable of finding someone more beautiful than I?"

It's crucial to me that my father couldn't even conceive of anyone more beautiful than I, even thirty years before he, literally, conceived me.

This is a daughter reading. This is a daughter looking for her father.

On the same day that I request *The Hibbert Journal*, at the very time that I'm reading "My Two Pastors," I check the catalogue for one of my father's magazines. It's called *Hot Dog*.

I remember exactly the moment I first came upon *Hot Dog* as a child. I was twelve, looking through my father's books. Stuck in a book—a volume of *The Catholic Encyclopedia*? a study of the priesthood or the Eucharist?—was a small magazine called *Hot Dog*. I knew it was my father's, so I opened it, looking for a trace of him. What I found was a photo of a bare-breasted woman, plaintively looking out at the camera. Underneath her body is the caption "Lover Come Back."

I was shocked and outraged. I ripped the magazine into many pieces and flushed it down the toilet, satisfied that at least I had destroyed the evidence.

But, in fact, I haven't. Long before that day, and even now, through the miraculously civilized enterprise of library conservation, there has been in this place where his body gave out, a record of his prior self. In the catalogue of the New York Public Library, I find a listing for *The Hot Dog Annual*, published in Cleveland in 1929. I experience the shock, the pinprick of the scalp, of the successful scholar detective. Again I have picked up the scent.

The Hot Dog Annual is on microfilm, included in a roll that is full of examples of pornography. I'm embarrassed when I have to ask the young Latina clerk to help me with the machine. Does she think I came to the library to look at dirty pictures? I wheel the film past a number of photos of naked women, all with captions in French. I don't stop to read them: they're all modern. Then I see the title *Hot Dog* and a series of drawings that can have come from no time but the twenties. Girls wearing drop-waisted dresses and fillets around their heads. Chorus girls bent over, their bums offered provocatively, but clothed in frilly pants. Bare-breasted women in stockings and garters. No photographs, and jokes whose titillations are merely pathetic, with the sadness of sexual jokes that don't time-travel.

When little Girtie Ginger was eight she socked her mother
with a stocking full of mush. When she was twelve she
kicked her father out of the house so her boyfriend would
have a place to sleep. When she was fifteen she murdered her
second husband and wrote the story of her life. When she
was eighteen, she killed two policemen because they said her
boyfriend was drunk. Now at twenty, little Girtie is in the
talkies earning 35,000 a week. Moral: virtue is its own applesauce?

Is this my father, writing this kind of thing, using words
like "mush," "talkies," "applesauce"? Can he really be the
writer of the caption underneath the picture of a bosomy
girl approaching a man in his underwear? The girl asks,
"How do you feel tonight, big boy?" and Big Boy responds,
"You ought to know."

Do I have to think of him in this new way, as somebody
stupidly corny about sex? As I had to rip up the magazine
when I was twelve? Do I have to try to understand that the
man who wrote aesthetic prose extolling the seventeenth-
century English parson as the model cleric, and rondels in
the manor of Ronsard, was writing about Little Girtie Ginger at the same time?

I ask the clerk to make me copies both of "My Two Pastors" and some pages of *The Hot Dog Annual*. I want to tell
her that my father wrote both of them. I don't think she'd
be interested. I'd like to tell someone, here in this room,
where I know he once was. But no one meets my eyes, and
besides, I wouldn't know what to say.

Because in reading *Hot Dog* in the New York Public Library, I can't recognize anything. In everything my father
wrote, I am looking for myself, for the place where I fit in,
the place that shows I was always in his mind, that he was
always thinking about me, that I was always with him, even

before I was born. But where is the place of the daughter in a magazine that's based on pictures of women she doesn't want to look at and jokes she doesn't think are funny? A magazine full of local bathing beauties that creates unbearable necessities in a daughter. The requirement to ask, "Which of these did you have?" The fact that I must feel relief at a pair of chunky legs, a flat chest, a too prominent nose. The anxiety when I see a woman with a body undeniably more beautiful than mine.

I am furious that my father has made me think about these things. That I have to think of him screwing girls who want to get into the magazine.

I discover, with the help of a librarian friend who does a computer search for me, that there are some copies of *Hot Dog* in the Brown University library. My friend puts me in contact with the appropriate librarian at Brown. While I am waiting for her to arrange for my visit—it will take at least a week—I decide to open the box in the closet.

I can tell by my handwriting on the box that I must have repacked the magazines when I moved to New York three years before. But I didn't look at them then; I just put them in plastic bags, and bought a special box so they'd be safe in the closet.

I begin with *The Children's Hour*, for 1953 and 1954. When I look at them, I am four, then five years old. I am on my childhood bed, in the room with the wallpaper of cabbage roses. I am holding *The Children's Hour*, the size and shape of *The Reader's Digest*. I am looking at the pictures, which seem to me the most beautiful things in the world. They seem serious to me, uncondescending, undomestic, unlike Hallmark greeting cards or the holy pictures nuns give out. They are ink drawings or woodcuts marked by high contrast, illustrating the classical, important, condensed *Children's Hour* texts. Portia with her finger raised. Aesop's fox arching his neck for the grapes. Three girls, characters in "Sleeping Beauty." One leans tenderly for a flower. One reaches for a butterfly. One is distracted, seen only in profile; we don't know what she could be thinking, what it is that she might want.

Forty years later, there's nothing I can say about these pictures to explain why they so captivated me. When I try to describe the power they have, it disappears. They're just pictures, ones about which I now ask, "Are they good?"

But when I lay on my bed, feeling the breeze from the streets, looking at the pictures, hearing the children outside playing, children I wouldn't have dreamed of joining, I didn't ask if these pictures were bad or good.

Nor did I ask that of the stories, which formed for me my deepest ideas of good and evil. Good was embodied in the figure of Brother Juniper, the companion of Saint Francis; evil is in "The Devil and Tom Walker," by Washington Irving. And the exemplar of the highest virtue, mercy, was the bird in "The Little Crow of Paradise," who flies all the way to Purgatory with a drop of water in his beak to relieve his master, and dies in the process, his heart broken from the effort.

"The Little Crow of Paradise" is illustrated by a picture of a large bird with an eye at once menacing and mournful. "The crow has a hoarse and melancholy voice because at the crucifixion, the crow, the Devil's bird always, did nothing but cry mockingly. Ha, ha, ha." But not all crows, the story says, have a cinder for a heart.

When I was a child, I didn't know exactly what a cinder was. I was confused about whether it was a dead coal or a blackened chip of wood or perhaps even an ash. But I knew it wasn't living, wasn't flesh and blood, was incapable of feeling or movement. And I feared that. Even at that age, four or five, I knew it was the greatest thing to fear. I could

see it, the cinder, stuck at first in the very bottom of what I
believed the heart looked like, not a valentine but something with two chambers on the top and a longer, fuller bottom chamber, a cross between a hot pepper and Mickey
Mouse's head. But the cinder sucked on what was the meat
of the heart and took it all into itself until there was nothing
in the empty cavern of the chest but this dense matter: coal,
wood, or ash, attached to the pelvis by a string made of itself.

I believed these were the choices, as I believed the choice
was between being the jolly and beloved Brother Juniper or
the gnarled praying sinner with the Devil crouched behind.

So it is possible to say that I learned what it was to be
human, or the only kind of human I was interested in being,
from my father's magazine *The Children's Hour*. I learned
what it was I wanted of the beautiful and the good; I found
images that fit my yearnings, yearnings I was too young to
be able to name, with a precision that was miraculous and
touched by grace. But I did not learn something that I think
he was using *The Children's Hour* to teach me. I didn't learn
what it was to be a daughter.

In the two issues of *The Children's Hour* there is a dispro-
portionate number of references to daughters. In addition to
the poem written to me, "A Poem for My Daughter," there
are three stories about daughters.

The first is "Miranda, Daughter of Prospero." The second
is "Rip Van Winkle's Daughter," the daughter as perfect
housewife, meeting her resurrected father's every need. The
third is a tale of Lafcadio Hearn's, "The Soul of the Bell."

Kuan-Yo, a mandarin, the most trusted adviser to the emperor, has been given the task of supervising the creation of
the most perfect bell ever yet constructed in the world. The
greatest bell makers are assembled; they do their work. But

when the metals are heated—gold, silver, and brass—they won't blend and the bell cannot be cast. In a rage, the emperor declares that unless the bell is cast, Kuan-Yo will be killed. He consults an old wise man in the mountains, who declares that only the body of a beautiful and spotless virgin will allow the metal to blend. Ku-Ngui, Kuan-Yo's beautiful daughter, hears this. Immediately, she knows what she must do. She goes to the vat where the molten metals will not blend. She stands at the side, and crying out, "For thy sake, O father," she jumps into the vat. When her father sees this, his friends restrain him from jumping in after her. The metals blend. "The glow of the metal seemed pale and whiter than before and there was no sign of the beautiful body that had been entombed therein."

The perfect life, the perfect death, the graceful fall into the boiling metal. "For thy sake, O father." She has given him everything. She has kept nothing back. Endlessly entombed, endlessly beloved, endlessly revered, the body turned to music, the perfection of the bell's tone repeats itself in the receptive and ecstatic air.

Is it possible, this sense that I have, that even at the age of four or five I was troubled by my knowledge that I was not like any of these daughters? Not the daughter of Prospero, or Rip, or the maker of the bell. Not any of the graceful girls in the illustrations of "Sleeping Beauty." Not the doe-eyed curly-headed child whose picture is at the head of "A Poem for My Daughter." It seems to me, now, that I recognized myself in only one place in *The Children's Hour*. On the cover of the 1954 issue, there is a reproduction of Goya's little prince, his gold sash gleaming, his lace collar transparent. His eyes are worried but his mouth is proud. When I saw it as a child, I thought it was a picture of me. I recognized his hesitancy, and his vanity.

. . .

When I see the images that pressed themselves into my mind—the face of the Devil, the face of the friar, the crow, the graceful girls, the little prince—I wonder what has happened to them in the time since I last thought of them. Where were they in my memory? Into what chamber have they disappeared, in what lagoon have they nearly drowned, waiting for me to rescue them, but hopefully, patiently, humbly, touched by belief in my eventual return? I hold these pages and I am back at the beginning of my consciousness: at the formation of the way I know myself as who I am, different from others. Forty years later, holding these magazines, which crumble in my hands, disintegrating into flakes the size of wafers, I understand that I am holding not publications but the past.

But even when I read them first, in 1953 and 1954, I had a sense of something called the past that my being born had ruined. A fragile screen, highly ornamental, that I burst through at my birth, creating as I went the modern age. The present ate up the past like an acid burning out the faces in a photograph, like spun sugar flowers on my tongue, so interesting, so desirable, then, in contact with my body, melting to nothing. The past was consumed before I had time to appreciate it. In becoming the present, the past grew valueless.

Now, when I hold copies of *The Children's Hour*, I see that I collected the past right there. I looked at the pictures in it obsessively. I savored them, taking them in slowly, putting them away to tantalize myself, to strengthen myself, then looking at them again. They did what art is meant to do: they left me fully satisfied and enlarged. I had a sense of a world greater than anything I had known or seen or been a part of, and which I knew very well I had no chance of entering. But for the time that I spent looking at the pictures,

looking was enough. There was nothing desirable in life outside them.

But now I don't find what the magazines offer at all desirable. Now, as I read them, not as a daughter reading a father, but as someone trained in the history of letters, I notice
the tediousness, the carelessness, the half-educated preser-
vation of the fantasy of the "best." Gross misinformation,
wishful thinking connected to no reality, or to a reality I've
tried to avoid: a prediction that the Spanish empire, resurrected under Franco's lead, will surpass the waning British
Empire, which stole the Spaniards' rightful place at the time
of the Armada. A description of W. S. Gilbert as

> a Christian gentleman living in the happy time of Victorian
> England, an England securely mistress of the world before
> the time when the atom bomb was invented as a proper pun-
> ishment for what the reds of our own time called "Fascist
> Japan."

My father is speaking about "the Reds." He is defending
the Japanese, who had been the enemies of his country less
than ten years before. This is happening in history. It is a
product of culture. And if I am trying to understand my father, I must stop reading him as a daughter. I must place
him in history.

As I read, hearing the phrase "the Reds," I remember the
terror that accompanied that time.

Unlike my image of the past, the present of those years
was filled with shadows: angles and dark faces. Every day at
Mass we prayed for the conversion of Russia: a special
prayer, composed just for that. So every day I thought of the
face of Stalin. And the face of Joe McCarthy.

And my father's face. He wasn't only my father, living in
a house with my mother and me. He was connected to the

part of life that included Stalin and McCarthy, that invaded my dreams and created daytime horrors: Suppose the bomb fell while he was in the city, unable to get back to me in time for us to die together. And the connection was closer. My father talked to me about Joe McCarthy. He said Joe McCarthy was a hero. He was going to Washington to speak to him.

I think that he phoned me from Joe McCarthy's office on my third birthday, but I may have made this up. He wrote some speeches for Joe McCarthy, but I don't know if they were ever used. He sent me a telegram from Washington that said, "Happy birthday, honey love," in faint Western Union type that I believed to be magical.

It's McCarthy's eyes that scare me, the look around them, the dark circles, his cruel mouth, which my father tells me is meant to be cruel in order that I can live in safety. But I don't feel safe from Joe McCarthy. His mouth could turn against me, and my father wouldn't be able to protect me. I know that Joe McCarthy is more powerful than my father. I think that he could turn. I see the way accusations come out of his mouth. I always stand ready to be accused, and I sense that my father is liable to accusation. I can tell this by the way people look at us, particularly by the way their faces go when they say the word "Jew." Joe McCarthy and the man who stands beside him, Roy Cohn, both with darkness under their eyes, both masters in the game of accusation and exposure, a game I very well understand. The game of hunter and hunted. I know I am the hunted: I see no possibility of anything else. And I know my father is the hunted too, but he doesn't understand this, and it makes me feel doubly unsafe.

Yet I am supposed to believe that these hunters with their dark eyes, their cruel mouths, are my protectors. They are protecting me against the communism of Stalin. Communists kill children; they will kill any child for speaking aloud the name of Christ. It will be my responsibility to speak aloud the name of Christ to the huge soldiers in their brown wool coats, their filthy boots, their steel helmets, their bayonets pointed at my tender breast. I am terrified that at the crucial moment I won't speak aloud the name of Christ and I will have to live with that. Or the worst thing: the gradual death of the slave's soul, the hardening over until the memory of the name of Christ has been forgotten, the memory of the purity of the friends of God (Stalin had been a seminarian) buried completely under the mountain of lies.

The murderous face of Stalin, the accusing face of McCarthy, both will discover me, expose me, and destroy me. I hear as if in a dream or through thick fog (I hear it when I am reading *The Children's Hour*) the news of the execution of the Rosenbergs. Mrs. Rosenberg in her boxy coat, her hat, her pocketbook, like anybody's mother. I am told she, too, is trying to kill me. She is a mother, but the deaths of children mean nothing to her. Even the death of her own children would mean nothing to her. She is a Communist. This is what Joe McCarthy and Roy Cohn are protecting me from. But every time I see electric wires, a chain-link fence with barbed wire on the top, or an electric power plant, sometimes even a water tower, anything sending something from one part of the official world into our private lives, I am afraid for Mrs. Rosenberg. For the electricity in her body. To save *me*? You don't need to do that to her, I want to tell everybody. It is impossible that people like me will be saved. We will eventually be found out, and we know very well that you will be the ones to do it. We don't know what we've done, but you know. Then we will join Mrs. Rosenberg. Then our bodies will be shot through with electricity. We will be shocked. (I have felt it when I touched the plug of the electric toaster.) We will be shocked to death.

. . .

Holding *The Children's Hour*, reading the words "the Reds," I remember that my father thought the Rosenbergs deserved to die.

The librarian from Brown phones to say everything is waiting for me. All doors, she assures me, are open; everyone is eager to help.

I have a wonderful idea: I will go to Providence with David Plante, my closest writer friend, who was born there. We will make a pilgrimage to both our pasts.

We drive up on a perfect May day. Every tree on the beautiful campus is in full flower; pink blossoms fall on the herringbone pavement at our feet. David, from a working-class neighborhood in another part of the city, would never have dreamed of coming to this campus as a child or a teenager. It is his first trip here.

We find the august Hay Library, a small Federal-style mansion with portraits of founders on the walls. I say who I am and why I'm here. There is something absurd, in these terribly serious surroundings, about asking for "the *Hot Dog* archive," but no one blinks, no one seems to find it funny. I am given a cardboard box. The librarian presses a secret button and I am shown through to a locked room.

I focus on nothing except the box. I hardly notice the paneling, the marble floors, the generous oak tables and green-glass-shaded lamps. Hungrily I open the box. There are a dozen copies of *Hot Dog: A Monthly for Regular Fellows*. And one bound volume, *The Hot Dog Annual: The Funniest Book in the World*. I open this one first. And there is my father in a pin-striped suit, a waistcoat crossed by a watch chain, with cloudy skyscraper shapes in the background. The credit: Bachrach, Cleveland. And underneath, a signature in thick script: Jack Dinnsmore.

But Jack Dinnsmore is my father. A "regular fellow," right at home in the twenties dream of plain, no-nonsense America. David Plante and I laugh at the incongruity of publishing a picture to go along with a pseudonym. But I can't really think of anything because I'm so in love with the beautiful young man. And fixated on a spot in the middle of his chest that I recognize: a spot where I used to lay my head.

It's all I can do to stop looking at his picture. I keep asking David if he thinks my father is handsome, because I'm always afraid that any judgment I make about him is untrustworthy, perhaps even insane. He assures me that, yes, my father is a very handsome young man. But he says he doesn't think we look alike. "Look at the eyes, the mouth," I say, insistent. "Well, yes, now I see," he says. David always wants me to be happy; I think that I have worn him down.

For two hours, I turn the dusty pages, trying to make sense of what is by any standards an odd mix. More jokes like the ones on microfilm in the New York Public Library. Photographs as well as drawings in this one. Film stars are included: Marion Davies, Pola Negri. But each issue has an editorial, and these are very serious. What unites them is a protest against "bluenoses," those killjoys who brought about Prohibition. The editorials also support religious tolerance, divorce, and women in politics. But they include references to Flaubert's *The Temptation of Saint Anthony*, to Saint Francis of Assisi, and to "a bally-hooer called Tertullian."

All this is next to articles like "Are Chorus Girls on the Square?" and one-liners like "Some men get married, others get by," and a picture of some chubby bucktoothed twins, the Marquette Sisters, who are part of what is described as the *Hot Dog* traveling tour. But what delights me most is pictures of my father dressed up: as a woman; with funny noses; in his underwear; boxing with a zaftig and marcelled soubrette in a gray wool bathing suit. This is the father I remember and love: the playful man who insisted, against all the evidence of where and how we lived, that we were supposed to have fun in life.

I put the magazines back in their plastic bags, indicating the pages I want copied. A young man, clearly overqualified, sighs at the number of pages I've marked. I feel very guilty: he didn't go to graduate school to make copies for me. I try to include him in the project. I point to a picture of my father dressed as a woman, with the caption "The Girl Who Had Her Legs Insured for Fifty Thousand Dollars." "That's my father," I say to him. "That's very interesting," he says, not looking up.

Hot Dog is here because the library has a special collection of humor magazines. On display is the work of a gay artist and writer who's died of AIDS. His series was called *Franny, Queen of Provincetown*. While I'm waiting for my copies of *Hot Dog*, the librarian shows us the exhibit, and some other, explicitly sadomasochistic drawings of this artist. "He should be more widely read," she says. "That's very interesting," I say, wondering if she thinks that my father and the author of *Franny, Queen of Provincetown* are the same kind of thing—part of her archive. I wonder what my father would say.

The next day, David and I, feeling we are undoing a curse, go to his parish church for Mass. He shows me the statue of Our Lady of Fatima, standing on a cloud that looks like whipped cream, but flecked with gold. As a child he thought it was the most beautiful thing in the world, so beautiful he's afraid to light a candle in front of it: it's still a bit too powerful. We remember our childhood prayers, prayers of anxiety and guilt. We knew ourselves to be impure, unworthy of the beautiful statues, of the light falling on the floor through the stained glass. In our separate churches, hundreds of miles apart, we were miserable children. But all that—the prayers, the statues, the stained glass—was what my father wanted for me. How did he get from *Hot Dog* to that place? Through "My Two Pastors?" Through *The Temptation of Saint Anthony?*

That night David and I swim in the pool of the Holiday Inn. Under the water, my father's face comes up to me, a Jazz Age beau, American, so American. Hopeful and large-hearted, amused and generous, a bit of a show-off. It's the 1920s: prosperity and Prohibition, flappers and flivvers. Scott Fitzgerald. *Bernice Bobs Her Hair.* The aftermath of the war. The Oxford of *Brideshead Revisited.* It won't last. But my father, the young man in the pictures, the one whose face will loom so intensely in the darkness of the hotel room later that I'm afraid to fall asleep, that man is someone who doesn't know it yet. Who hasn't yet heard the bad news.

But even underwater, I can't rest with the pleasant dream of my pleasant, fun-loving father. The librarian gave me a page from a scholarly book, *American Humor Magazines and Comic Periodicals.* I have to think of the way it describes *Hot Dog,* even as I swim and dream of my twenties father.

> *Hot Dog:* One of the jollier and sexier of the skeptical regional humorous commentators. Jack Dinnsmore was editor of *Hot Dog* throughout its run in the 1920's. The "regular fellows' " monthly was a twenty-five-cent digest-size publication 6˝ by 9˝ and thirty-four pages, in breezy slang. . . . Humor included limericks, short gags and one-liners and some longer jokes of the comic tough-guy type. . . . By November 1933 Dinnsmore was in New York City . . . and had

cheapened both his paper and his image with more nudie photos and cartoons and somewhat increased political content.

All the copies of *Hot Dog* that I'd found were from its early stage. So while I read the jokes and looked at the picture of my father dressed up as a woman, I could forget what I knew had to follow. But I knew that the "increased political content" was going to be something distressing, something I hoped might not be there the next time I went back. I've always known I would have to face it. And the time has come.

Before I put David Plante on the train to Boston, I call David Sloane, the editor of *American Humor Magazines and Comic Periodicals*. He lives in New Haven. I ask for an appointment, saying that my father was the editor of *Hot Dog*. "So you're Jack Dinnsmore's daughter," he says. For a moment, I can forget what I'm afraid of.

Three days later, I drive to New Haven. David Sloane has a small store in a depressed section of town. At the back of the driveway are men with tattoos wearing bandannas around their foreheads; their hungry, dangerous dogs are tied to the fenders of their pickups. The men loiter and stare as I get out of the car. I knock on the door of the American Flag Store. David Sloane shows me in. The *Hot Dog* file is waiting for me.

The store is a little oasis of gentility in this run-down neighborhood. I sit at an antique desk and look at shelves of books and magazines separated by markers that say things like "Southern regionals," and "crackerbarrel humor." It still amazes and unsettles me that someone else has been reading and thinking about my father. Even writing about him. Someone from a university, the University of New Haven, where David Sloane teaches, inhabiting a world similar to mine.

The issues of *Hot Dog* from the twenties show me nothing different from what I saw at the New York Public Library and at Brown. But then I open the June 1933 issue. And there it is: the picture I ripped up when I was twelve. The bare-breasted woman is still crying "Lover Come Back." Nothing has changed. Nothing is unrecoverable. The past is a fiction, the passage of time is nothing to fear. It hasn't passed. It has stood still.

The model is a thin, dark, rather morose-looking young woman with small breasts whose long dark nipples are childishly un-erect. Perhaps she is very, very young. I keep wondering if my father knew her. I keep wondering whether, if he saw us both, he would think she was more beautiful than I. I'm angry at him for making me imagine him looking at her, for making me worry about my own breasts in relation to my father, a thing a daughter shouldn't have to do. Why did he put that picture in? Where is the man in the fake noses, the fright wigs? Why can't he stay in a place where it is easy to love him.

The Jack Dinnsmore of the thirties is much less amusing than he was ten years before. He's trying too hard. Prohibition is over; the bluenoses have all jumped off buildings or are selling apples on street corners; Calvin Coolidge is long dead, and Roosevelt isn't nearly so satisfying a sitting duck. But humor magazines aren't doing so well in a country where there's less money to be spent on entertainment. The tone is much more shrill, self-righteous: there's no playing with the enemy; it's a fight to the death. At the same time, the pictures and jokes are much more sexual. Nude photos. A cartoon of a peacock with his head held between a woman's legs, an ecstatic smile on his face as the woman stabs him and, underneath, the caption, "Oh, death, where is thy sting."

Under the heading "Interesting People" is a caricature of

Albert Einstein writing a mathematical formula on a small slate. His hands and fingernails are grotesquely long; his eyes crossed and mad-looking. The article begins, "This genius of a Jew-boy is the most likely of anyone living today to achieve immortality."

I feel panic. What is my father doing? Doesn't he know what's implied in calling someone a "genius of a Jew-boy"? If he does, he's someone dreadful; if he doesn't, he's someone I have to worry about. It's the thirties. We know how the story ends.

The article continues in the same tone:

Another ham-hater, Max Baer, licked Schmeling. But Einstein licked the old astronomer, Newton. Newton is dead and Schmeling isn't so strong these days, either.

What this baby can do with figures makes Flo Ziegfeld turn over in his grave.

His favorite recreations are fiddling and inhaling noodle soup.

Einie says the world isn't round after all. We advise him to go on a good American drunk and he'd find out he's all wet.

As a globe trotter, this baby runs a close second to Post and Getty. He left Berlin for California to observe sun spots. He's the greatest proof in history that education doesn't make a man smart.

Einstein has a string of learned degrees after his name longer than the list of your mother-in-law's symptoms. But what did this reputedly clever bozo do when he hit Hollywood? Did he go swimmin' in the moonlight with Thelma Todd, as you or I would have done? Did he go out to a cabin in the Sierras with Joan Crawford to get away from it all? Did he make himself a nuisance at the filming of bathing beauty pictures?

He did not. He spent his time in California looking at sun spots.

Don't send your boy to college.

I'm tempted to rip this up, as I ripped up the picture of
the nude woman when I was twelve years old. If I destroy
the evidence, no one has to know my father wrote something like this. No one has to know he was so intent on being
a "regular fellow" that he called Einstein a Jew-boy and Max
Baer a ham-hater, because regular fellows in the thirties had
turned anti-Semitic and anti-intellectual. Was he so afraid
of drowning that he did anything to stay afloat, even something this ugly and stupid? It doesn't help me to know that
this dreadful stuff is the cry of a drowning man. He knew
better. He knew who he was. A Jew-boy, a ham-hater. I remember that when I was little, he refused to eat ham (the
only meat I liked) because he said it "didn't agree" with him.
He said it always made him sick. Now I allow my mind to
drift away from the father who wrote "Jew-boy" to the father who cut up a ham steak to make a sandwich for me, and
was screamed at by my mother because that ham was dinner and "money doesn't grow on trees like you think." I'll do
anything to get back a father I can love.

But because he was a writer, because he's left evidence
that anyone can read, because I know now that there is
someone else, a professor, who has read what my father
wrote, I can't leave it, or pretend it isn't there or pretend
that it's something I've made up.

David Sloane asks if I can finish reading at his home; he
has to take care of his young son. I meet his wife, a funda-
mentalist Christian, who is wearing many layers of concealing clothing and has a kerchief on her head, although the
day is warm. All over the house are religious drawings the
children have done. Mrs. Sloane has to go to the D.M.V. to
get her registration form renewed. She is in a hurry and runs
out the door, leaving a sponge mop on the wet kitchen floor.
That mop, its damp yellow-gray face curling toward the
ceiling, stands for everything I feel. I would like to run out

the door behind her. I suppose she'll come back, pick up the mop, finish the job. I would like never to come back. Never come back to the father who called Einstein a Jew-boy. Only come back to the father in the twenties, wearing the fright wig and false noses. The handsome man in the pin-striped suit and watch chain in the Bachrach photograph. But that man is really dead. My father killed the Jew-boy. Did he kill him before the regular fellows could kill him, or kill him because he knew how much they wanted to? In any case he was made to die, and that murder was the end of the only father I could love without difficulty.

The fiction of my being the Common Reader of my father breaks down again. I'm not reading him as anyone else would, and I'm not reading what he wrote as I would anything else. I've been reading *The Children's Hour* and *Hot Dog* the way I read *Jane Eyre* as a young girl. Each time I read it, I thought that Jane and Rochester's wedding would go through, that the woman in the attic would be not the mad wife, but an old retainer, a distant relative. I was reading my father this time hoping the record would have been expunged. Or that I had read him wrongly in the past—when, for example, I read his biography of Claudel—and what I'd thought was dreadful was merely a rhetorical tic, a joke I could now see through.

But nothing has gone away or disappeared.

Now I must follow him into the thirties, to read what he wrote that I know partakes of madness or of evil. It was a decade of madness and evil in history, too, of extreme positions, of lies and murders in the name of truth.

I suppose he thought of the thirties as the decade of his rebirth. They were the years of his conversion. When I think of him in those years, he is lit by Warner Brothers. My father as *film noir*. It's the lighting that fell on John Garfield,

Edward G. Robinson, Paul Muni. Jews in trouble. Playing characters who always inhabited a semidarkness, whose actions always seemed partly invisible, partly incomprehensible to me. They had once lived some other life that explained what had happened to them and how they now behaved, but I would never see it.

I don't know the story of my father's conversion: who he met, where he was baptized, and by whom. What he kept from me is part of the shape of the fiction he made of his life. But I can reconstruct the stage for the drama of silence and darkness. I can build the base for the missing statue. I can create the empty frame. I know just how to do it; I have known for years.

He converted in 1937. The Spanish civil war is raging. The Moscow trials have taken place. *The Life of Emile Zola* wins the Oscar for best picture. Jack Benny is on the radio. But running him a close second in popularity is the radio priest Father Coughlin. Father Coughlin, from Royal Oak, Michigan, a suburb of Detroit, a first-generation Irish priest with a tongue of gold. He takes the country by storm with his garbled message: populist, xenophobic, obsessed with the iniquities of international bankers, anti-Semitic, and, although Coughlin started out supporting him, later fanatically anti-Roosevelt. Every Sunday afternoon, millions of Americans gather around their radio to hear him. I know from an article about my father in a 1942 issue of the *Cleveland Press* that my father was a member of Coughlin's League of Social Justice. But was he a member before his conversion? Was Father Coughlin his first priest?

And how did he meet Father Leonard Feeney? The dark poetic Jesuit, the aesthetic right's darling, with the burning eyes and the long upper lip, the high-rhetorical prose style, the friendship with Hilaire Belloc. My father wasn't the only one to come under Feeney's sway. He had an impressive list of visitors to his center, St. Benedict's, near Harvard

Square: Robert Lowell, Robert Bly, the theologian Avery Dulles, even Daniel Ellsberg for a while. People who were at Harvard during the thirties and forties tell me about seeing white-faced, rapt young men and women, followers of Feeney, carrying six-foot crosses across Harvard Yard.

Most people grew out of their Feeney period. They rather quickly saw that despite his charismatic powers, Feeney was too extreme, even mad. My father didn't grow out of him. But when Feeney was excommunicated in 1950 for saying that no one who hadn't been baptized in the Catholic Church would be spared damnation, my father didn't follow him out of the Church. A proof of Feeney's power is that he started the only schism in the modern American Church. But my father didn't join him, didn't join his cult, the Slaves of the Immaculate Heart of Mary. Even though my father thought Feeney was right, he believed he had to be obedient to the pope. What does this say about my father? That he needed the Church, loved the Church more than he loved reason and the individual conscience? Is this something I admire?

Leonard Feeney was my father's mentor throughout the thirties. He was literary editor of the Jesuit magazine *America*, its conservative voice. He hired my father to write essays and poems for the magazine; this is why I have so many examples of what he wrote at this time.

There was another literary editor at *America* at the time: John LaFarge. He was a descendant of the John LaFarge who started Henry James on his writing career and was a convert who insisted upon the morality of racial integration early in the thirties. My father allied himself with Feeney against LaFarge. In their contest for the editorship of *America*, LaFarge won, and by 1940 his name is on the masthead of *America* and Feeney's is not, and my father is no longer writing for the magazine.

Feeney's biographer sent me a sheaf of articles and poems

my father had written for *America*. He also sent me an ex-
cerpt from an interview with someone I remember from my
childhood: Charlie Rich, another Jewish convert, unedu-
cated, a professional mystic; he was supported by the Jesuits
at Xavier High School on Sixteenth Street, working as their
doorkeeper so he could spend the day in prayer.

These are Charlie's words, taped by Feeney's biographer:

> Feeney was very devoted to Jewish converts, Jewish peo-
> ple, yeah, he told David Gordon—David Gordon, I knew
> David very well for years, and he told David, David told me
> that "Father Feeney told me if I don't become a Catholic I'd
> go to hell." So he had that kind of strict, rigoristic philoso-
> phy. But that impressed David. Because David couldn't be
> reached except for this terrible fright, you know. That's the
> type of life he lived because he lived a very dissipated life.
> And because he lived that life, background, Feeney was
> afraid he'd go back to that life. But David told me he was
> very bad off financially. He couldn't get a job. And he would
> never go back. But I think Feeney was afraid he might go
> back to the life of editing magazines that wasn't exactly
> kosher.

Charlie Rich's tone makes me impatient. I want to flick
an imaginary cigar like Groucho Marx and say, "You're
right, it wasn't a kosher *Hot Dog*." To get away from the pain
of all this, of having to think of my father as someone bul-
lied by the bully Feeney, someone terrified, someone afraid
of hellfire, I want to tell him that there is no hellfire. But he
wouldn't believe me. And I know the fact that he believed
in hellfire and I do not makes us as different from each other
as it is possible for two people to be.

Fifty years after my father wrote for Father Feeney, one of
my closest friends, Gary Seibert, a Jesuit, arranges for me to

go to the headquarters of *America* on Fifty-sixth Street, off Fifth Avenue. He introduuces me to the editor, Father Pat Samway, who offers me access to the archives.

Gary helps me find all my father's articles and poems; he helps me xerox. He holds my hand when I start to cry. He tells me not to be embarrassed or upset by what my father wrote, to remember that he's writing as one newly converted.

As Gary and I are going through issues from 1938 and 1939, Pat Samway comes downstairs, looking amazed. He's writing a book about Walker Percy and is listening to tapes of conversations he and Percy had. He's been doing this for some months. And just now, as I am sitting two floors below him, Pat hears Percy mention my name on the tapes. He says he thinks I'm a pretty good writer. Percy's wife gets furious; she says I'm not a Catholic at all. Percy tells her gently to calm down.

The room is full of ghosts: my father, Leonard Feeney, John LaFarge, Henry James, Walker Percy. But I'm interested in only one of the dead, my father, and I am looking in these archives for a man I can understand.

I start reading an essay in which my father defines himself rhapsodically as a convert "who is not afraid to avow that we converts have access to special gifts." He is more blessed, he says, than cradle Catholics, who can't "know of the thrill of escaping inadequate theophanies." How, he asks, can those blessed at birth "experience the Resurrection feeling of Lazarus?"

I think I understand. All the unease at the disreputability of *Hot Dog;* the attempts (unsuccessful) to raise the tone; the tough-guy insistence that the truth be told, that real values be valued; most important, the anguish at being a Jewboy—all these can be put to rest. He has a mother, a bride.

He has buried the "inadequate theophanies." He's found a place where everything equivocal, ambivalent, is banished. And they've let him in! Not only have they let him in, they've named him as a prize. All that was required was that he murder his past.

But in 1937, he writes this poem to his mother, on the anniversary of her death:

A Prayer for my Mother (Bessie Robins Gordon, who passed from this life April 29, 1933)

Mary! Who once wert a Mother in Israel, look now, I pray thee,
Look to the soul of this dear one, a mother in Israel too;
Hear how my prayers are commingled for her sake to you;
Branchy and holy in intertwined Motherhood: who shall gainsay
    thee
Plenary power for shriving the souls who on earth did not know
    thee by name?
Mother art thou of my soul, Deipara, now pray for my poor
    body's mother
Keeping the Old Law, this giver of flesh to me, like to another,
Anne of the Old Law, thy parent, she tended the flame,
The Flame of the Promise, the half-light by Prophets denoted
Thy Prophets, Mary and my Prophets, she too did love them:
David, Ezechiel, Elias and holy Isais.
Jonas and Daniel and Enoch and grand Jeremias:
Yet in my babyhood, lisping the gold Hebrew vocables, after her
    their words I quoted
and prayed to the Father above them
Magnificat anima mea Dominum, thou saidst it, I say it, she said
    it,
Each in the tongue we were born to, each by the Spirit enticed.
Pray, therefore, Mary, ask the Redeemer of all of us,
Pray that at Judgement day, when there shall come that dread
    call of us,
She shall be called with the Justified. Glory to Jesus Christ.

Why couldn't my father have kept writing like this? Why couldn't he have been the sad and tolerant and loving son, regretful of the riches he had left, yet fixed on the new story he had chosen? How could he have forgotten his mother? Why, in the very same year, 1937, when he was writing the poem to his mother, and in the three years after that, the years of Feeney's editorship, does he have to publish all these letters to the editor in *America*, the same place where the poem was published?

I myself think that Mussolini's Italy is today the best governed large nation in the world. And I can continue believing so and be in temper with the Church and the Pope. But the back-handed compliments toward Marxism of the collegiate Catholics put them on dangerous ground.

Popularity with the "civic" people who send Jewish soldiers to Spain to help murder nuns in Lincoln's name is not worth having. My Uncle Ike used to say: "Onions will build you up physically but they will drag you down socially."

I am neutral, I confess, not because I am against bloodshed—there are crueller men than soldiers; men who slay souls rather than bodies. I am neutral because in a conflict between two pagan and brutal forces, I can wish for no decisive victory for either of these forces.

I detest Hitler's *Rassensucht*. But I equally detest the clammy ideal of the utterly Christless English gentleman. I would not want to see a victory for the kind of Germans who, within the memory of living man, closed Catholic schools in Bavaria. Neither do I want to see a victory for the kind of English democrats, who, within the memory of living men, shot Irish grandmothers simply for going to mass!

If only I could keep from knowing these things about my father! That he supported Mussolini and Franco, and reviled the Lincoln Brigade because it was full of Jews. And, more terrible, that he saw no difference between the Nazis and the English and (was he insane?) defined the worst work of Hitler as closing Catholic schools in Bavaria. I know that neutrality was a popular position in 1939, in the year he wrote that letter, and people didn't know about the concentration camps. But he did know about the *Rassensucht*— even the word *Rassensucht*, "race sickness," betrays his awareness—and knowing that, he failed to cry out in the name of his people; worse, he downplayed the horrors he did see, horrors carried out against his own people, people like his mother, whom he begged the Virgin to take to heaven.

How can I love the man who wrote those letters? Who is he? Is he the man who taught me to read? Is he Jack Dinnsmore, the regular fellow? The man who saw the face of God?

I am losing my father. He is disappearing. I am running to keep him in sight as the forties approach and all the lights go out.

It's a hot day in August when I open the cardboard envelope I marked—more than ten years ago—"*Catholic International.*" This is the name of a magazine my father published in the early forties. Like *The Children's Hour*, *Catholic International* lasted only two issues: Advent 1942 and Spring 1943. The titles are incoherent. It should be Advent and Lent, or Advent and Eastertide. Or, alternatively, and more simply, Winter and Spring.

I'm in Cape Cod, in a house I've rented for the month, a house that once belonged to John Dos Passos. Is it safer for me to read what I'm about to read here because Dos Passos turned to the right like my father?

From my window I can see Edward Hopper's studio.

Hopper's America was the America my father took no interest in, wanted no part of. I wonder what my father would think of my summering here, among prosperous artists, writers, psychiatrists, old bohemians turned squire, intellectuals of the left.

Catholic International is meant to be a journal of cultural and political thought. It's chock-full of a certain kind of Catholic writer: politically right-wing, inclined to aesthetic embellishment—Belloc, Wyndham Lewis, Father Coughlin—as well as writers whose names reverberated only in the small recusant circles my father revered: Caryl Houselander, Christopher Dawson.

There's a sketch of Chesterton, which includes something that I think might be a clue to the way my father thought. The article quotes an inscription Chesterton wrote in a book to a little girl: "Stand up and keep your childishness / Read all the pedants' screeds and strictures / But don't believe in anything / That can't be told in colored pictures." Nothing my father believed couldn't be told in colored pictures. That's the problem with both his life and his magazine.

So in *Catholic International* there are articles on interfaith movements (against), old Quebec (still French and still Catholic), Madame Blavatsky (she is absurd), God and gardens (in favor of both), government philanthropy (against) vs. Catholic Charity (for), and medieval Christian Ireland (utopia). It's full of an aggressive and obsessive parochialism, which springs up everywhere. In an essay entitled "Autumnal," Rev. Michael Earls, S.J., can't write about the beauty of the season without pointing out that Protestant and pagan poets can express their joy in only a limited way.

I suppose I have to believe that the fantastical re-creations of the world presented in the magazine are offered in good faith. "We find practically no permanent marriages whatever in Marxist circles in Greenwich Village, N.Y. . . . The

Catholic slums of Vienna are full of Catholic marriages." I recognize the old tough-guy trick, the one from *Hot Dog*, of mixing high and low. In the twenties it was that "bally-hooer called Tertullian"; now there's a mythical bartender, T-bone Reilley, who explains what's objectionable about Eleanor Roosevelt by saying, "I wouldn't let her in my bar." A boxer named Kingfish Levitsky, who never won a single fight, is called up to explain my father's failure to hold the day against liberals. This is followed by a list, naming names, of Catholics who were neutral about or supported the Spanish Loyalists, those murderers of Catholic priests and rapers of Catholic nuns.

I can't imagine a foothold for myself in this magazine. There is nothing that I can find myself in, nothing that doesn't alienate or scandalize me, nothing that allows me to feel I can possibly have any connection to its editor. Then I come upon a feature common to both issues: "The Catholic Home Front." It reminds me that the magazine was written in wartime. But there is more: The name of the author jumps out at me; she is someone I knew in my childhood, someone who played an important part in my life.

I remember her very well. Always, my memory of her name is associated with my parents fighting. My father accuses my mother of not being enough like this woman. He is saying something like "She has seven children, and she still has time enough to read." My mother, at the end of her rope, shouts back, "Her husband has a job. She has a maid." My parents walk away from each other to separate parts of the apartment. The woman's face shimmers in the air between them. I hate the presence of this stranger, and I blame my father for introducing her. For once, I'm on my mother's side.

We visit her and her family only one time. They live in Westchester, in a white house with many sparkling windows and deep, rich lawns. The children are older than I, mostly grown up, except for the two youngest girls, teenagers at the time we visit. They seem like nobility to me, gentle and graceful girls with long hair, flat shoes, and loose dresses.

My mother is right: They do have a maid, who seldom moves from the large kitchen, where the dishes are kept in cabinets whose doors are windowpanes and where the spotless appliances hum the unclouded melody of money unassailed by insecurity or doubt. The father, the woman's husband, is a lawyer, and years later I hear from somewhere the rumor that some of his clients were "shady." I am glad to hear that, even if it isn't true, for it reassures my sense of things that such a luminous solidity might be built on rubble.

I hate being in that house. I'm afraid of breaking something, spoiling something, and I don't budge from my father's side while we're there. I've never experienced anything like it, anyone like that woman, coiffed and manicured, wearing a dress and high heels in her own house in the middle of the day.

And I've never seen my father quite so comfortable, as he sinks into the expensive furniture, affable, calm, unjokey and unplayful, not himself. Although he'd never ignore me, insists, in fact, that I recite poetry and prayers and sing Latin hymns (which I do, with mixed pride and abashment), I can tell, as I rarely can, that he is interested in something besides me.

I find a way to pay him back. I am in a period when I find his desire to kiss me excessive, and I particularly dislike the wetness of his kisses, a by-blow of his toothlessness. I turn to the woman for succor, in mock desperation. "Could you please tell my father not to kiss me on the mouth," I say to her. "I don't like his wet kisses."

"Why not just kiss her on the forehead, Dave, like this."

She kisses me, marking me with the mark of the traitor.

"You try it now, Dave," she says. He does, and I am doubly marked.

I hate standing beside my father, in front of her. I want to run back to the big kitchen with the maid, or upstairs to the dark, empty room where the girls' old toys and games have been laid out for me, in case I should want to play with them. But I don't go anywhere. I stay next to my father until it's time to go to dinner in the dining room, where we are served by the maid.

It's the first time I've been brought dinner by a servant. While we eat, I'm longing for the car ride back, the Merritt Parkway, with its decorative overpasses, and the lights of the expansive Whitestone Bridge. I want to be asleep, or dead, or banished, anywhere I can atone for my betrayal.

When I get home, I say to my father, "I didn't mean what I said about the kisses."

He says no, I was right. And the woman was right.

But he forgets. In a few days, he kisses me too much and too wetly again, and I don't like it any more than I did before that woman told him to stop.

But I have done what my mother couldn't do. I banished that woman's face from the air of the house.

That woman made a place where my father and I can stand together, even in *Catholic International*, the most unbearable of his texts. It is a place of jealousy and punishment and deep female revenge. But it is better, far better, than nothing. I have to be grateful to this woman, my enemy. Not only because of my memory of her, but because of something she wrote.

The first of her articles is full of ideas my father couldn't find fault with; it's anti-contraception, anti–Eleanor Roosevelt. But in the second there's a little headnote: "The views expressed in this department are those of the author and not necessarily those of the Editor of *Catholic International*." The last four words are in capitals. What my father is taking exception to is the author's assertion that women should get out of factories, where they are doing war work, and get back home, where they belong. He's refusing to go along with the idea that a woman's place is in the home. We're on the same side. Of course he likes me better than that woman.

There is another small place for me in the pages of *Catholic International*. A couple of moments of meditation when my father is not fighting with anyone but is thinking of the face of God. There's a piece called "The Advent Hush," which my father translated from the German.

The words of the article bring back the anxious hush of winter evenings. Advent, the cold darkness, the shock of the early disappearance of the sun. The Gospels mentioning "The abomination of desolation," a phrase that calls up for me fears of nuclear disaster, of wandering, of confusion, of lostness. But, unlike my fear of nuclear destruction, the vision of the Gospel of Septuagesima Sunday offers a possibility of final triumph. After the roar of the crowd, the virile and victorious Christ the King arrives, to a blast of trumpets, to claim his own. I can imagine, after the terror of the blast and the roaring of the wind and the waves, the quiet placement beneath the cloak of the triumphant God.

I can rest with my father in a vision that seems tragically beautiful in its acceptance of death, its insistence upon death as the distinguished thing, the ennobling thing. But I can't rest long. Even in this meditation, there is an assertion of Jewish inferiority. It's cloaked in regret, but the inevitable assertion of Catholic rightness, Catholic superiority, towers over the pastel outlines of regret like the Madonna who dwarfs the tilling peasants in the background of a van der Weyden, a van der Goes. The German priest pities Jews for their benighted quest for the Messiah, "their eternal unfulfilled Advent twilight," when they could experience "the full light of Christmas morn."

Always, the vision must be buttressed by the face of an enemy. Even my father's thoughts of the joy of Easter must call up the dangerous lion, seeking whom he may devour.

> Christ is risen, what difference does it make at last that the traitor is at the gate without and the enemy has wormed his way within. . . . *Absorpta est mors in victoria!* Death is swallowed up in victory.

The words "Advent," "Easter," the sound of the Latin phrase, make me remember a time when my life was marked by liturgical seasons, because my father insisted on such marking. Winter was Advent: the darkness; spring was Easter: the white light that followed darkness. Cycles of blackness and illumination, the silence, the lamentation coming out of silence, the first fire with its shock, its joy. Cold stone against my knees, the scent of hyacinths, and the promise that death will be swallowed up. Which I believed. Which I no longer believe, because death was victorious, swallowed my father up, and in so doing was victorious over me, marking me as one touched by death, as one belonging to a dead man.

I am my father's daughter. I am reading what he wrote as his daughter, desperate not to lose him because of the words he sent out to strangers, to the world. But how can I fail to lose him, reading what he wrote? He is writing in 1942, 1943. Too late to say he didn't know what was going on in Germany. He *did* know about the concentration camps: he printed a piece about a Catholic boy in Auschwitz who has

the Jews join him in singing the Gloria as they are jointly
brought to death. He knew everything there was to know.
And he was saying it wasn't so bad, it wasn't the worst thing.
He was insisting on the perspective that the worst thing is
what is done against the Church. The deaths of the Jews
must be kept in perspective. He quotes Christopher Dawson saying, "The Nazis have yet to persecute the Church as
much as have the French Masons."

More important than Jews being murdered by the millions is that Jews are poisoning the world he is trying to save.
In 1943, he writes an article called "Can Christianity Survive Hollywood?"

> The trade is in the uncontrolled hands of non-Christians.
> This is what nobody denies. It exerts as much influence on
> the adolescent mind as the schools do. No one can deny that.
> We do not allow Jews, even of the highest caliber, to control
> our schools, but we allow the worst class of them to control
> the mind-molding amusement of old and young, boy and
> maiden, indiscriminately.

And he insists that the Jews be blamed for the death of
Christ. I find this in one of his editorials.

> A high tone non-Christian literature professor named
> Jacob Zietlin is the author of an essay diffused through many
> American newspapers through one of its feature syndicates.
> This essay demands that the Catholic Church change its in-
> fallible teaching to suit certain non-Christian social
> gospelling groups.
> Professor Zietlin argues in this essay that both the *New
> Testament* and the Catholic Church are wrong in teaching
> that Jesus Christ was done to death by the Jews. It wasn't the
> Jews at all, says Prof. Zietlin—in defiance of two millennia of
> the infallible Catholic *Depositum Fidei*—it was the Roman

capitalists (it's always the capitalists who are the villains among such as Professor Zietlin)—who crucified Christ.

I finish typing this and I go to sit in a spot where I have always been happy: a sandy rise, overlooking the bay. The breeze blows my hair; it sweeps through the reeds that grow here on the rise. I don't want to be writing about my father anymore. I don't want to be thinking about him. My dog, wet, her fur like feathers, stands at the top of the rise. Why can't I just enjoy it? Why do I have to go on with all this?

I give it up. For two days I try to live as if I didn't have to write all this. As if I could be not a person marked by my father's death but someone who can think of him or not, whatever she likes. Someone who wonders if he is worth thinking about anymore, so long dead, so unimportant. Someone who has forgotten him. Someone who would have to dig him up, who wonders if he is worth digging up, a man I can only expose if I speak of him, and why expose him if he is mad, pathetic, a failure? Not really interesting, except perhaps as representative of an incoherent turmoil, a hodge-podge of historical times. Or as a fictional character for whom I make up an explanatory inner life.

But I know it's blasphemy to invent an inner life for a father, whose inner life, literally produced you. Blasphemy, all these years after the Holocaust, to invent an explanation to make what he wrote seem comprehensible, pitiable.

A fatigue comes over me. A desire to sleep. Not to speak about him anymore.

Then I become afraid. I'm afraid of the closing-over of the heart that ends in the equivocal embrace, or the impossibility of embrace. I'm afraid of making him a failure in what he imagined was his last enterprise, the one that would make up for everything. The making of ME. The daughter who loved him.

What he wrote, what I have made myself read, what I have waited so long to read properly, has taken away what I used to have: my joy in being with my father, with the man who took me to the city, who bought me books, wrote me poems. Before, I could be alone with the image of a man who was the source of my knowledge that I have been loved unto death.

I waited a very long time to give my father a proper reading. When I look at the copies of *Catholic International*, I know I've touched them before. The look of the pages, the print, the illustrations, are not unfamiliar. But if I ever read what he wrote in the magazine, I didn't take it in. This is the story of my reluctance, of my flinching from the loss I knew would follow the truth. Before now, I allowed nothing of what my father wrote to penetrate my dream of him.

But now it has. And I can't silence the voice that is hateful to me. My father's voice saying: "*Perfidei Judei* . . . our Yiddisher democracy." It isn't that I wouldn't like to. But I can't.

My father left me in what he thought was a great, good place, the place ruled by my mother's arch-Catholic family, the place he dreamed of, where the Church was at the center. He thought that my mother's family knew everything important to be known. The most important thing they knew was that they were always right, and anyone unlike them wasn't.

Because of him, I'm a Jew, and the people he left me among—my mother's family, the Catholic neighborhood—wouldn't allow me to forget it. Did he think they'd forgotten it in his case? Didn't he know they despised him? Didn't he know they would take everything of mine that came from the place where he and I had lived together and would destroy it, leaving me nothing? Didn't he hear them saying of me, "That's the Jew in you" and "You have book learning,

but you have no common sense. You'll never get anywhere"? Didn't he hear their hatred when I used a word
they didn't understand, when they caught me, as if I were a
criminal, reading, dreaming? Didn't he see that he left me
alone among them, marked as a Jew and therefore tainted in
their sight? Didn't he see that his scheme didn't work, that
I was the only victim of his fantasy of a safe haven?

But I won't domesticate it. What's at stake isn't my personal history. I am someone alive after the Holocaust. It's
essential that we, those living now, name ourselves as people who know what went before. That we mark our understanding of the effects of hatred of Jews. That we say that
the hatred is not forgivable, even if it emanates from one
who is a Jew himself.

I know what his ideas led to. My silence about his part in
the evil would be a sin. Against the commandment "Thou
shalt not bear false witness." The first commandment of a
writer. I am my father's only witness. Either I must be silent
about him, or if I speak, I must expose him.

I won't speak of him as a generality, a type. A self-hating
Jew. A self-hating man. A victim of something or other. I
speak of him as a daughter, as someone who had her origin
in him, who was marked by his love and his death. His love
and his death must be on my tongue with every word I say
about him. But I am no longer a child; I waited too long to
be able to speak as a child. So knowledge must be on my
tongue. And the responsibility of the witness.

But who has called for the trial that requires a witness?
Who, if not myself? Not the millions of dead Jews, who
don't even know his name. He did no damage because he in-
fluenced no one, because he wasn't a good enough writer.
This is the other information I have now got. A friend said
to me, "The only thing that matters about your father is if
he's a good writer." But my father didn't bring me up to live

with ideas like that. It's because of him that I can't forgive him, as Auden says history "will pardon Paul Claudel, / pardon him for writing well." But even if I believed writing well was grounds for forgiveness, he wouldn't be a candidate. Everything he wrote or edited was patched together, cobbled together, not very smoothly, not very well. I'm not even left with the pride of the daughter of a fine stylist. He was far from great; he wasn't even very good.

Does the fact that he is, by every standard, a failure, relieve me of the responsibility of exposing him? And the fact that he is dead?

I wake up the next morning at five. There is a thick mist, and I walk to the rise blindly, unable to see the water. I speak to my father in a mixture of love and fear: I am unable to say which dominates. In this atmosphere, in which it is impossible to make distinctions, I say to my father, "I will not leave you as one dead."

Yesterday, when I was putting the *Catholic International* back into its box, I found another envelope. In my childish handwriting are written the words "Daddy's letters from the hospital."

The white sun breaks through, falling on the tough grasses—hog cranberry, bayberry—the small, hard fruits—beach plum, rose hips—the colorless and endlessly absorptive sand. I decide I must leave this place and go back to New York to read the letters. Another text, the final one. I will go back to the Forty-second Street library, where I can always be with him.

I take a small plane in bad weather. We fly through a storm and I believe it's possible that I will die. Always when I feel myself in danger of death I tell myself it won't be so bad because at least, dead, I'll get to see my father. But today, as the plane careens and lunges, it doesn't seem enough. I'm no longer sure that the most desirable thing is to be with my father for all eternity.

Back on the ground, back on Fifth Avenue, back in the high, beautiful rooms of the library, I am with the father who is dying. That day in the library, January 14, 1957, he must have known that he was dying. Perhaps he knew it even before that day. I have a memory of him in our apartment, a memory that begins at midnight, a memory of being awakened from sleep by hearing him groan.

He is in his blue bathrobe. I can hear him groaning. I have never heard anyone groan before that, and I have not heard it since. It is the sound of dread, and even though I am a child, I recognize it as that. No human could fail to; no human could mistake that sound.

It is past midnight. He is sitting in our kitchen, our cheerful kitchen, which, in the style of the times, is full of objects in the shape of something else—salt shakers in the shape of roosters, orange juice glasses in the shape of an orange, a nut dish in the shape of a peanut, corn holders in the shape of ears of corn.

My father and mother are sitting in the dark. He is holding a shot glass full of whiskey. She is sitting across from him. His legs are opened, spread apart. The chair is black leatherette. I hear him groan. He is saying, "My heart is killing me."

I know he won't be able to resist death.

He sees me and knows that I heard.

We had bought the blue bathrobe he's wearing at Grant's, a year before, at Christmas. I didn't like Grant's, but I admired us for shopping there. It was a no-nonsense store, no glamour. The prices were good. Exactly the opposite of the stores on Fifth Avenue where my father and I occasionally wandered—Lord & Taylor, Best and Company—where I knew we couldn't buy anything. At the same time I knew those were the stores where we belonged. I knew we didn't belong at Grant's, but I prized the ideal of humility, the right values (my mother's) that placed me there.

It brought me no joy to shop at Grant's. I disliked everything on display. The corduroy shirts stacked tightly on top of one another, the work boots, the boys' shoes, the girls' underwear. What was called ladies' lingerie, but I knew it wasn't lingerie—it was too serviceable, too durable. I understood the word "lingerie": it was a thing of the moment only. What was bought at Grant's was meant to last.

The stores I liked spent money on decoration. At Christmastime, silver cherubs hung from the ceiling and ardent reindeer leapt above the elevator, heading somewhere cold and innocent, landing in the dead of night. At Grant's, a few desultory ropes of red and green tinsel were draped here and there. A plastic bell hung down from a light fixture. My mother said Grant's was the place to buy a present for my father; he was hard on clothes. Did anyone else speak about a husband's and father's body in the way we did? We talked about his missing teeth, his rundown shoes, the holes in his socks. We never praised anything about his physical life.

The robe I chose for him was like a blanket, something like an Indian's, dark blue with a lighter, almost invisible zigzag running through it. There was a thick, twisted silken cord with a fullish tassel for a sash: it was at odds with the heavy fabric of the robe.

I loved his body in that robe. I could forget the outlines of his chest and limbs and concentrate on the thick warmth of the undifferentiated outer surface. He told me that God kept babies in his bathrobe pocket, then reached in and placed them, one at a time, in the stomachs of mothers who prayed for children. I knew that God's bathrobe was exactly

like my father's, so I felt no need to ask for a further explanation of my origin.

He is groaning in his blue bathrobe. He is dreading the approach of death. He sees me standing at the door. He sees
my face. He knows that I am worried.

"Don't worry," he says.

"But I heard you say your heart was killing you."

"It was just an expression."

This sounds so sensible, so much like the kind of conversation we habitually have, that for a second I am reassured.
But only for a second. After that, I have to pretend to be reassured. I know he is dying.

The memory of that groan has never left me. Because of
it, although I have never known terrible physical suffering
(except in labor, when I may have groaned; I don't remember), I feel that I know something about the suffering of
prisoners and slaves. Those who are waiting for the inevitable. Waiting for the worst. The animal's revolt against
its fate. The animal's hopeless bearing of witness. I have had
a hint of the dread of those under the sentence of death. I
understand the language of the darkest of the psalms, words
of affliction and abasement and despair.

I know these are the words he heard, the words that lived
inside his skull, that bloomed inside his chest. Does it matter that he was wrong to hear them? Does it matter that he
heard them alongside the words of hate, and used them to
justify his hatred? That the words he spoke were words of
evil?

Is it possible to speak evil words and not be an evil man?

What is justice to the dead?

After he left the room in the Forty-second Street library
where I am now, he became a dying man. He didn't speak
any more words of evil. Certainly he didn't write them. The
only words I have after he left this place are words of love.
Love, literally, unto death.

He knew that he was dying. I know from another of those sources—someone who reads what I say about him and gets in touch with me—that in the hospital he was in terrible pain. I got this letter in 1985:

Dear Miss Gordon:
A friend of mine was narrating the life of a fascinating friend of his. He ended with these words: "On his deathbed from a horribly painful death, this man said he was offering all this so that his beloved daughter would be a saint." As it turns out, you are this beloved daughter.

Suppose I said to my father, "I don't want to be a saint." Would he believe me? He would be both right and wrong to believe me. But suppose I said, "I can't be a saint because I have to be a writer. And I have to be a writer because of you." Would he forgive me? Does he forgive me now?

I know that he forgives me because of the letters he wrote me, letters written in pain but written so I wouldn't worry about him, so I could be happy while he was dying. With those words he made a place from which we could begin again if he lived, if he came home. In those letters, there is always a place for me. I am never unforgiven, never without a home.

But after he became ill in the library, I never lived in our home again. After the first news of his heart attack, they brought me to my grandmother's house. No one paid attention to me. It can't have happened this way, but in my memory I spent the whole time in only one room, her dark first-floor bedroom, fearing, for a while, that it was possible for my father to die, and then growing hopeful: he would never die. I believed them when they said he was getting better. They said when he was up and walking they would take me to the parking lot of the hospital, and he could stand at his window and wave at me. I am in the dark room, waiting to be allowed to see him, to wave to him. I have always been. I have always been waiting. I have always known that if they let me see him, he will never die. I know what the sight of me means to him. Everything.

Now I am in the Forty-second Street library, but I am in that dark room too, and I am reading his letters:

Letter from Hopsital (Mommy told me how to spell it right. Ekscuse yesterday's bad spelling.)
Dearest Miss Mary Catherine Gordon Honey Love Darling Daddy's Sweeatheart (Spelling) I am gitting so healthy here I pester all the nurses for kisses and they say to me: "Mr. Gordon, do not pester us for kisses. You have a daughter of your own to kiss." So I say: "Nurse, My Honey-Daughter is very stingy with Daddy-kisses." So the nurse said, "Just wait till you git home. You will git plenty kisses from your daughter now." The end.

It was one of the things he did—pretend to need my help correcting his spelling—so he would misspell words and I would return the letter to him corrected. I would also correct his penmanship. On the reverse of this letter, in my very childish printing, are the words: "David F. Gordon. Please practice your writeing." I weep to see my own printing. And his humor, his charm, his imagination, his extraordinary love.

Dearest Honey
I just signed your report card. What a wonderful student you are!
I'm so glad you got one A Minus. Otherwise you would not be a girl but a machine.
When I was in second grade I got so many D's on my report card that your Grandfather, my father called me [crossed out] said to me: D is not for David, my son, D is for Dunce.

And here my own daughter gets so many A's. I am sure proud of you.

I am sending you a poem about your Patron Saint.

Love,

Daddy.

Dearest Honey Love:

This is February First and—since I forgot to make my good resolutions on January first last month—I am making them now and here they are:

Number 1: No more pestering my honey daughter for kisses (except on Saturdays, Sundays, and holidays)

Number 2: No more corny jokes (except on Tuesdays and Thursdays)

Number 3: No more dirty feet (except in Winter and Spring)

Number 4: No more bad English (except when I forget, which is most of the time)

These four good resolutions will make me almost an angel, so if I grow wings I will not be able to hug you. How is that?

Dearest Father's Honey:

I miss you so much and I love you so much that I am losing my new big belly. Guess what I did all day today? I practiced spelling. Here is some homework.

Vowyools a-e-i-o-u

here-hear	red-read	blue-blew
here-hear	red-read	blue-blew
here-hear	red-read	blue-blew
here-hear	red-read	blue-blew
here-hear	red-read	blue-blew

The end. Love and Hugs. God Bless you. Healthy Daddy

Dearest Mary, my sweet child

Tomorrow is First Friday and—you know what? If you go to Communion this first Friday it will be your Ninth First Friday Communion (I believe). Now ... ask Mommy or Granny to tell you about the twelve (12) sure promises Jesus made to all who make nine (9) First Friday Communions and you will be very happy. On the next First Friday I will probably be home and Healthy (spelled right?) again and you and I and mother May? go to Communion together.

Well, if not next First Friday, it will be the one after next. If you have time this weekend, send me some homework, because this helps me very much.

Love, No Pestering Daddy.

Dearest Little Chicken:

About your spiritual bouquet:

I loved it and God loved it because God loves to hear the prayers of children for their fathers.

My spiritual bouquet for you is this:

All the 7 years of your life I have said at least 20 prayers a day for you at Mass and Communion and other times. So here is the arithmetic: 20 prayers a day = 20 × 300 (about) days every year = 6000 prayers × 7 years makes altogether 42000 (forty two thousand) prayers I have said for my honey love. Say many prayers for Daddy and I will say many for you. A nice priest, Father McCarthy brings me Communion every day.

Love and Hugs. The End. Daddy.

Dearest Little Honey:

I wonder where Mister Buttons disappeared to? But it really doesn't make much difference because when it snows again you can make Mister Buttons the second.

You can have your cousin Tom baptize Mister Buttons the second if you can catch him before he melts.

Tell Tommy I am very grateful to him for being so kind to my daughter.

When I get home you and I will buy Tommy some cigarettes

(spelled right?) but because it is a secret, find out quietly what kind of cigarettes he smokes.

I wish I could see your face just one minute. Not yet, but soon.

Love, Father

.   .   .

My father died in winter. I remember how I always felt on the day of his anniversary. My mother and I went to early Mass. It was dark when I woke up, but for once I didn't mind waking up early because it was a day of honor. February 13. The deep end of winter. A somber time. Lent to look forward to. Sometimes Ash Wednesday followed soon after. And Valentine's Day, which the day of his death always overshadowed. Clearly mourning took precedence over ordinary romance.

I would often cry on the day of his anniversary, or stoically hold back tears. It was a secret only my father knew: the depth and constancy of my sorrow. But I was trying to be a saint, and the saints kept their sorrow to themselves. After the Mass, in the car, our Rambler, with my mother, I drank hot cocoa from a thermos and ate an egg sandwich: This was my rushed breakfast (we had to fast between midnight and Communion) between Mass and school. I was proud of it all: my early-morning hunger and alertness, my furtive breakfast, my position as a public mourner, and the unknowable depths of my real mourning.

On his anniversary day, I knew exactly who I was, as I know exactly who I am when I read his letters. I am the daughter that he loved. Not witness, not critic.

This is an impossible position for me, reading everything else he wrote.

Because, reading what he wrote, I have to understand that he did other things in his life than love me.

.   .   .

When I knew him, we were a father and a daughter, and the world was nothing to us. Then he died, leaving me a hunger for a living man. I looked for this man in what he left me. But what harm would there have been if all the words he left me had been made to disappear? Wiped out by a benevolent, obliterating wing. The angel of erasure. The angel of forgetfulness. What harm would there have been if I had been able to make everything up, to rely only on memory, or on objects, with their malleable testimony, their cut-out tongues?

If only he hadn't been a writer, leaving a trail. If only I had no other words from him than his letters from the hospital.

If he hadn't been a writer, would I have been one? It was because of him that I never doubted, as many women do, that I had a right to be a writer; it was because of him that it never occurred to me to be anything else. I am a writer because he was one, although reading what he published sometimes embarrasses me, sometimes tears my heart.

If only neither of us was a writer. If only we were both saints.

If only I could think of him as the writer of one sentence: "I wish I could see your face just one minute."

I am trying to make a resting place for him in words, a place that won't be torn apart by the words he insisted upon using: words that make me feel I have no right to love him. That I must bear witness against him. But then I want to run into his arms, headlong, like the child who was the only one to know him as a father. I want to say, my tearful face resting against the place on his chest that was to me the place of safety: "Let those for whom you wrote those other words, those published words, let them condemn you. Only the words in your letters are mine. Only they are my text. To be commented on, illumined, and interpreted."

But what am I to say of those crumbling magazines that

fall apart when I touch them, those pages that turn to flakes that I could put upon my tongue and melt like the Communion Host. They, too, fit into the gear of the machine that produces the image of my father. I know also from the sound of those words who he is. The sound of the words, the worlds they created, are a way I came to know him after he was dead, even if I abandoned them, misplaced them, was unable to persevere and finish them, refused to hear them, radically misremembered them, forgot the first thing they said. They were a way I knew my father and a way I knew myself.

I am a writer because he was one. And not only that: I write the way I do because of the way he wrote. Some dream of purity, or style. Some way of naming and distinguishing. Some taste for exclusion and embellishment. And a desire for a point of silence, emptiness, and rest.

But he does not allow me, the reading daughter, the writing daughter, a place of rest. I hear him speak in tones of ecstasy and madness, of foolishness, vulgarity, love, hatred, humility, devotion, destruction, desperation, joy. The waters of his contradictions rise around my head and I am drowning in the seas that surround me. The sea of the impossible love of a child for her father, the sea of oblivion, the sea of a daughter's shame.

This is the story of my father I must simultaneously read and write. This is what it is to be his daughter.

III

Tracking My

Father:

In the Archives

DEPARTMENT OF COMMERCE AND LABOR—BUREAU OF THE CENSUS
THIRTEENTH CENSUS OF THE UNITED STATES: 1910—POPULATION

THE UNITED STATES OF AMERICA

No. 4708364

TO BE GIVEN TO
THE PERSON NATURALIZED

Petition No. 85498

OFFICIAL

THE UNITED STATES OF AMERICA

Northern District of Ohio   Hattie Bohn
1037 Parkwood Drive   Cleveland, Ohio

Northern District of Ohio
Cleveland, Ohio

thirty nine
sixty four

PAPERS RECORDED
JUL 17 1911
CARD OF ELECTIONS
CLEVELAND, OHIO

(SECURELY AND PERMANENTLY)

Hattie Bohn

EDGE OF THE PHOTOGRAPH

Seal

REGISTRATION CARD   3367   No. 81

Form 1   1493

1. Name in full   Alsard Israel Gordon   23

2. Home address   2194 - E 68 - Cleveland Ohio

3. Date of birth   March   25   1894

4. Are you (1) a natural-born citizen, (2) a naturalized citizen, (3) an alien, (4) or have you declared your intention (specify which)?   Alien

5. Where were you born?   Vengie   Wilna   Russia

6. If not a citizen, of what country are you a citizen or subject?   Russia

7. What is your present trade, occupation, or office?   Newspaper advertisor

8. By whom employed?   Self
   Where employed?   505 Superior Bldg, Clev. O.

9. Have you a father, mother, wife, child under 12, or a sister or brother under 12, solely dependent on you for support (specify which)?   Father and Mother

10. Married or single (which)?   Single   Race (specify which)?   Caucasian

11. What military service have you had?   Rank   None   branch   Nation or State

12. Do you claim exemption from draft (specify grounds)?   Sole support of Father & Mother

I affirm that I have verified above answers and that they are true.

David Gordon
(Signature or mark)

On the morning of March 25, 1994, I took the Number 1 train to Houston Street, a block away from the federal office building where the National Archives, Northeast Region, is housed. It is also a place where immigration cases are handled, so before I am let in, I must stand behind agitated-looking men and women, wringing their hands, answering impatiently, anxiously, suspiciously, when the guard asks them questions and passes them through the metal detector. He doesn't ask me any questions: I am white and middle-class; I simply sign my name. I pass the photos of the president and the vice president and take the elevator to the twelfth floor: the National Archives Research Room. The clerk tells me I'll have to leave my coat and bag in a temporary locker, for which he gives me the key.

The clerks in the National Archives are all pale, reluctant, bored with the exultant gasps and the crestfallen sighs of failure that are the staple of their clientele. I suspect them all of being Mormons, who have a particular stake in genealogy, since they feel that they must save the souls of everyone who ever lived, by mentioning their names.

The clerk explains the procedure for getting the microfilm of the census you want. It is so complicated that I know I'll never learn it, so I stop listening halfway through his explanation. You have to find something called a Soundex code, which suggests something having to do with spies on submarines. You begin with the name of the place your people lived in. Then you work out the code for the family name. But the microfilm of the card on which the original material was recorded is filed not under the family's last name but in alphabetical order under the first name of the head of the family, then alphabetized by the last name too. So my grandfather, Joseph Gordon, is listed after Joseph Gardner and before Joseph Grand, but nowhere near other Gordons whose names are not Joseph.

I follow the procedure and find Joseph Gordon, a dry-goods merchant, and his wife, Bessie, living in Lorain, Ohio. These must be my grandparents. But there is no David. There is a Hattie, an Israel, a Rosa, and an Annie.

Israel's date of birth is given as March 25, 1894. My father's date of birth, according to his marriage and death certificates, is March 25, 1899, and his birthplace is Lorain, Ohio. The birthplace of the family of Joseph Gordon is listed as Vilna, Russia. Their native tongue is Yiddish.

I start to break out in a sweat. Where is my father? Where is David Gordon? Is it possible that he is Israel? Or that there was another Joseph and Bessie in Lorain, or that my grandparents neglected to include a son David? Why do they have a son Israel, with the same birthday as my father, but born five years earlier than he said he was?

There must be some mistake. I get the microfilm for the 1910 census (ten years later). There are Bessie and Joseph and Hattie. But now there is a Rose, with the same birthdate as Rosa, a Dorothy with the same birthdate as the child who in 1900 was listed as Annie. And Israel has become David.

My hands are shaking so that I have great trouble getting

the microfilm off the machine. All I want is to be outside of that room, in a place lit by natural lighting. I run as quickly as I can into the air.

I cannot find my father.

Or perhaps I have.

I was looking for David Gordon. Seeing the name David Gordon always gave me an extraordinary joy. It inscribed itself in my brain; part of my brain was a palimpsest with one text only: the name David Gordon. Repeated over and over, successive layers of the name, crudely written or embellished, illumined or nearly blotted out. Engraved in happiness, in unhappiness, in longing, in celebration, cut into the surface desperately because I was alone or lightly, playfully, because I knew my father was always with me. David Gordon, four syllables, two trochees, which could possibly be the cord bounding someone else's identity, not my father's.

But I didn't really believe that. Every time I saw the name David Gordon in print anywhere, I was sure it stood for my father. Or that the man whose name was David Gordon was only pretending to be him and understood that the real David Gordon—the original, for whom all others were only stand-ins—was my father. I rejoiced in the name because it was a proof that I did not make my father up. Proof that he did not emanate from me. Proof that I could believe in what seemed too good to be true: he generated me, he came before me, he was waiting for me, preparing the world.

But what proof do I have now?

And who is Israel? Israel who gave birth to David. Israel, born in Vilna in 1894. I was looking for David Gordon, born in Lorain, Ohio, March 25, 1899. But I found Israel, who turns into David, and his sister Hattie, whom I knew of, and two new sisters, whose names were also changed. None of them were born in America. In 1910, none of them spoke English. Native language: Yiddish. Citizen: No.

The weather is terrible: a wet snow, the flakes flat as wafers, landing in plops on the filthy sidewalk. I give in to simple self-pity: an animal in foul conditions. It's all I can think about: how cold I am, how wet it is.

Who am I, if my father is not himself? I won't allow myself to think about this. On the subway I keep saying, Don't think about it, don't think about it, you can't think about it yet. The farther I am from the building where I found the news, the more unreal it seems. The dark room with everyone silently bent over their microfilm machines had the dreamy quality of a movie theater when you enter in the middle of the film. Perhaps, I tell myself, what I saw on the screen of the microfilm machine has no more to do with my life than a movie or a dream. There's a mistake. Would my father have lied about so much? I don't argue.

I walk through the door of my apartment and I am greeted by my children, whom I know to be real. I embrace my daughter, Anna. She has the family eyes, her grandfather's genetic code. The code of all the people I have just discovered today. Hattie, David, Rose, Dorothy. Or Hattie, Israel, Rosa, Annie. All of them are her people as well as mine. I allow myself to lose my fear in the solidity of her thirteen-year-old body.

I tell her what happened. I ask if she will come with me the next day, since she has no school.

"Of course, Mother," she says.

So that is who I am—I'm someone's mother. Someone recognizable. The vector of generation does not travel in one direction only. It goes forward. From me.

Vilna, Dorothy and Rose. Israel. Mary. Anna and David.

I make my children a thick soup, full of root vegetables. Each carrot I chop is an act of deliverance, I don't exactly know from what. Perhaps my unconscious is so vulgar it wants to give them new roots: carrots, parsnips, straight from the soil, plain.

In the dark room I have run from, past the metal detectors and the official portraits, is the information telling me I am not who I was. I am not David's daughter, I am Israel's.

Now, I am sure, all the lights in that building are out. The security guard is snoozing at his desk. All the information is now inaccessible. Perhaps tonight it will be stolen. It will disappear. Perhaps tomorrow when I go back with my daughter, it will have vanished.

The next day, when I take my daughter with me, I have to learn how to use the Soundex code all over again. When I'm trying to put the first film, the 1900 census, on the microfilm reader, I do something clumsy and the film unrolls across the floor. My daughter understands immediately that this is the kind of thing that makes me fall into despair. "I'll deal with it, Mom," she says kindly. "You just sit down."

I watch her. She's calm and competent. She reads the instructions on the microfilm reader and follows them without a problem, without my shaking hands, the ribbon of sweat that runs down my back. She's thirteen years old and can easily do things I will never be able to do. I watch her peaceful face in front of the machine and I think: She's an American. I have never felt really American, or assumed that my parents were. Americans were Protestant and we were not.

She's at home here because I married her father, whose ancestors have been in the Appalachian mountains for two hundred years. There is a statue of my husband's great-grandfather, a Union hero, in the center of the town of Marion, Illinois. My husband's grandfather was the president of that town's only bank. His father built houses on the shore of Lake Michigan. When my daughter was born, my mother-in-law said, "She's the first person in this family to have brown eyes."

I married the American my father could never become. My husband is an inheritor of the America of no foreign languages, no name changes. The America of nothing that needs to be covered up.

When I compliment my daughter on her handling of the machine, she says, "Just seeing your father's name makes you get emotional. It doesn't mean the same thing to me. You keep forgetting I never knew him. I only think of him as someone who was your father. So it's not hard for me to do any of this. I just want to help you."

I am simultaneously touched by her and angry with her. I don't understand why my father doesn't interest her in himself. Can't she see how interesting he is, how original, how vivid? I don't want him to exist in her mind only as my father. I want him to be a source of valorous pride for her, as he is for me.

I understand for the first time that this won't happen.

She reexamines the films of the 1900 and 1910 census to make sure I haven't made any mistakes out of anxiety. I haven't. She recopies the data into my notebook. Her handwriting is neat and legible, but still a child's.

We look at the 1920 census. There is no Joseph Gordon, but we find David, in Cleveland; he is the head of a household consisting of his mother, Hattie, and Rose. His profession is listed as author.

So my father was once head of another household. One consisting of himself, his mother, and his sisters. Responsible. An author at twenty-five. I assume that his father has died.

Israel, born in Vilna has become an American author.
This is recorded by his granddaughter, who has in her veins
the blood of Union soldiers. She holds my hand on the subway to comfort me, but she doesn't know what has happened that puts me in need of comfort. I can't tell her,
really, because I'm not sure myself.

It's not finding out that my father has lied about his past
that causes me this anguish. Almost as soon as he was dead,
my mother and I discovered that he'd lied to us. He'd told
us both that he was an only child, and then, the day after he
died, a woman named Hattie Gordon who said she was his
sister called our house and asked to have his body sent to
Cleveland so he could be buried in the Jewish cemetery
with his people. "My husband is not a Jew, he's a Catholic,"
my mother said. I know I heard her say those exact words.
    My mother and I never talked about this sudden sister
again. I don't know if it disturbed her, but it didn't bother
me that my father had lied to me about being an only child.
I believed that he had done it for me. I had felt almost freak-
ish about being an only child; it was a stigma in the Catholic
world of the fifties, a world of almost universally large families. So I renamed the lie back then; I called it a gift, a kindness. I never thought about the fact that he'd lied to my
mother, too, and that it couldn't have been a gift to her.
    But perhaps it *was* a gift that he lied to her about not hav-
ing been married before. If he'd told her the truth, there
would have been complications about their being married in
the church. I think they would have been able to get some
sort of dispensation, but it would have been both embar-
rassing and unromantic. People liked the idea that my parents had found each other in middle age. It would have
ruined things if people had to think that he'd once belonged
to another woman, instead of waiting for my mother.

When I got the news that my father had been married before, I wasn't troubled by it, and I never thought of letting my mother know. I think I was excited by the idea that another woman had chosen my father and then left him, or been left by him.

I was nearly thirty when I heard of my father's first marriage from the man who was his stepson: the child of his first wife. He phoned me in 1978 when my first book was published. He said his name was Walter Lister, that he was a producer for CBS TV. He had wonderful memories of my father, who had been a loving stepfather to a little boy whose father had abandoned him. He said my father had been tremendous fun. I was thrilled that someone knew and liked my father, that the task of remembering him happily wasn't entirely mine.

I found out that Walter's mother, Miriam, was Protestant, the daughter of a Methodist minister; had been to an Ivy League college, Brown; and was a flapper, a free spirit. She and my father were a Jazz Age couple. But after a while she couldn't stand his deliberate flouting of gentility, respectability. That might have been what broke the marriage up, although it could have been the Depression. They had met because Miriam's first husband was trying to write for *Hot Dog*, but he wasn't good enough. Her marriage to my father lasted less than a year. I discovered, too, that my father kept in touch with Walter and Miriam, that they lived less than five miles from us on Long Island, that he went on visiting them after he had married my mother, perhaps (though Walter wasn't sure; he had left home by then) even after I was born.

Walter and I meet for lunch from time to time, to talk about my father. I am a little in love with him because he gives me details about my father when he was still a dashing bachelor. He tells me about going to my father's hotel in

Times Square in 1938. My father invites him to play Ping-Pong in the basement and lets Walter, who is still a teenager, win, and says it's a close shave. But in a little while Walter realizes that my father is only humoring him. My father and his girlfriend, who had been watching the game, begin to play. It's a fierce match; my father holds nothing back with his girlfriend and only narrowly beats her.

This story excites me. Fifty years later, I am inflamed by the idea of my father and his girlfriend, whom I imagine as Joan Crawford in *Grand Hotel*. She has a little job, a little dress; she's a stenographer, a receptionist. Like my father, she's from the Midwest. She shares a flat with another out-of-town girl. At night, their stockings drip above the bathtub. My father sleeps with her when her roommate is out on a date. Their clothes fall on top of each other on the floor. Perhaps he holds his socks up with garters. Her stockings are darned. For fun they play Ping-Pong. She is proud of my father, grateful that he is introducing her to Walter, who may be going to college soon. She leaves my father to marry someone else and move back to her hometown.

Why is it that I was undisturbed by the news that my father lied about a sister and a wife but am shaken that he lied about his place of birth? And particularly, that he first spoke another language? The answer may be simple. I thought there was no other human being whom I couldn't displace: no other woman—wife or sister—whom he wouldn't consider inferior to me. And the domestic world, the official world, marriage and family, wasn't the world we shared. So another wife, a sister, didn't matter in the least. But these lies I have just discovered do matter. The world we shared was a place of images and words, and what I have learned is that he was formed by images and words that he kept from me. So all the time I thought he was with me, he may have been going to a place I could never have gone.

He could travel someplace I could never follow. He could
have been remembering things I had not even thought to
imagine. He could have been going back to places I had
thought of as inhabited only by strangers. The place of Cha-
gall's dancing cows, dark men in dark fur hats, hawking,
shouting, praying to a God who has no son or mother. Ellis
Island. An abashed face, side curls marking him a Jew. He is
in the Great Hall with thousands of other immigrants, but I
can't pick him out, as I can't see him on the streets of the
shtetl.

And now I have to hear him speaking words in a language
I don't know. Among others speaking the same language,
telling stories to outwit the Cossacks, cursing each other:
"May you die like an onion"; "May you live like a chande-
lier." Words without Latin roots, insults not intended for my
ears, utopias to which I will not be invited. I have to wonder if my father once spoke with an accent. My grandparents must have. Were they ashamed of the sound of their
own speech? Was he? With every word his parents spoke,
did he see a town with one mud street, ox-drawn vehicles,
no hope for advancement, families crowded into a suffocat-
ing house, a soup made of goose grease and cabbage leaves,
chickens in the front, money saved bitterly to get out, to get
to America. Did he hear the word "America" spoken in the
Yiddish tongue and dream of a sea voyage? In reality, not
the sea voyage of his dreams, but the nightmare of steerage?

Now I have to imagine sounds other than the words he
spoke to me, sounds other than what I hear when I read
what he wrote. Sounds in a language other than English,
which I have always thought of as the one birthright we
were both heirs to. So he can think thoughts he can keep
from me if he wants to. At any moment I can be abandoned
as he disappears into Yiddish. It may have happened many
times, and I didn't even know it. There is nowhere I can go

in language that he can't follow. I have no language that is safe from him. And this is as it should be: there should be, between us, no impermeable borders, where the spirit is impeded as though it were alien flesh.

How can he have done this? It's as if he'd had another child, perhaps even a daughter before me, whom he visited regularly without my even guessing her existence. His knowing Yiddish without allowing me to know it is a shocking act of faithlessness. The sign of all he kept from me. It may be he thought I was too good for it, like the legitimate daughter kept from the love child. Of course the lawful one will die suspecting that all the time it was the other he loved best.

For the first time, I realize that I have spent very little time imagining my father as a child. My imagination of him begins with the picture of him as a young man that I have always treasured, the picture I found after his death among his framed prints of the saints. It is printed on heavy cardboard, the edges degraded, the image dusty, blurred with dirt. One Christmas I asked my mother if, as a present, she would have a copy made of this photo, and she did. As an object, I kept it near me; as an image, it was the lodestar by which I could always locate myself.

I didn't want to go back beyond that photograph. I was too lonely to start such a journey without a face to accompany me, and too weak to invent a face. The face in the photograph eliminated the possibility of an inglorious past. It was a prosperous face. The careful haircut. The arrogant just-try-it look. He fears no one; he apologizes to no one. Jewish enough, but not too. Not so you'd have to think of anything dangerous or distressing, like steerage or the shtetl. No need, looking at that face, to think of unhappy ancestors, ancestors in trouble. Perhaps this is why I've had very little

inclination to look up the histories of my maternal grandparents: her Irish roots, his Sicilian ones. And it explains my
reluctance to undertake the project I am involved in now:
looking for the facts. Why do I need facts? The face in that
photograph is my only family history. There is no need for
anything more. Only that face, which I can carry with me
into every room I ever live in. Portable and inviolable and
entirely sufficient: the past I can bring anywhere and live
with, however I choose to live.

But he did have a life before that picture. A life full of
sounds and images that proved he was capable of leaving me
for a place I couldn't go. Perhaps he was always leaving. No
wonder I have always felt alone. No wonder this new reve-
lation makes me feel the sting of having been deceived.

The rest of the information I need requires that I travel to
Ohio. I want to know details about his education. I will start
in my father's hometown, or what I thought was his home
town, now the town I know he lived in only from the age of
six, after his arrival in America.

I have always known my father was brought up in Lorain.
Why didn't I ever go there? Why didn't I go in the adventurous sixties, when I couldn't have imagined anything I'd
be afraid of, or in the seventies, when I was a young woman
thinking of having children? Why haven't I brought my own
children to discover their roots? Always, I must confront my
own reluctance, my resistance, the fear that must have been
born of the stories that didn't quite hang together, of the
people appearing in my life with contradictory reports, of
my need to have my father to myself, created by me, untouched by history, unverifiable.

But now I board a plane to track him down.

I arrive in the Cleveland airport in the middle of an ice
storm, having left New York in spring sunshine. The hotel

in Lorain has sent a van to the airport to fetch me, and I travel alone in a vehicle meant for nine, or perhaps twelve. The driver wears red suspenders and an Abe Lincoln beard. He is completely silent for the whole trip, which takes about an hour.

I found out about the hotel, called the Renaissance Inn, from Toni Morrison, who is also from Lorain. I used to wonder if her family had gone to my grandfather's store or saloon, when I thought that was his business. Her family came to Lorain thirty years after mine, the next wave of immigrants to feed the mills. But the boom times were over; the story of the blacks in Lorain is another story, another America, with a grimmer face.

And the current face of Lorain is certainly grim.

When we get off the highway we enter a ghost town: one of those dead zones, a victim of the seventies, or whenever it was that work went out of the industrial heart of the Midwest. But The Renaissance is an eighties fantasy: some investors' dream that the dead bones of the town might once again be made to live. I don't share the dream. The windows of the shops on the wide main street have the downhearted half-emptiness of businesses that will never serve the prosperous.

I have brought the wrong clothes: a dark blue leather coat I recklessly bought because I thought it might make me feel Italian and, in a bad patch, cheer me up. But the plan has backfired. I'm covered with anxiety that the storm will ruin my beautiful coat. As I unpack, it's all I can think about.

In the hotel restaurant, there's some attempt to serve a with-it cuisine: chicken, fish, and pasta dishes called "heart easy." The hotel also has a health club with a pool. I order a heart-easy pasta dish and take a swim. Then I buy a Milky Way from the vending machine that is, disastrously, outside my door. I get into bed with my Milky Way and watch a movie with Robert Redford and Demi Moore. A movie I would never go to in a theater.

When I wake the next morning to the same weather, I transfer all my reluctance to look for facts about my father to distress about my coat and self-castigation for my vanity in bringing it. By the time I finish my heart-easy breakfast (bran muffin, fruit, coffee with skim milk) the storm has turned severe. I look out the window at the ruined town, covered with wet and cheerless snow. I go back to bed and literally shiver under the covers. I don't want to be here. I don't know what I could possibly be looking for. I want to go home. I seriously consider it, but realize there's no way I can even get out of town in this weather, and flying is clearly out of the question. What, I ask myself, shivering under the man-made fibers of my blanket, what is knowing? Pilate's question, with only a minor change. And with the question come two simultaneous answers: First, there is too much to know, and I can't stay around long enough to know it. Second, there is no fact in the world that will help me understand my father's life.

I have brought his picture, and it glows like a sanctuary lamp in the room I've darkened. Does he want me to go home? To leave him in peace? To allow to stay concealed what he worked so hard at concealing? At the same time, my great love for him, my conviction that he is the center of my life creates a desire whose tooth is as sharp as lust's to be in contact with anything to do with his past. I want to be with him, more than anything I want to be with him, and I think it's at least possible that I can be with him more completely if I have more information about his life.

But I keep thinking about my beautiful leather coat. I haven't even brought an umbrella. I phone the front desk and ask if they can lend me one. I'm hoping they'll say they can't, so I'll be trapped in my room. But they can. I dress, piling on all the sweaters I've brought, so I look stuffed and feel absurd, almost grotesque, far from the Continental dream I had of myself in my leather coat. I take the umbrella and walk a block to a drugstore that sells everything from caramel popcorn to lawn mowers. I buy an umbrella and a hideous translucent plastic raincoat with a hood. I return the other umbrella to the desk clerk.

I am walking on my father's streets, and all I can think is that I look so unattractive he'd be ashamed of me. Wrapped in plastic, stuffed with sweaters, my sneakers dark and wet. I can hardly see the two blocks to the library. I turn up Sixth Avenue, a street where my father and his family, according to the census, once lived. But everything from that time is gone: the houses that are there now were built in the fifties, tract houses with blue or yellow or brown shingles. An African Methodist church. Several vacant lots.

The library is on Sixth Avenue. It is not the building whose stone arches I had imagined my father entering as a young boy, ardent, eager for the smell of books. It's a functional two-story structure built in the sixties. The place where my father might have read is gone.

But the library is a lively place, the liveliest place I've seen in Lorain. People of all ages and races are taking out books, on auto repair, on how to write a résumé, on the state of the market in the last lean years before the millennium. Perhaps they are also taking out poetry, or books on astronomy and medieval art. But those are in the back section, the section I can't see.

Upstairs, in the local history department, which is also the reference department, a man in his forties, wearing a knitted ski hat and a flannel shirt whose buttons leave gaps, is pounding his fist on the table. He swears that he can crack the Whitewater case if he can just get into the right data bank. "But they don't let you. They keep it from you. They keep everything you need to know."

I let him finish his tirade before I speak to the librarian.

He is the local historian with whom I'd had an unsatisfactory correspondence before I left New York. He'd told me he had some things to show me, city directories that had mentioned my grandparents. But he said he was swamped with genealogical requests, and he worked only part-time. I'd imagined a white-haired, white-mustached retiree, someone who'd once been in mutual funds. But the local historian is another one of those pale young men who might be a Mormon. He shows me the city directories, the records of Ohio residents who fought in World War I, a volume commemorating the building of the new synagogue in the thirties, including the history of the congregation. He opens a locked case and lets me take any copies of the Lorain high school yearbook—*The Scimitar*—that I want.

I find my grandfather and all the members of the family in the city directories for 1905, 1907, 1910, 1912. The business address and the residence address are always identical. The family always lives on the premises.

So this is another new way I have to think of my father: as someone who lived in the back of the store. Or maybe, if times were better, above it. But the idea "if times were better" indicates a sense of progress, a movement toward prosperity, and I don't have any evidence for that. I don't know how to make sense of the family's frequent changes of address: is it movement upward or downward, or was it just something that happened all the time? Nor do I know what kinds of dry goods my grandfather sold. "Merchant." "Dry goods." None of these words seem to have anything to do with me. My grandfather was a merchant. My grandfather was a dry-goods merchant. Nothing resonates in the part of my memory where I formerly imagined a man with a beard spinning glasses down the smooth surface of a saloon bar, which is what my father said he did.

And what kind of dry goods were they? Fabric? Under-

wear? Shoes? Coats? Sheets and towels? And of what quality, what style? And to whom was he selling? To native
Protestants? To other Jews? To a mixed stew of immigrant
customers?

I never imagined myself living in back of a store. I grew up
not knowing the exact meaning of the term "dry goods." Of
all the harsh fates I imagined for myself—primary among
which was prison or reform school—living in back of a
store was not one. So how could it have been my father's
fate? How could he have been living a life I couldn't imagine?

The new facts challenge me to make a setting for them,
the setting of imagination. Now that I'm too old for my
imagination to roam freely, now that imagination would in-
volve creating a face for my father differentiated from the
faces of history, of photographs of strangers. The Lewis
Hine photographs of immigrants. Is that how I have to place
my father? In those dark eyes? In those ill-fitting clothes? Is
that what I have to do now because of these new facts?

Facts nose their way into what I thought was the past like
a dog sticking his nose under a lady's skirts. How I resent the
insidious, relentless, somehow filthy nudging of these facts.
Yet I cannot ban them. Just in case my father should appear,
like a flame bursting suddenly from a pile of oily rags. His
face in the center of the flame. Illumined. Entirely visible.
No longer in shadow.

But as I look in the directories, 1905, 1907, 1909, I see no
faces, only names: Joseph Gordon, dry-goods merchant. His
wife, Bessie, his children, David, Dorothy, Hattie, Rose. By
1909 Hattie is gone. Out on her own? On her way to prosperity?

When I come to the directory for 1910, I see something
that I'm sure is a mistake. There is a David Gordon, living

at the same address as Joseph and Bessie, listed as a stenographer for the Baltimore and Ohio Railroad.

I know this can't be my father. In 1910, he was only sixteen, a sophomore in high school. After high school he went to Harvard. How can he be working as a stenographer? And I can't think of anything he would be less suited for. He was so disorderly, so impractical. Perhaps it's some relative, also named David, living with them while my father was still in school.

I turn to the yearbook of the Lorain high school. It's soft-covered, more a magazine than a yearbook. It includes poems of an inspirational type, short stories, long, gossipy alumni notes. Only one class picture, no individual shots, a list of the graduates. I look in the yearbooks from all the years 1912 to 1917. There is no David Gordon. No Israel Gordon. There is a Benjamin Gordon, but when I find him in the group picture, I can see that he is not my father. My father is not in *The Scimitar*. There is no place where his name appears. But the name David Gordon does appear in the city directory. A sixteen-year-old employee of the Baltimore and Ohio Railroad.

I am filled with an urge to rip everything up, the city directories and the yearbooks. Especially the yearbooks. I ask the local historian if there can be any explanation for my father's absence from the graduating class list. He looks at me in a puzzled way, but not kindly, as if I were idiotic or mad. His look enrages me. I want to tell him it's his fault. He's made an error, some kind of pernicious error, in failing to include my father's name in the graduating class of 1912. I want to ask him what kind of place he thinks he's running, what kind of operation could be so careless, so malign in its irresponsibility. Then, slowly, like the realization in a dream that you are wearing no clothes, I understand something that is the last thing I would have thought of in my father's

history. He didn't graduate from high school. He was working as a stenographer in the years I imagined him walking
around Harvard Yard.

I leave the library and walk into the freezing air. I step in
puddles, letting my feet get soaked. My father, my intellectual father. Not in the classrooms of George Lyman Kit-
tredge, of Irving Babbitt, of Alfred North Whitehead,
studying alongside T. S. Eliot and the nephew of Henry
James. Nothing like that. He's an autodidact. Stealing time
from his office job to read at the public library. Looking in
the public library for what he thinks are the important
names, beginning with *A*, reading through to *Z*. His writing
makes sense in a wholly new way. The name-dropping. The
incoherence. The dream of the great, exalted, culturally em-
bossed world.

It makes perfect sense and it makes everything incomprehensible. I feel nauseated, and the ground below me seems
unstable. If my father's an autodidact, he's at best an admirable freak, at worst pathetic. But then, I ask myself,
where did I get the idea that he went to Harvard? Did he
ever really tell me that? I can't remember the exact words,
or a place we were when he said them. Where did the idea
come from? Where have any of my ideas about him come
from? They were simply something I always had, like the
color of my hair, the shape of my mouth.

I have to understand, walking down the empty streets of
Lorain in a sleet storm, past wig stores and shops selling cut-
rate liquor and cigarettes, that everything I thought about
my father might be false. That I don't even know which
were his lies and which my inventions. And these ideas were
the things I based my life on, scenes I played over and over
to place myself in the world, to give myself stature and protection. It was terribly important for me to imagine my father a student in the teens of the century, walking around

the quad, arguing with his fellow students, enduring their genteel anti-Semitic slurs, ignoring them, or silencing them by his wit. I even invented a rationale for his self-hating anti-Semitism: it was the contempt of the Harvard boys, so unbearable he absorbed it to be free of it. I compared him with a similar case, Walter Lippmann, who would have been there at the same time. Lippmann, arguably the most powerful journalist in the country during the thirties and forties, was so eager to pass among the goyim that he made a point of downplaying the threat of Hitler. Walter Lister told me that my father had said to him once, "That Jew Lippmann is pretty good."

I imagined my father in his high collars, sneering at his Protestant classmates with their gentleman's Cs, leaving them behind for Europe, where he found his dream of the greater world.

But none of that happened. He was working at the Baltimore and Ohio Railroad. Reading on his own time. Furtive. Yearning.

It is unbearable for me to think of him in this way. If he is yearning, then I am unsafe.

I ask myself which I would prefer: that I invented everything, or that he lied.

Then I remember, I didn't invent the Harvard story. Charlie Rich, my father's mystic friend, told me my father said he'd spent four years at Harvard drinking a bottle of whiskey and seducing a different woman every night.

I'm relieved. I would prefer that he lied to me than that I made everything up. At least he gave me something, at least I was involved. That way, I'm less alone.

I have lunch at an overlarge diner in a shopping mall where half the stores are vacant. The woman in the booth across from me has a black eye. Her hair is stringy; I think she's younger than I, but she's so haggard it's hard to tell: she could be anything from twenty to fifty. The man she's with, who has a greasy ponytail and is wearing a leather jacket, is saying, quite loudly, "You understand why I have to do it? You understand, right?" And she is nodding and nodding and telling him to be quiet, but not too firmly, and finally she stops and lets him go on. "I just need to know that you understand."

I want to say the same thing to my father. I want to ask him for the same kind of understanding, the same forgiveness. I order a Swiss burger, something I don't even like. I can't finish it, and the coffee is very bad. I go out again to the unbearable weather, back to the library. I make a few notes in my notebook, but they aren't really necessary: what I saw is burned into my skull. I go back to the hotel; I'm about to be interviewed.

"I had to do it, I had to do it," I say to my father, whose eyes stare at me from the picture I brought. I brought it as a kind of map or marker in case I met someone very old who thinks of my father as a young man because he never saw his face changed or aged. "I'm sorry," I tell the face, the face that is my origin and my source, my placement and my safety. "Above all, I'm sorry to be talking about you to strangers. To a newspaper. But I'm trying to find something out." I can't even use the words "the truth" to my father. What I can say is only this: "I am trying to dig up the bones you buried."

The editor for the book section of the *Cleveland Plain Dealer* comes herself to interview me. Her questions are insightful; she is impressively well prepared. She has beautiful, merciful blue eyes, and she's even brought me a winter coat because she was worried about me in the unseasonable weather. We're both hoping that her article will bring some people forward who knew my father. I want to give her all possible information, but at the same time I want to sit in silence. Am I one of those modern people who doesn't know the difference between the public and the private? One of those people on *Oprah* or *Geraldo*, one of those transsexual doctors or dominatrix twins who can't wait to tell their tales? Am I squandering my legacy by putting it out in the open, on the trail, where it can be consumed, like Hansel and Gretel's crumbs, by passersby? I *am* doing that, of course, because part of my legacy is the encrustation of my father's defeats and cover-ups. This is what I'm exposing to the elements. And who will care? Will it be just another interesting story, a curiosity for people who have curiosities enough?

When the photographer who accompanies the editor takes my picture, I want to hide. The last thing I want is to be subject to the camera's eye. The photographer says to the editor that my picture and my father's should be printed side by side. What I hope is that when people see the pictures together they'll say, "Doesn't she look like her father?" I'm hoping that people will be able to see that we have the same face.

After the photographer and the interviewer leave, after my pasta primavera and Snickers bar, I decide to follow up on some calls I'd made from New York. I phone the Lorain synagogue. The woman who answers the phone is friendly and concerned but says that she can't help me. They have no records that go back to my father's time. I am so disappointed that I can't hear correctly; I seem simultaneously to hear her saying that there was a fire, and that the records were lost when they moved to a new building. I am cast down not to be able to trace the record of my father's bar mitzvah—a record I never thought of looking for until a few months ago. I feel like an ox who has been stunned by a blow to the head with a mallet.

The woman at the synagogue suggests that I call a member of the congregation who is in his nineties and is the congregation's unofficial historian. When I speak to him, he says he won't be able to see me because it is the week of Passover. I allow him to think I am an observant Jew; I don't question him about the Hebrew words he's using that I don't understand. He says that anyway he has no memory of anyone in my family, he has nothing to tell me.

I feel I have been cheated of the trace I so desperately need. The sign of reassurance that my father was, in fact, alive before I knew him. Before I made him up.

What did I think? That because I was looking for records, they would be there? That information would be lying like Sleeping Beauty, waiting for the enlivening kiss of my attention?

Of course that's what I thought.

I hadn't made a place in my calculations for bad luck, the bad luck which is the careless wing of time. But in the course of this attempt to find the facts, I am also occasionally brushed by the wing of good luck. At a reading I'd given at Goucher College in Baltimore, I'd mentioned that I was looking for genealogical information about my father, who came from Lorain, Ohio. A woman rabbi in the audience said she could put me in touch with a Jewish genealogist in Cleveland.

Why was this woman sent to me? An angel, an angel in the form of a woman rabbi, sent to me by my father, who is disappearing into shadow, who has been dead too long. My father is with me, is watching over me. He wants me to be doing this. I'm doing nothing wrong.

When I finish with the old man from the synagogue I call Arlene Rich, the head of the Cleveland Jewish Genealogical

Society. The rabbi has called her with the information I'd
given her about my family, and Arlene has already gone to
work. I'm amazed at what she's done in my behalf. She's already found a Ronald Gordon in Lorain, and spoken to him.
She tells me to call him; he thinks we might be cousins. She
also tells me to go to the Case Western Reserve library in
Cleveland, which has extensive holdings in local history,
and particularly Jewish history. She tells me which hotel to
stay in and how much it will cost. Too much, she says, but
it's very convenient to the library. She tells me there's a
meeting of her society at the nursing home, once called the
Jewish Old Home, now called Menorah Park, where my
grandmother died. I say that I'll rent a car and come to the
meeting.

I call Ronald Gordon. He says he's heard of me before. His
father, who died in 1986, wrote me a letter when my first
book was published, explaining our kinship. Ronald has no
idea what the details of the letter were. I never got the letter.

Ron and I are both hoping for a connection. Two Gordons, coming from Vilna, to Lorain. There must be a relationship somewhere, we both agree. He and his wife invite
me to dinner in Cleveland. We will meet in the lobby of the
Renaissance Inn the following night.

That night, I put myself to sleep dreaming, for the first time
in my life, of kinship. Hoping that Ron Gordon and I will
look alike.

The next morning, before I leave for the library, I make
several more telephone calls. They are all to old people who
might have known someone in my family. They've all heard
of me, from the synagogue, or from Ron Gordon, or from
Arlene Rich. None of them remember anyone in my family.

Not Bessie or Joseph or David or Hattie or Dorothy or Rose. Or Israel, Annie, Rosa. They remember other Gordons who "did well for themselves." They mention Meyer Gordon, Ron Gordon's father, a lawyer, and Benjamin Gordon, a lawyer who settled in Cleveland, whose picture I remember from *The Scimitar*. And a Sadie Gordon, who was "very, very clever."

But my family has left no trace. They didn't "do well for themselves." They were in no way memorable. In a town of only forty Jewish families, everyone says the same thing about them: "Nothing rings a bell."

Instead of that chime, that sound of a target being hit, there's silence. Instead of a mark made, a blank. Instead of Harvard, the B&O Railroad, which I never even wanted in Monopoly.

After my phone calls, I decide that I will spend the day in the library creating an impersonal frame. I will read "local history," as if my relatives were people who had nothing to do with me. As if they were people in a group photograph, background figures, unidentifiable, instead of people with whom I share a name, blood, DNA. As if they had nothing to do with the man in the photograph in the hotel room, in whose gaze I have lived and moved.

Lorain, I learn, was a boomtown in 1900, when my family arrived. There were so many jobs available at the new steel plant—National Tube—that there was no place to house the workers. Three men in line for every conceivable bed. In the photographs of Lorain from 1900, the streets are wide, there are no sidewalks. It looks almost like a town from a Western. It is full of people from all over the world— Poles, Slavs, Germans, Irish, even Jews. The old people I spoke to said anti-Semitism wasn't a problem, there weren't enough Jews to be threatening to anyone. Everyone, they said, just got along. But I discover that a local ordinance required that "foreigners" had to live in segregated areas until the beginning of World War I.

My father was one of the foreigners.

The first synagogue in Lorain was opened in 1901. My grandfather was one of the first sixteen members, the secretary of the congregation from 1902 to 1905. A Hebrew school was started in 1902. The children were instructed by a rabbi whose family was, the next year, brought over from Russia to join him, at the expense of the congregation. My father must have gone to this school, held in the rabbi's house. Did he like it? Did he enjoy learning Hebrew? Was the rabbi benevolent? Did he encourage my father? Or was he a humiliator? Did my father resent having to learn this foreign tongue or adore it? Was he the star of the class, or the clown, or did he once again fail to make a mark?

The congregation grew and so did social pressures. The South Lorain Jews and the North Lorain Jews couldn't agree. They split into two congregations, one more orthodox, the other more reform.

Which did my family belong to? Did my father pray? How? What did he believe?

And whatever he believed, how did it fit into the "real" America recorded in *The Scimitar*, the real Americans in the graduating class of 1913, the class he should have been part of. The class of William Beverley, Harold Bennett, Oliver Becker, Daniel Gray, Frank Norcross, Charles Patterson. The Lorain that opened its arms to the immigrants who fed the mills—the Slavs, Poles, Italians, Irish—did not encourage them to graduate from high school. The class list for 1913 has no foreign-sounding names. And the stories in *The Scimitar* are all about boys on their way to college, with worries that have nothing to do with proving you have a right to be in America. I read one of the stories. "Algernon Green stood before the glass trying desperately to fit into a collar two sizes too small. At last, the feat accomplished, he turned his perspiring face to his college chum Freddy Archer and said, 'She's a peach, but I haven't the nerve to ask for a date.'"

These are the people the high school was for: Algernon and Freddy, their chums, the peaches of girls. Not for people with dark eyes and accents. You had to be unusual to make a place there. Like Benjamin Gordon, class of 1914, or Meyer Gordon, class of 1917. I guess my father wasn't unusual. I look up the statistic: only 10 percent of Jewish immigrants in the Cleveland area graduated from high school in the year 1910.

So that's it, then. My father wasn't unusual. Just another Jewish boy whose parents couldn't afford to keep him in school. Dreaming, over his clerk's job, of the Algernons and Freddies and their peaches of girls. And the books they are allowed to spend all day reading.

That my father was in anything not unusual is something that never occurred to me before. I never imagined that he conformed to a pattern. Or that the pattern he conformed to wasn't the one of creative self-invention but that of anonymous lack of distinction.

So that is who he is.

He is disappearing further into the shadows, taking his place with other faceless Jews. Pitiable, envious, part of a story I never imagined I was part of. I thought I would find in Lorain evidence of a small prosperity. Instead, I find a failure to make a mark. A failure to connect. And he has become someone with whom I can feel no connection.

And if I am not connected with him, who am I?

If he's not a person I can recognize, I can no longer recognize myself.

. . .

That night, the snow becomes a blizzard and I'm afraid to
drive to Cleveland. I call Arlene Rich to say I can't make the
meeting; she understands. But now I have nothing to do. I
take a long bath. I visit the candy machine and watch Jack
Nicholson in *A Few Good Men*. I do not read my Proust, my
Walter Benjamin, my novel by a Pole living in Italy. I fall
asleep with those books on the bed beside me. Before I turn
out the light, my last vision is my father's face, in the photograph on the night table, which, despite everything,
makes me feel accompanied. And still proud, because, after
all, he will always be a beautiful young man.

The next day, the weather breaks and I can walk around the
town. I try to imagine my grandfather, my father, in one of
the stores on the main street, but I can't relive the surge and
bustle of 1900, the promise of a limitless America. Off the
main street, I see the large houses that belonged to the mill
owners and executives, beautiful houses that must have
seemed palatial to a boy from Vilna. The numberless windows, the generous porches! I try to imagine his awe, his terror, his gratitude, his hopelessness. Did he walk around
these streets, looking at these houses, practicing being an
American? Or would he have been afraid even to walk past
these houses? Did he look at them in hatred or in love? And
what determination did they build in him? That he would
live there one day? That he would get the people who lived
there to talk to him? That one day they would understand
his superiority and acknowledge him? Did he know that he
would never be able to keep from them the knowledge that
he had lived behind the store?

The wide streets. The porches with room for a summer
swing. The dark boy passing them on his way to where? To

school? To deliver a package for his father? To the synagogue? To the Baltimore and Ohio Railroad?

Knowing that I was going to Lorain, my father's stepson,
Walter Lister, told me he would express mail some photographs he'd found of my father and him, as well as some
others of his cousin, who is now living near Cleveland. He
told me to phone her while I'm in the area: she might remember my father.

When I get back to my hotel, an express mail package
from Walter is waiting for me. In all the photos, my father
is clowning with the children. He's wearing a twenties
bathing suit, down to his knees. I look at his bare legs; I
don't remember them.

The woman in the picture, my father's wife's sister, is a
cute button-nosed flapper on the Zelda Fitzgerald model: a
tawny blonde with a cloche hat. I wonder if she was in love
with my father. I wonder what she thought of her sister's
marrying a Jew. Such an obvious Jew, sticking out of the
otherwise perfect Jazz Age scene. His large nose, his darkness. What's wrong with this picture? The Jew in the middle, playing with the children as if he belonged?

You don't belong with them, I say to my father in the pictures, you belong with me.

I remind him that the place I make for him is, more than
ever, his only proper place.

When I phone Walter's cousin, she tells me she remembers
very little about my father. She was very young when he and
her aunt divorced and he went "off the scene."

"He was very handsome," she says. "I remember that. If
you look like him, you must be a good-looking girl. Of
course he could never hide what he was, you know."

I say I know.

"Not that he tried. Not that he wanted to. But he couldn't have, even if he wanted to."

That evening, when I go down to the lobby to meet Ronald Gordon, I find a man who looks nothing like my father or like me. He's tall and slender with well-cut silver hair, a well-cut blue blazer, and gray flannel pants. He looks like a Wasp.

He, his wife, and I drive into Cleveland, and we tell each other our ages, our children's ages, our education, the histories of our careers. His father, Meyer Gordon, four years younger than my father, was a young man when Ron was born, so Ron is nearly twenty years older than I. He tells me that his father took himself to New Haven and talked his way into Yale, and into a scholarship. After Yale Law School, he came home to Lorain to practice law. He married a Protestant.

Ron practices in his father's firm. His wife is a Jew, and he recovered his lost Judaism through her. His daughter is a third-generation Yalie. He tells me he's writing a series of articles for a conservative magazine on why welfare has failed.

His grandfather was a peddler. Max Gordon took sheets and towels into the countryside in his horse-drawn wagon to sell to the farmers. Ron was embarrassed by his grandfather, who, even when there was no need for it (his son Meyer was prosperous), insisted upon walking around downtown Lorain with a pack on his back.

The question that cannot be answered: Why did Meyer Gordon get himself to Yale and my father only get as far as the Baltimore and Ohio Railroad?

Ron tells me these stories in a steakhouse, where we eat asparagus and filet mignon. The restaurant is in a former train station, turned, in an attempt to revive the dying downtown, into a glitzy mall. It's called Terminal Tower; the name seems ominous to me. As Ron speaks, I have an image of his grandfather, Max, with a pack on his back. I have an image of his father, Meyer, in New Haven. But my own grandfather is darkness to me. I imagine Kafka's father, the father in Henry Roth's books. I imagine a father who frightened his son, who failed to make his son feel safe. What did Joseph Gordon, my grandfather, fail to give his son—besides, that is, money to stay in school, to go to college? And how did he so fail to leave a mark that no one remembers him? I have a photograph of my grandmother, and my father told me stories about her, probably all lies. It is unlikely that she was, as my father said, a concert pianist. And her maiden name was Rabinowitz, not Robins, as my father's records say. At least, though, I have something from him of her. But there are no photographs of my grandfather. And not a single story about him. Behind my father, a dark father, in silence. A shadow, failing to provide.

I sign Ron's wife's copy of *Final Payments*. I am moved by their generosity to me, but my instinct is we are not kin.

Before I leave Lorain, I call the high school to see if they will give me a copy of my father's records. They say the records, even that far back, are sealed. They say I'll have to get a court order.

I leave the town enraged, driven this time by a chatty van driver, whom I lie to because I don't feel like saying what I've done. I leave town without contacting Toni Morrison's friends, because I can't bear to talk any more about what's happened to me. It was bad enough to talk to a newspaper reporter. But I'm afraid of turning my father into a "character." An eccentric. An American "type."

I have lost a tremendous amount in these days. I came to Lorain imagining a father whose proud family came together with others in the community to send him to Harvard. I imagined a father surrounded by shy relatives, seeing him off on the train with swelling breasts and baskets of food and tear-filled eyes. The family prize sent East. Of course I imagined a family that had a place. I have had to give up the idea of family that made a mark. A mark of any kind.

The Renaissance van leaves me at the Glidden House in Cleveland, right on the Case Western Reserve campus. It is the former home of the Gliddens of house-paint fame, now a bed and breakfast. Another American failure? Each of the rooms bears the name of one of the Glidden family members, to make us feel at home among the four-poster beds and Laura Ashley wallpaper.

In the Case Western Reserve library, the librarian steers me to the appropriate records: the Cleveland city directories, the necrology files. "Necrology file" sounds perverse, as if I'll find it in a tomb, visited by white-faced searchers carrying tapers. I am given the index of marriages. The index of Jewish newspapers. The index of magazines published in Cleveland.

I can trace my father in Cleveland through the city directories from 1914 to 1931. In 1914, Bessie, Hattie, and David are together. But not Joseph. Where is his father? Why is my father working as a salesman? What is he selling? In 1917, he's living with Rose and working for an advertising agency. In 1918, he's employed by the J. R. Gordon advertising agency, whose place of business is the same as his home. In 1919, he isn't listed, although Rose is. In 1920, he's living alone, working as a clerk. In 1921, he's living with Hattie and Rose, a salesman again. In 1922, he's alone, but is president of the Merit Publications Company, which published *Hot Dog*. He's listed as editor and publisher of Merit

Publications until 1929. In that year, the listing for Merit Publications includes a name I recognize, Charles Rothman. Charles Rothman was a figure from my childhood, a broad, bald man who smoked a cigar and who had an apartment on Central Park West that I knew, even at the age of three, was luxurious. When my father took me there, I ate cookies with a maid in a large, dark kitchen while he and my father talked about money. There is a picture of him at my fourth birthday party. Then he becomes one of the villains in the story of our family life. He stopped supporting *The Children's Hour*. He bowed, my father said, to the pressure of B'nai B'rith. It was because of him, I was led to believe, that my father had to take the jobs as a taxi driver, a bartender.

I am surprised to learn that he was backing my father's magazine in the twenties, that my father kept up the connection for thirty years. So the break with his past, which he portrayed as total, inviolable, occurring at the moment of his conversion, is another lie.

There is no record of my father in the city directories after 1931. I imagine that he went to New York then.

I find the certificate of his marriage to Miriam. His date of birth is listed as 1894, not 1899, as I had always thought. But he lists his place of birth as Ohio.

The librarian directs me to the files of the Jewish Old Home, where my grandmother died. It was the most orthodox of the charity homes for old people. The records are handwritten, in a loose-leaf notebook. I see that my grandmother entered the home in February 1932 and died a year later. Next to the entry concerning her death are two mysterious lower-case letters: p.o. I try to understand what "p.o." might mean. Payment owing? Pretty orthodox? Particularly obnoxious?

And I try to understand why my grandmother was sent there. Where was my father? Why did he leave her to this?

Where was Hattie, where was Dorothy, where was Rose? Why weren't they taking care of their mother? It's the thirties; daughters take care of their mothers. Bessie had three. And a son.

What did it mean that none of her children could care for her, that they allowed her the shame of being a charity case?

I try to imagine my father in New York, trying to resuscitate *Hot Dog*, feeling guilty about his mother, his sisters, whom he has left behind.

This is another way I have never had to think about him: as the guilty, abandoning son and brother. I was happy to see him listed as the head of the household in the census record of 1920. Head of the household: responsible, perhaps, as he had never been for my mother and me. But where is he in 1932? Sleeping with chorus girls in New York? Thinking about converting, while his mother is in the poorhouse and his sisters are God knows where?

But it is 1932, the middle of the Depression. Perhaps none of them had the money to take care of their mother. Perhaps it was a more common story than I'd known. Yet another way I have to think of my father: as someone touched by history. Not just sleeping with chorus girls, not just walking around New York in his George Raft hat. But as someone if not poor, then temporarily impoverished. A victim of his times.

I find a folder of applications to the Jewish Old Home, including the ones for the year Bessie would have entered. The applications are quite detailed; there is a long section in which the family must explain why they are sending their parent to the home. My heart races. I will find the story of why my grandmother became a charity case. I will discover the narrative of the family's collapse.

I go through every application in 1932 and 1933. I keep going through them, again and again. I am sweating with frustration. I must be pulling on a string of amber beads I'm wearing, because, as I'm flipping through the pages, the string breaks and the beads scatter all over the floor: a scandal in the orderly silence of the reading room.

My grandmother's application isn't there. The librarian looks blank when I ask her, trying to keep my voice from sounding frantic, if there's another place where missing applications could be. Kindly, she goes through the whole file with me, but the only references to Bessie Gordon are her date of admission, her date of death, the location of her grave in the charity section of the cemetery, the letters p.o.

I excuse myself and go into the ladies' room. I sit on the closed toilet seat, rock and cry. The record is lost and I am helpless. Nothing I have found does anything but make them all recede, more unknowable than ever, less mine.

I wash my face and go back to the applications. If I can't find my grandmother's, I will read the stories of others. The official language, masking tears, renunciations, lacerations, threats. "Daughter and mother cannot get along because daughter and family will not keep proper Kosher Home." This is a rather frequent tale: "The children won't accede to the parents' demands for orthodoxy." "Son says he cannot afford to keep mother although mother insists he rents out a room for money which she could use." And the old familiar tale of the one who has lost all her connections. "No family. No one to take responsibility. Lives alone."

That night I go to dinner at a good restaurant down the street from the Glidden House. When the waitress tells me she doesn't have the chicken with mushrooms, I lose my temper and tell her they have no right to suggest that they can provide what they are unable to provide. I am not the sort of person who loses her temper with waitresses; I'm shocked at myself and I apologize. "I've had a very hard day," I say. She nods, not looking at me and tells me the daily specials. Swordfish. Baby quail.

The next day I am able to turn up nothing but a death notice for Rose. She died in 1959, two years after my father. Her death is marked by three lines in the *Plain Dealer*. Sister of Hattie. Date of death. Place of burial.

So I suppose Rose never married and had no children. That is something known. But not much.

I have come to the end of the archival material in Ohio that could supply facts about my family. No, that's not it: I've come to the end of what I can bear to do. I could search out birth certificates and wills, but I've lost energy and faith. Information has brought only disappointment, loss.

I turn to the local history of Cleveland. At the library I pull from the shelf a book of photographs of Cleveland in the twenties, the years my father lived there. It is, in those years, the *locus* of American success, the town of John D. Rockefeller. The mansions of Euclid Avenue—Millionaires' Row—are the envy of the world. It is the center of the American auto industry. By 1920, 70 percent of the population is immigrant. And there is little or no ethnic conflict; in this time of prosperity, there's enough room for everyone to be himself. Anti-Semitism seems not to be a large issue, at least not the kind coming from the native population. The biggest problems occur between the more recently arrived Eastern European Jews and the more established German Jews, who are terrified that the new immigrants, in their poverty and disorder, will blacken their hard-won image of respectability, gentility, achievement, their ability not to stand out, not to make problems or a fuss.

Where is my father in all this? Walking in the bustling downtown to his jobs as a salesman, clerk, advertising man? Where is my father in this city where the machines pump, bang, turn out products at a dizzying speed, putting money, endless money, into the open hand of John D. Rockefeller? Is my father, too, dizzy with activity, dizzy with the promise of success?

I look at a picture of Public Square where he once had an office. I imagine him walking there, on top of the world, full of hope. What can stop him? He has lost his accent. He has read many books. He has found a prose style that has both dash and cultivation. His photograph is taken by Bachrach of Cleveland. What can hold him back?

But in fact he lives not in the smart section of Cleveland but in Glenville, the Jewish section, and moves uptown only gradually, until he is on the border of the still Jewish but more prosperous Cleveland Heights. I look at pictures of Glenville. I see Orthodox men in stores with Hebrew lettering, old men sitting on barrels. Many synagogues, women in black kerchiefs, the thick web of the old country still intact in the prosperous American twenties. My father is the dashing young bachelor in his downtown office, but at night he comes home to his mother and sisters, who cook him kosher meals in Glenville.

And then what? He marries a Protestant. He leaves Glenville for her neighborhood, the neighborhood of her people. He divorces. He moves back to Glenville, then to Cleveland Heights. The Depression comes. He leaves Cleveland. He goes to New York. His mother becomes one of the poor.

And I can do nothing to fill in the blanks. I have a picture of Bessie, but no faces to go with the names Joseph, Hattie, Dorothy, Rose. No faces. Only facts. Demographies. Photographs of streets and stores, in which I have no way of placing my family. No way to form a whole.

That night, when I return to my room at the Glidden House and call my family, I learn that a friend of mine has committed suicide. Death enters in a new form. A violent one.

The bereftness of this man's son and his wife, my friends, friends of my children, blots out my own bereftness. The darkness of death ceases to be monochrome. My father inhabits one area, but he is accompanied by me; my grandmother is near him. In a room without illumination are Joseph, Hattie, Dorothy, Rose. But in another place, not a room at all, nothing so tender as a dwelling, my friend the suicide sits upright, his eyes open with the shock of his own act. He is consigned to the blasted, bombed-out site that is the abode of those who died by violence, not abandoned or forgotten but appalled.

And so, I ask myself, what does it matter who they were, what the details were? All of them—my father, mourned and beloved, my unmourned relatives, my friend the suicide—all are among the dead. Life is over for all of them. We will not have them back. Whatever I learn about my father, I will not see his face or hear his voice or feel his hand taking mine, as I often pretend to, stretching my hand out in the darkness.

We have lost our dead. They are no longer ours.

The shocking news of my friend's death makes me torpid, and I can't look at any of the material I've xeroxed and brought back to my room. But Arlene Rich, the genealogist, is not a victim of torpor. All day she has been telephoning in my behalf. I have many messages from her. She locates the niece of someone I thought was my father's cousin, Sam Zieve, the man who wrote to my father's friend Eddie, "I knew Dave had a daughter." The man I never wrote back to, ensuring the darkness would hold sway. This woman, also named Arlene, remembers my father, but she doesn't seem interested in him or me. She was bothered by his anti-Semitism, she says; the family didn't want him around the house. I can't seem to jog her memory to give me any details.

"So you're a writer," she says. "Could you tell me how someone would go about getting an agent?"

I can't bring myself to go back to the Case Western Reserve library. I go instead to the Art Institute and look at the Asian collection. I am looking, for consolation, at the impassive, merciful Buddhas, who have seen everything and are disturbed by nothing. Who have no interest in details. I pack and take a cab to the airport. I've done it. It's over. The fact that I don't know what "it" is will be the thing that I will have to work to understand.

When I get home, there is a message from the amazingly energetic Arlene Rich waiting for me. Following a lead from Ron Gordon, she's discovered a very old man in Cleveland who is related to the Lorain Gordons by marriage. He's still working at his business: aluminum siding and storm doors. He remembers my father; he's willing to talk to me.

"Your father was a *meshuggener*," he says. "A Communist and an anti-Semite. You can convert, nobody says you can't convert. But you don't have to be nasty about it. He was nasty about it."

He was married to a sister of Ben Gordon, a Lorain boy of my father's cohort, who became a successful Cleveland lawyer, representing RKO when Cleveland was a movie center. "Ben Gordon threw your father right out of the house when he came to Cleveland," he says. "We didn't need anyone like him around. The Gordons were scholars. Philanthropists. They were in every Jewish philanthropic thing going. What did they need that *meshuggener* for? They threw him right out on the street."

As calmly as I can, I ask what year this was.

"The forties. I married my wife in 1938. You know, I

could have married her in thirty-six, but I didn't have the money."

I feel as if I'm talking to Mel Brooks's two-thousand-year-old man. He is garbling information. But the information he's garbling is horrifying and crucial to me. Once again, I am simultaneously on my father's side and on the side of his enemies. I can't like anyone who would throw my father out of the house. At the same time, I can perfectly well understand why they would do it.

"I think I remember your grandfather," he says. "He was skinny, with a beard."

But the next day, Arlene Rich calls to tell me she's found my grandfather's will. He died in 1927. My father was the executor. I call the two-thousand-year-old man and ask if he could have known my grandfather before 1927. "No," he says, "I didn't meet any of the Gordons until 1936. I told you, I could have married my wife right then, the minute I met her, but I didn't have the money." When I tell him my grandfather died in 1927, he says, "Well, I couldn't have met him. I must have been thinking of someone else."

So the figure of the bearded grandfather, stooped, thin, alone, has to be erased. As does the two-thousand-year-old man's credibility. My father was never a Communist, I'm certain of that. My grandfather was dead ten years before the old man claimed to have seen him.

Was my father really thrown out of the house by his cousin Ben? Or is this yet another new father I must meet now, the father of other people's fables, the character created by people who hardly knew him, but for whom he served as a bogey, a *meshuggener*, someone to be warned against and kept away from.

"Your father didn't do well for himself," the two-thousand-year-old man says to me. "But you seem like a girl who did well for herself."

I would like to beg him not to say that. When he says it I want to say, "Everything I am is because of my father. I couldn't be who I am if not for him."

But I can't because he thinks my father was a *me-shuggener*. A *shandah*. A blot on the shining surface of the Gordon name.

Arlene Rich finds a death notice for my aunt Dorothy. She died in 1914, at the age of sixteen, of scarlet fever. A sealed history, the end of which I can contemplate with sadness, but without shame. The dead young girl. The one who made her way out of the family intact.

Arlene tells me that one thing she found in my grandfather's will gave her pause. She says that my aunt Rose's address is listed as Massillon, Ohio. Massillon, Arlene tells me, is the location of the state mental hospital.

She's phoned ahead and got the names of the medical directors. They won't give her any information. They need to speak to me, the next of kin.

How can I be next of kin, how can I have any authority over anything having to do with someone whose existence I learned of only a month ago? Someone whose face I can't even begin to imagine? What is this claim I seem to be able to exercise?

I press the claim. And in doing this, I become someone I don't know: Rose Gordon's niece. I can't imagine what that might mean.

But I say the words to the medical director. My own name and then, "I am Rose Gordon's niece." She comes back with information. Rose Gordon, sister of David and Hattie, daughter of Bessie and Joseph, was admitted to Massillon State Hospital in 1922. She was transferred to Cleveland State Hospital in 1946. There is no other record, no diagnosis, nothing to indicate why she was transferred. That kind of record, they tell me, is destroyed after ten years.

When I call the former Cleveland State Hospital, they tell me the same thing. They have no diagnosis, only a record of admission. Rose Gordon was admitted in 1946 and died there in 1959.

I hang up the phone and go into my bedroom. I close the shutters. The room is completely dark. I get into bed and cover my head with the sheet, blanket, and quilt.

I am trying to call up a face. I am trying to call up a face I can comfort. A face to whom reparation can be made. But I have nothing to go on. I can call up only a thin body in a gray overwashed dress, shoes without laces, blue or tallow-colored legs. The figure is wringing its hands, is gibbering, is moaning, rages, is restrained, is put in a straitjacket. Then is silent. Gives in. Goes on for thirty-five years. The hair that was dark in 1922 becomes gray and frizzled. The shoulders bow, the ankles thicken and grow mottled, the shanks wither, the hands twist into claws.

I am the next of kin.

And with the current emphasis on genetics, the question of kinship takes on new meaning. I must ask myself the obvious question: Does this new information about a mad aunt raise fears in me about my own potential madness? And I have to answer: It does not. I never thought myself susceptible to madness, probably because of a kind of peasant toughness I have inherited from my mother. But also because of a combination of appetite and distractibility that is my father's gift. This has sometimes led me to fear that I am perhaps not imaginative enough, not free enough to go mad. A workhorse kept to the plow. I thought this in the mid-sixties, when I was trying to write poetry like Sylvia Plath's.

So I don't fear my own madness. The bad seed, the tainted blood. Rather, Rose's fate makes more real to me the possibility of my father's madness. It makes me go back to look at his face in the photographs. Of course there is madness there; it stares at me. As does the sense of his growing up in an unstable place: a hospitalized sister, a missing father, a mother left to live among the poor. What it gives me is a sense that the blood in my veins is full of a history of bad luck, a series of misfortunes, but that my father's love for me was the filter that changed it from a deadly poison to something merely weakening, something that slowed me down, did not drive me mad. Rose inspires in me neither identification nor fear but an immense pity. A sense of what was lost in the trip across the ocean. Of the demands of the bustle and hum of America that crushed the more fragile ones, like my poor aunt Rose, who found herself a job for a while in the Cleveland Public Library, perhaps looking for refuge in books, as my father did, as he would teach me to do.

But because I have neither photographs of her nor stories about her, I mourn Rose not as herself, an individual, but as a type, as representing something. I cannot pretend to know, her. Rather, I feel the responsibility to bear witness to the loss, the wreckage inflicted by the remorseless engine of boomtime America. Not only the boom of the drum that set the pace for the parade to prosperity, but the boom of the American cannon that annihilated flesh and bone. To bear witness to the darkness that, for Rose, for many others, became the only refuge. The place to hide the shameful wreckage from shining America.

To keep it out of sight.

What happened, my aunt Rose? Were you one of those unmarried women who was locked up for being too eccentric? Did you wear the wrong hats, talk too loud or to yourself, refuse to go to parties? Or did you try to harm yourself or kill your mother or set the house on fire? What did you do to be consigned to a darkness, a darkness I can't save you from because I can't call up your face? Why couldn't my father save you? Or your own father and mother, or your sister Hattie, or anyone else in the bustling, prosperous city of Cleveland?

Why were you left to die alone, a death it took thirty-five years to accomplish?

Did you hear voices? What were they saying? Were they the same voices my father heard? Is this the secret, the explanation for his life: that he had to live as he did, create this fantastic carapace, to keep out the voices that stole your life?

I would like to pray to you or for you. But I don't know to what face I would make such a prayer.

I close my eyes and pray into the darkness. To a darkness without a face.

Forgive us all.

Protect us.

I hear from Arlene Rich almost daily. I look forward to her calls; I have come to depend on them. When I come home and play back the messages on the answering machine, I'm very disappointed if there's none from her.

She's been unbelievably generous, avid, intelligent, in her activities. But she keeps hitting blank walls. We agree that my family was unusual in the extent to which it failed to make connections, leave a mark.

But by tireless calling and checking, Arlene finds two Cleveland lawyers, A. B. Glickman and Chester Gordon, who are related to the Lorain Gordons. A. B. Glickman is the grandson of Edith Gordon, sister of Benjamin, who did or did not throw my father out of the house. He is a partner in the law firm Benjamin started.

He looks for information in the firm's extensive files, and another piece of good luck comes my way. He finds the files of Hattie Gordon. He tells me that she died an incompetent in a nursing home. His father was her legal guardian. Among her few effects, removed by his father from her room in the nursing home after her death, are several pictures of me, spanning the years from my babyhood to age five, with notes on the back from my father. He tells me as well about two letters his father, in his capacity as Hattie's lawyer, wrote to my mother in 1966, the year of Hattie's death. The letters name me as heir to her estate of $3,600, since I am the only surviving relative and she died without a will. The firm tried to find my mother, but they were looking for an Anne Gordon in Manhattan. Certified letters were sent to every Anne Gordon in the Manhattan directory. But we weren't living in Manhattan; we were living on Long Island. My father must have given Hattie only his business address, one of those temporary offices he rented from time to time in midtown. He must have kept his wife and child's home address from her. In case she would try to get in touch? Did he feel unable to trust her discretion? Had he let her know that he had told his wife and daughter he was an only child, and she mustn't blow his cover? Was he afraid that in a moment of weakness, of a desire for kinship, she would try to find me? Was he trying to keep me from her or her from me? And why?

Whatever his reason, he succeeded. The letters never reached me. But if they had, I would have had to give the money back, because later a will was found in Meyer Gordon's office in Lorain. Hattie left her money to "The Golden Agers at the Jewish Old Home."

So I was not her heir after all. The Golden Agers were.

I try to imagine what it would have meant to me in 1966, as I was preparing to go to college, to have discovered (even if it was a discovery I'd have to give up) that I was my aunt's heir. It would have created a huge storm that would have blown open the door on all the life my father had so carefully sealed off. The family he said had sat shiva for him and declared him dead. Once again, I try to remember how I learned this, and I can't. Once again, it's something I seem always to have known. But it isn't true. He and his sister were in communication. She died in a room with pictures of me that he had sent.

Why didn't she get in touch with me? Was she obeying her brother? Was her failure to connect with me proof of her loyalty to him, her understanding that he couldn't have his wife and daughter know about his past? Or was her silence a sign of her own fear and shame?

A. B. Glickman sends me the xeroxes of Hattie's files. My father's notes on the backs of the photographs are all intimate and informal, in the handwriting I love: "From Mary Catherine Gordon, age 8 months, to her Aunt Hattie, with love. Hattie: she looks like her grandmother, our mother. Dave." "To Aunt Hattie with love from Mary Gordon, October 1952. Excuse the lollipop."

There is a copy of my parents' 1953 Christmas card, with a picture of me and Santa Claus and a printed message: "David, Anne and Mary Gordon wish you the blessings of the season promised to those who inerrantly believe."

I want to shout at my father: What were you doing, sending your sister a card like that? It names her as one of the excluded, one of the denied. And what were you doing using the word "inerrantly" on a Christmas card? Was sending her that card an act of carelessness, or cruelty, or madness? Or did you simply like the picture of me and Santa so much it was all you saw?

But when I turn over the last two pictures in the pile my anger disappears. One picture is dated January 1953; I am standing beside my doll and her carriage. My father has written on the back: "To Aunt Hattie and Aunt Rose from Mary, who loves you." I imagine Rose in her colorless dress, in her shoes without laces, holding this picture in her hands. I am grateful to my father for lying about my love. Or perhaps he did once ask me to say, "I love Aunt Hattie and Aunt Rose," and I have simply forgotten.

The last picture in the pile is a baby picture. I am sitting up in my parents' bed, on a spread I can still remember: a rose-colored brocade whose differences in texture—the alternating smooth and rough—were a constantly renewable source of tactile satisfaction and surprise. On the back of the picture my father has written: "To the Aunt Rose I do not yet know but will ever love. Mary Catherine Gordon, age 8 months, August 1950."

I weep for Rose's pain, for my father's having to live with a buried sister in his heart, live with his worry for her, his shame for her. And what else: his hope that she and I will meet, embrace, cover each other with healing kisses and pledges of constant love? My father, the brother who offers his lost sister a gesture of impossible hope.

And what could the picture, the words, have meant to Rose? Did she sit in the hospital, holding my picture? Did it matter, was there enough left of her so that it mattered, the false pledge of eternal love?

Aunt Hattie and Aunt Rose. They knew of me, thought of me, had images of me. But I had nothing of them. Because of *him*. And because I don't know what they were really like, I have no way of knowing whether he did it from kindness, a desire to protect me. And I have no way of knowing what it was he wanted to protect me from. Or if it was himself he was trying to protect. Or them.

· · ·

The picture I have of Hattie in the copy of her naturalization certificate included in her file does not, I must admit, draw me to her. She's far from beautiful; she has her mother's wide face and broad nose, but her expression has none of Bessie's sweetness. Her eyes are ringed with dark circles. The corners of her mouth are deeply turned down. It is the face of disappointment. Chances never taken, opportunities not presented or passed up. There is no joy or liveliness in that face, no trace of humor or appetite. Did my father steal all that from his sisters? In order to give it to me? Am I not the lawful heir but the daughter of the family embezzler?

Hattie's picture doesn't make her seem to be someone I would have been proud to know. Even her signature is childish and unlovely. Unlike my father's, of which I am always so proud.

Then I think: She was naturalized in 1938. Was she afraid of a Nazi victory? That they would come to America and hunt down foreign Jews? Did she think that if she could name herself a real American she'd have less chance of being put to death?

She looks like a woman who knows she has no possibility of being singled out for special protection. Who has never been singled out. A worker. No one's ornament. No one's prize.

At the time of the photograph, her mother, her father, and one sister are dead. Her four-year marriage, to someone named Herman Bohn, a dry cleaner, has ended in divorce. Her sister has been shut up for seventeen years.

And where is her brother?

Nowhere that will do her any good. Nowhere from which he could be called upon to help. A *meshuggener*. A betrayer. Perhaps you would pretend to the cousins that you had lost touch with him, so as not to forfeit at least that little place.

So perhaps the ruse was mutual. Perhaps both my father and Hattie agreed to keep their contact secret, out of fear of what could be lost.

The other Cleveland lawyer contacted by Arlene Rich, Chester Gordon, who may be a cousin, phones to tell me he remembers having seen Hattie when he was still a child. His family, too, is from Vilna, via Lorain. He says he remembers Hattie from the early forties, when he was a child. She would visit a cousin of his mother's named Yetta Barker, who lived across the street. Yetta Barker was known for her kindness.

Chester says that when the children heard Hattie was coming they would hide. He says she had frightening hair, the kind of hair that alarms children. His ability to say this sentence makes me like him very much. Most adults forget that there is a kind of hair, that is to say, a category of hair, that frightens children. He says her hair was wild, obviously bleached blond. Wrong-looking. Out of control. And she behaved like a kind of "dizzy blonde," in a way that made the children want to hide, and the adults let them do it because they, too, knew she was strange. Something to keep the children from. As if the sight of her could bring a kind of danger, a suggestion that the world might not be as their parents said.

But I look at Hattie in her naturalization picture and I can't imagine that woman being a dizzy blonde. The severe bun, the harsh, rimless glasses, the sour, downturned mouth. There is a gap, and I have no way of knowing whether the gap is the result of a great transformation taken on, undergone by Hattie, a misremembering on Chester's part, or simply a misleading photograph taken by a bureaucrat recording a moment of anxiety and stress: becoming an American.

I am constantly being presented with information that takes away more than it gives.

Chester is coming East for his son's graduation from Brown. I invite him and his wife and a second son to dinner. The son who is coming to dinner is named David Gordon. He is twenty-six, and was born with Down's syndrome.

I'm not usually comfortable with Down's people, but David Gordon immediately wins my heart. He radiates an extraordinary joy and interest in the world. He is playing basketball with my son, David. My David, who is ten, lets him win, as if he were a younger child. There is something terrible and wonderful about the beautiful, whole child, playing with the earnest, damaged one. Both of them bearing my father's name.

David's mother, Stephanie, tells me that David's particular kind of Down's syndrome is described as a "mosaic." There are certain areas in which he is not deficient but is actually in possession of superior knowledge. An uneven savantism, alongside areas of retardation. David's two fields of expertise are opera and Greek mythology. He is delighted when I produce a board game called By Jove, a game based on Greek mythology, which I too optimistically bought as an educative tool, and which my children have rarely played. David Gordon beats my David, David Gordon Cash, hands down.

If I had invented a family for myself, it couldn't have been better than the Chester Gordons. Chester, whose mother died when he was young, went to Harvard, worked in Kennedy's campaign in Cleveland, defended civil rights activists, is involved in Democratic politics, and raises orchids. His wife is Croatian, born a Catholic. She converted to Judaism after twenty years of marriage: the end of a long spiritual journey, she says. She's devoted her career to studying learning disabilities, about which she speaks with eloquence.

We are happy doing the dishes in the kitchen, as if we'd been doing them together after holidays for years.

I tell Chester and Stephanie all the details of my father's story I've been able to discover: the lie of the origin, the early death of one sister, the madness of the other, the missing father living apart from the family, the mother in the charity home, my being listed as heir and next of kin to people I'd never met.

"Gee," says David Gordon. "It sounds like a Greek myth."

Everyone at the table laughs and he basks in the glory of an archer who has perfectly hit the mark. He claps for himself. We all clap, with and for him.

Arlene Rich calls to tell me that she's found the Gordon connection with Lorain. It's not through the male Gordons, Meyer's line, but through the female Gordons, a Sadie Gordon who married an Abraham Gordon; they became the parents of Benjamin. Gordon, I've discovered, is not a name changed at Ellis Island; it has been a native Lithuanian Jewish name for three hundred years. Some people think it goes back to a Scottish merchant who moved to Vilna, married a Jew, and started a dynasty. Sadie Gordon's obituary of 1922 mentions a brother, Joseph, living in Lorain. Why wasn't he in Cleveland with his wife and family? Arlene searches Sadie Gordon Gordon's tombstone to see if she and Joseph had the same father, Israel, whose name I knew from my grandfather's death certificate. The tombstone inscription is full of errors. Sadie is referred to as "he" and their father's name is spelled "Asrael." So even what is literally carved in stone is not dependable. That's the end, Arlene says, there's nothing more to find.

But little bits of information dribble in. A copy of my father's school transcript, an undistinguished one, ending in tenth grade. My father's draft record: he was exempt from

World War I because he was the sole support of his parents. But where was his father, and why, at the age of fifty-seven, did he need support? I get Rose's death certificate: the cause of death is listed as coronary thrombosis, but secondary causes are "schizophrenia of the paranoid type."

A group that specializes in searching passport files determines that my father never had a passport. So all the stories about his walking among the dreamy spires of Oxford and sitting in cafés on the Left Bank are also lies. I had placed my father in Europe, and in doing that, I could place myself there. What would it have done to my imagination of myself if I had known that Europe was not a place my father had gone before me? If I had known he never went to Europe?

No, that's wrong: he never went back. Back to the place I didn't know he came from before my hours of undigging the bones he'd buried so thoroughly, so imaginatively, for so long.

What was I doing digging in the archives? What was I looking for, and was my search in any way an act of love? Was it a vengeful act, like the uncovering of Noah by his drunken sons? Only worse, because it was done deliberately, scientifically? If I had loved my father above all things, would I have turned detective?

As I use the word "detective" to describe myself, I think of a poem by the Russian Marina Tsvetayeva, a passionate cry, not about the loss of a father but about the loss of a lover. No matter: it is about all and any of our dead.

> There are blanks in memory . . . All is a
> whiteness. (My spirit is one
> uninterrupted wound) . . . You
> are unique. And love is no detective.

> Let some neighbor say whether your
> hair is black or fair, for he can tell.
> I leave that to physicians or watchmakers.
> What passion has a use for such details?
>
> You are a full unbroken circle, a
> whirlwind, or wholly turned to stone.
> I cannot think of you apart from
> love.

"You are unique and love is no detective. . . . All is a whiteness."

I couldn't live that way. I couldn't create a poetry of blanks. I couldn't endure the incoherence, the torture of not knowing what had once been where the blanks were. If I had been acting only from love, if I had been willing to enter with my father into the whiteness of passionate love, love without question, love beyond understanding, if I could not think of him apart from love, perhaps I would have been able to bend the knee to erasure, erosion, illegibility. To accept a fragmentation, such as I have seen on the walls of cloisters in Italy, where they hang next to each other a Roman funereal inscription, the partial face of a saint, the pediment of a column, the toe of a hero's foot. Perhaps I could have devoted myself to the heartbreaking beauty of the broken, the caesura, the silence that will not yield. But that wasn't enough for me. I was tortured by the emptiness between things, the failure of things to join up.

I experienced a loss of faith in my father, a loss of hope in the sufficiency of our love. Perhaps this wouldn't have happened if my father had been someone I could love because of his writing, not in spite of it. If he had been someone whose writing didn't call for exculpation, a need for someone to blame or to excuse.

Is that who I was looking for in the archives? Is that why

I turned detective: to get my father off the hook? To present the evidence of innocence so that the verdict of guilty, also rendered by me, could be revoked?

The detective who is also the judge is in an impossible position.

The detective in love with her client usually ends up murdering or murdered.

Both have happened to me. I am both the perpetrator and the victim of a crime. I would have avoided both if I could. But I can't, because I am no longer capable of that love that silences questions with a kiss or a sigh.

A crime had been committed. I was looking for evidence.

But I went to a place where I was not the only one. I entered rooms that buzzed like hives, throbbed with the drone of workers collecting the honey of what could be learned. The swarm of a desire to know the past, a past that was theirs, theirs only. Almost a mania now in close-to-the-millennium America; two thousand genealogical journals were published in 1994. All races, all classes, on the trail, dreaming of who-knows-what. In rooms brimming with records, rooms ornate through the generosity of plutocrats, or governmentally plain, rooms rising above the ground with the encoded yearning of their information and the fission fuel of searching, recognition, and lost hope, rooms unlike any in all the other libraries I worked in: democratic, practical, and yet fantastical as any room in Borges, shimmering with the blue light of expectation, fogged by the dank smoke of failure to connect.

Who are all these people, and how could I be one of them? What are they looking for? What is the evidence they need? Are they trying to find lost kin, or details of a family once prominent, now temporarily fallen from grace? Or maybe someone with money, the money that can change their lives?

I told myself I wasn't like them, these men with Ban-Lon shirts tucked into their pants, these women with big hair, wearing sweatsuits and too-new sneakers or polyester dresses and big heels of a too-vivid color. I wasn't looking for family, or money. Or if I was looking for family, it was only to find out about my father. I didn't want to add more family to my life—my life was overfull; I didn't want anything from kin but information about my father. If there were others connected to my father by blood, that would only dilute the purity of my connection. I would be contacting them against my will, because there was no choice; there would be no joy in it, no tearful hugs and greetings, no sense of relief or rest.

And I wasn't like them in the way I went about finding information. I wasn't just anyone walking in off the street. None of that amateurish questioning for me. None of that apologetic, provincial, kittenish or bearish joking with librarians and clerks. I knew what to do. I'd been told by professionals. Academic historians. My colleagues. My friends. Those other people had no connections. I was privileged; I had experts on my side.

But I have had to learn that these distinctions are only minor shadings. I have had to understand that all of us are doing the same thing. We are all trying to find a past that belongs to us. To assure ourselves that we are not alone. Thinking we can shed light on the darkness that was the world before our birth, that will be the world after our death. Perhaps that is what is unbearable to all of us, in all the libraries and archives, sifting through census records, manifests, wills, birth certificates, marriage records. What is unbearable is that the world went on before our births. Perhaps that is the crime we are on the trail of.

Or perhaps it is not a crime at all. Perhaps it's a new land we're after. Perhaps we are all Columbus looking for a new world that we call the past. A world that has always been waiting for us, waiting only for our acknowledgment of it to come alive. Americans dreaming of America. Looking for the face of America, made in our image and likeness.

We are, of course, looking for stories of success. We aren't looking for Hattie or Rose, or a father who didn't go to Harvard. We're looking for people whose prosperity makes failure seem an aberration, an easily correctable error, a recoverable slip. We want the log of a voyage with a happy ending. The story we don't want to hear is the story of disintegration, diminishment, humiliation, loss. This is the America that we cannot imagine. And may, despite the evidence, refuse to see.

All of us in the archives are acknowledging the insufficiency of memory. The falseness of the myth of continuity. The loss of living speech. Our own inability to live with the blanks. To live in the enveloping whiteness of imagination and of love.

Do we think that facts can make up for all this? Did I?

I no longer remember why I was looking or what I thought I'd find.

IV

SEEING PAST

THE

EVIDENCE

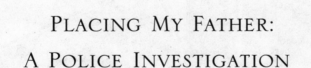

PLACING MY FATHER:
A POLICE INVESTIGATION

TELLING STORIES TO MY FATHER

EZRA POUND

HENRY ROTH

H.L.
MENCKEN

BERNARD BERENSON

PLACING MY FATHER:

A POLICE INVESTIGATION

I

SCRAPS OF EVIDENCE

Those were·the stories he prized above all others, stories he loved: of enchantment and delicacy, of princelings and fair princesses. So often the princesses were not only fair, but they were the fairest in Christendom. You couldn't help that. Maybe they wouldn't mind if he was Jewish. And King Arthur's knights, they sought the Holy Grail, the radiant vessel like a loving cup out of which Jesus had drunk wine. So everything beautiful was Christian, wasn't it? All that was flawless and pure and bold and courtly and chivalric was goyish.

—Henry Roth
MERCY OF A RUDE STREAM

Jews . . . as commonly encountered, lack many of the qualities that mark the civilized man: courage, dignity, incorruptibility, ease, confidence. They have vanity without pride, voluptuousness without taste, and learning without wisdom. Their fortitude, such as it is, is wasted upon puerile objects, and their charity is mainly only a form of display.

—H. L. Mencken
TREATISE ON THE GODS

By study of Jewish institutions and literature . . . we shall
begin to understand the puzzling character of the Jews; begin
to understand, I say, for comprehend them we never shall.
Their character and their interests are too vitally opposed to
ours to permit the existence of that intelligent sympathy between us and them which is necessary for comprehension.

—Bernard Berenson

"CONTEMPORARY JEWISH FICTION"
THE ANDOVER REVIEW, DECEMBER 1889

The kike . . . has herded the Slavs, the Mongols, the Tar-
tars openly against Germany and Poland and Finland. And
secretly against all that is decent in America, against the total
American heritage. This is my war all right. I've been in it for
twenty years—my grandad was in it before me.

—Ezra Pound

BROADCAST ON ITALIAN RADIO, MAY 5, 1942

II

THE FACTS OF THE CASE

My father was a Jew.
My father was not born in America.

My father was a Jew who hated Jews.
My father was a Jew who became a Catholic.

My father was a Jew who dreamed of a Europe that would
always have excluded him.
My father never went to Europe. No, I keep forgetting. He
was born in Europe. What I mean is: he never went back.

. . .

My father is dead.
My father is a dead Jew, like the six million Jews killed in Europe, by European hands.

My father was not a citizen of the United States.
My father was American.

I was born American and baptized Catholic.
I am, in some sense, a Jew.

My father is dead.

I am trying to understand these things.

III

PROCEDURE

I am trying to understand my father. I have come to the end of memory, the end of information, of what can be learned from the record. What can be surmised from what he wrote, and what can be gleaned from all the facts in all the documents.

I am trying to explain the behavior of a ghost. I am trying to get answers from a shadow. I am trying to understand a skeleton. I am trying to make a context for dead bones.

I have used the language and the methods of several professions: scholar, critic, historian, detective. None of them give me what I want: an explicable villain.

I will not allow my father to be the villain of his own life.

I will create a face, a stranger's face, a villain's face, from a multiplicity of features. A nose here, an eyebrow there. This will be my final methodology. The last profession I will enter in his service. I will become a police artist, presenting an invented face to the witness, who saw only a fleeting glimpse of the running criminal, and that in the dark. A police artist. That's it, that's the next step for me. A police artist. Inventing a criminal from incoherent features.

And what is the nature of the crime? Murder, of course. The crime of murdering the father I could, without difficulty, love.

IV

TO CATCH THE CRIMINAL, I DECIDE TO IMPERSONATE MY FATHER

Before I begin, I have to do one last thing. I must become my father. I must, finally, begin to understand what it is to be a Jew.

"You must realize," says a Hungarian woman, a historian of the Holocaust, "that for most Jews throughout the history of the world it was impossible to be a Jew."

I must become that impossibility, the Jew, my father. I must hear what he heard: a buzz, a hum, accusing and tormenting.

Then the escape from that, transport to sublimity. Now I must be with him in torment and in transport, not beside him, but absorbed into him.

I will become a filament, an X ray, the negative of a photograph, the chalk outline on the sidewalk after the dead body has been removed. I am knife-thin, or iridescent, or composed entirely of shadows. Ready above all for absorption and interiority. Incorporeal, waiting only for embodiment. And yet every cell is shot through with intelligence, every atom supersensible with understanding. The surplus allows me to say the word "I" and know it is applicable to two beings. Or perhaps three. My mind. The ghost I have become. My father.

I can easily walk where he walks. But I cannot allow my mind to be swallowed up in him. His body pleases me. The body of the beautiful young man in the photograph. The young man in the pinstripe suit, the vest, the watch chain, the strong chest I can lay my head on, any time, for comfort. But I am frightened of his mind. A breeding ground, a place of seething.

If I see what he saw, hear what he said, reduce myself to a ghostly outline tracing the outline of his body, can I keep my own brain, sound and white, not seething, not fevered?

Can I understand my father without becoming him?

Can I understand my father without losing myself?

Can I say "I" and be speaking not of myself but of my father?

Can I say "I am David Gordon," or are these words I cannot say without knowing that I am mad?

I will do it.

I will take what I have learned of his life from hints, memories, documents, photographs. The unlucky sister and the mad one. The picture of my grandmother, the lies about her, her sad end. Then, the shadowy grandfather. There are no stories of him, no photographs; the documents are full of empty spaces. So I will make things up. I will make up a tyrant father for my father. The age was full of them. The monster in the house.

I will speak as my father spoke.
I will become my father.

V

I AM MY FATHER

*I am a boy in Vilna, Lithuania, or Poland, or the Kingdom of
Russia. The new century has not yet started.*

*A figure trails me. Stalking, shadowing, hissing or insistent,
offering me drinks in poisonous bars, telling me to sit down, rest
on dust-filled, worm-ridden couches when I am exhausted, offering me infested clothing when I am freezing, proffering ban-
dages filled with pestilence when my skin is flayed.*

*Sit here, drink this, put this on, and then this. Now listen to
me. I will tell you who you are. "The Jew," he says, but he can
hardly say the words because of the disgust they cause to rise up
in him. "The Jew." "The Jew." Yet he seems to need to repeat the
words "The Jew," turning the J into a sibilant grown pointed,
then spreading, from contempt.*

*I cannot refuse this stalker. He always knows when I will be
susceptible. Then he approaches. The smile of understanding
softens his lips. His voice insinuates itself into a whisper I can
only think of as the voice of wisdom.*

*The tormentor hisses remarks to me in Yiddish. He has
learned my tongue in order to torment me. Or I overhear him
in Polish, in German, words I need to learn because of what
they lead to. Surely I can leave the tormentor behind in the flat
country of Lithuania, the dark country with its meager trees. I
am going to America. The hiss that says it has a right to my
death will not be audible in this new land. Here in Vilna, in the
Kingdom of Russia, I must always be looking over my shoulder*

*for men on horseback, or women who will tell their husbands I
am a danger to their children, whipping them up into a frenzy
to close their hands around my throat. I am afraid to pass a
church at night in the dark. I have heard that the ghosts of dead
goyim appear, to choke the life out of any Jewish child who has
the effrontery to appear on the streets of their habitation. My
head is down, my eyes are shielded. And in the house, my father says it is my fault. Everything is, and I believe him. He has
gone before us to America; perhaps when we arrive he won't be
there. I wish this and do not. I fear him, but without him we
would starve, because the world would prefer that we did not
live. There is no one but him—his bony hand, his thin beard,
the insults, endless—telling me I am the cause of every known
misfortune and those that cannot even be anticipated; only he
is between me and the world that calls out every moment for my
death.*

*In America, my father will not insult me. In America, he will
be forbidden to raise his hand. But by whom?*

In America, I will not be terrified.

*This is who I am: a child who is terrified. This is what shapes
my bones, the skinny legs my mother worries over. Terror. I am
a child who lives in terror. Because of the large fair man on the
horse, holding the whip that at any minute can come down on
my face.*

And because of my father.

*The man on horseback will not follow me to America. His
horse will be unable to approach the ocean, over which I will
sail. He will be unable to find me. On the shining streets of
America, I will disappear in a blaze of light that will burn his
vision and consume his eyes.*

*We land in Baltimore, Maryland. We are going to Ohio. A
word like a wail: a good place for a Jew. To arrive in the place
of mourning, of lament. No, it's not lament. Lament is not
known in America. It is the whoop, the war cry, of Red Indians,*

who will take me among them. I will live among Red Indians. I will become a warrior. Now I will ride horses, shoot arrows that in a whizzing moment will strike my enemies to the heart. The Red Indians will capture me under my father's eye. They will take my mother, my sisters; we will be allowed to stay together, but my father will be alone, unable to find us. He will believe it is my fault. But it is not my fault. It is the doing of the Red Indians.

We gather as Jews, in hiding. The place here in Ohio where we pray has no sign on the door, is a landmark for no one. Our congregation has a name that no one needs to know. In the darkness, in the house of the rabbi, whose wife speaks no English, in a dark tongue we do not even cry out. We beg and lament, rock back and forth, as if in torment. The swarming of our prayers is joyless and bereft of hope. On Sundays I pass the tall buildings with their signs, their legible names: Good Shepherd. Saint Mary's. First Presbyterian. I can hear the songs of light and power: "All is ours, we ask only for more."

And we, in the dark, nameless house whose location no one in Ohio, in this town, Lorain, can tell you, we kiss the grimy fringe of our old tallises, unfresh after the passage, we buzz in a low rumble like the working songs of insects: Spare us, protect us, do not take the little that we have.

On Sundays, girls leave churches with joy and hope. Clip, clip, their heels go on the streets. They take each other's arms; they walk behind their mothers. Their talk is full of hope. Each one of them is beautiful.

My sisters and my mother do not link arms and walk full of belief in progress. Their heads are down, their eyes are lowered. Their wide noses spread like misfortune over their dull faces; their unhappy mouths speak of a grievance they can not forget.

My father says that it is all my fault. How could I not believe him?

And the buzz inside my skull keeps saying, "You will never live without this torment. Everything you are is wrong."

Wrong, wrong, I am filled with my own wrongness. Yet I am clever; I can understand what is needed. Unlike my sisters, I can understand.

Walk quickly, keep your eyes ahead, miss nothing, learn the jokes, take a drink. Read books. Remember what is in them. Forget nothing. Move. Above all, don't drag your feet. Lift up your eyes. Keep moving. Do not partake of heaviness and darkness, all that you were born to. Keep moving. The sound of your shoes on the hard pavement, click, click, click, drowns out the buzz that names you "wrong."

Above all learn their language.

I walk into the library, looking for something that will drive out the buzzing noises that say, from the first moment of my wakefulness, "Remember, you are always wrong."

The ceilings are high; there are marble pillars. Once there was a time when all dwellings were like this. Once there was a time without darkness. Without the cramped, smoky houses of Lithuania, the packed rooms above the store where we live now in Ohio, all of us, crowding one another with reproaches, disappointments. Once there were no rooms like the rooms I have always lived in. Once there was a time without Jews.

The librarian likes me. She is a sad, pinched woman. Can she be born of the people who walk triumphantly out of the churches—Good Shepherd, Saint Mary's, First Presbyterian? Yes, because her eyes do not apologize or ask leave. She is not quite kind when she speaks to me, but I do not require kindness. Wonderful books she gives me. No, I will not say it like that— that use of words, that word order can give me away. I must remember always: the subject comes before the verb. I must avoid the telltale variation.

Perhaps she thinks that I am handsome. She likes me because she doesn't know what being a Jew really means: the opposite of everything in the beautiful books. She likes me because she hasn't seen my father. If she saw him, or even perhaps my mother and my sister Hattie, she would no longer like me.

When I tell her I must leave school to get a job, she looks disappointed. But she tells me I must not give up my reading: the library is open Saturday afternoon, when I don't have to work, when I don't have to sit next to ignorant boys, coarse men, who shove pieces of paper under my nose and call me slow, reminding me always that I am a Jew, so they hate me whether I am clever or stupid. It makes no difference to them: anything is a cause for hate. But it is worse than that. They don't know my value, my superiority. I am a boy who reads Matthew Arnold, reads Walter Pater. I am not the brother of my sisters, even my sister Rose, who comes to the library with me but is afraid of the librarian and reads only the books I get for her. Certainly not the brother of my sister Hattie, underbred, working in the knitting factory. I am (I must be forgiven for this) not the son of my mother, who wrings her hands in fear of what my father will say next. In fear that I will raise my voice against him (I will not, for I am weak). I am not the son of my father or my mother. I am not the brother of my sisters. I am a boy, reading.

Reading of a place and time finer than any of my people know. And yet this time makes a place for me. The open spaces of Rome, the dappled woods of the Middle Ages, the majestic palaces of the Renaissance. These are my habitation. Not the smoky rooms of Lithuania, the cramped rooms above the store. These are only the places where I have appeared to live. The rich words, the embroidered words, the words that jump with such speed, such entirely enviable velocity (I am slow, weighed down with Jewishness), these are my home.

My home is not Ohio. Ohio is a land of gods. Gods of two sorts: those who have won divinity by birth and those who have made themselves as gods. I watch them in longing and in desperation, also in contempt, because there is a darkness I know and they will never notice. How I swing back and forth; how I am tossed up and down on filthy waves in this leaky boat built up of adoration and contempt. Never, though, even in the mo-

ments when I suspect that I am better, do I give up my adoration, my knowledge that the areas in which I may surpass them are not the important ones. Then the buzz of hatred, of anger, of impossibility can make me drown.

All day I work, hearing the click, click of the telegraph, the insults of the other clerks. I dream of Europe. But I am not a European. I am an American boy, reading, dreaming, of Europe. The place of the Cossacks was not called Europe. It was the place where I was born, but I don't know its name. Perhaps: the Kingdom of Russia. Not the Europe I have found in the so beautiful, so hopeful books.

The place where I really live is a place that has not known darkness, lamentation, and upbraiding. A place without insult, where the buzzing voice is silenced, swallowed up, annihilated in the bright heat of the incandescent air.

My mother and my father and my sisters will always be Jews. I can see by their faces that there is nothing they can do about it. But things are not so fixed with me. In dreams I plan, over and over, my escape. One day to awake to a rich, saturating silence. One day to awake without reproach.

VI

I AM NO LONGER AN IMPERSONATOR.

I BECOME A WITNESS

I cannot bear to be my father. I sink down to my own identity: his daughter. My body takes its shape. The hum and buzz release me. Now I, the daughter of my father, see him in the distance. He is silent now. He has become a "he." That is to say, one of many.

He is dreaming of Europe. Boys all over America are dreaming this dream. Sometimes on farms, but more frequently in minor cities, in provincial houses, houses with large rooms full of family furniture, with many windows, with porches, with comfortable chairs, with kitchens as well equipped as laboratories, and as sterile and unfleshed. Boys dream in isolated towns, in mean houses with two or three small rooms. Boys in tenements are also dreaming, in hallways smelling of dinners of which they are ashamed. The air of the real Europe saturates these hallways, but this is not the Europe of their dreams. The Europe they have found in books and pictures does not smell.

Boys dream of Europe even in mansions when their mothers leave to go to Europe with their fathers. Boys dream this dream, and because of it they are rude to their mother. Or they treasure and protect their mother vow to take her with them. Take her away from the insufficient father, the father whose threatening voice causes the mother to put her hands up to her ears. The mother who plays the piano. The mother who would have liked to play the piano but never had the money or the time. The mother to whom the son makes vows—One day I will buy you a piano—as he sits in the kitchen, watching her work, knowing he can do nothing to help her. Speaking of his dream of Europe is, he thinks, a way of carrying her through the deep waters of her fatigue. Boys dream of Europe for dead mothers, who died without it. Boys dream of Europe to save careless or foolish mothers who don't understand that although their sons are in the house, they have left for good.

And yet all these boys are dreaming as Americans; they cannot dream as anything else. They are Americans who think they do not love their country, who would leave it if they could. But they don't leave, they only dream of leaving.

· · ·

Now I step back and see from a greater distance all these boys collecting (but they think they're alone), approaching a still point where they believe there is prepared for them a vision of such fineness, such unusual distinction, that no one they know (even their mothers) can even begin to discern its outlines. At the head of them I see a bald figure, a paunchy figure, leading the dreaming boys who think they do not love their country.

They are wearing the wrong suits, the wrong shoes; the bald man is not. But they, thank God, have not noticed the difference. They are looking for a solitude that is not lonely, a chaste beauty tested over time. They say it is not America they hate, not the real America, the old America, but that America is gone. It has been replaced by clamor and cheapness. The clamor and cheapness of machines, of money, the clamorous, cheap bodies of women, overlarge and thrusting, irresistible, refusing peace.

What can they do but fear the future? If they suspect that the Europe of their dreams is dried up now, unlike the overripe world they inhabit, that is all right. Dried up as well, if they could only be there, would be their fears and failures. There, they could dare to hope. To imagine a future permeated by the past like a dark sky after a hurricane. A future that is not made up of striving faces, grasping hands, taking and ruining what these boys believe is theirs, or could be. Slavs. Poles. Hungarians. Of course, Jews. Even if they are one of them they do not call themselves one of them, but an enemy to all those others who are.

They cannot live in America. But they don't have what it takes—money or courage—to live in Europe, as the short man with the bald head, the paunch, the beautifully cut suits has done. Follow me to a world of endless emendation, the bald man croons, rocking on his heels, nursing his

wounded hand. The mist rises on the meadow; the boys
swoon with yearning in their dream of Europe. My father is
among these boys, swooning and dreaming, begging someone—it cannot be God—for the one distinguished thing.

The meadow is split by a cleft. On the other side of the
cleft from the swooning boys, other boys run in all directions. They are crying the name America. The hands of man
are sacred, they cry out, and sacred are his works. Down
with the overfull rooms of Europe, the too-tame rivers, the
diminished trees. Down with the silences and lies and killing
pressure of decorum. Oh, our boyhood, our untainted boyhood. Only to be allowed to do as I please. Only not to be
silenced and hushed up.

Women open their arms to us, their haunches heavy with
longing. Truth is a silver fish moving, always moving, in the
waters of American forward progress. The future is ours, I
sing the body electric, they cry out, myself I sing. Striding
behind their leader with his hat, his streaming beard. Nothing to be afraid of. The future is limitless, is ours.

My father looks across the cleft, uncomfortable, suddenly, in his tight shoes. Jokes, drinks, the clip, clip of feet
on pavements, the refusal of distinctions, of judgments, all
these make him remember he is, after all, young and handsome, lively, and an animal, a male. The boys across the cleft
offer him daring, bustle, and the thrill of motion. But he is
afraid. Movement becomes clamor. Clamor is accusation.
He will be swallowed by the hordes; he will be mistaken for
one of them. Soon he will hear reproaches; reproach is always the tone underneath the clamor, the buzzing message:
"Everything about you, everything you do is wrong.

He will not even look across the cleft. I am not a democ-
rat, he whispers softly, placing himself beside the swooning
boys dreaming of Europe, a Europe that would never have
him, that he has made himself forget as origin and source.

My father walks out of the meadow to the marble building. He is light with feverish joy but his forehead is cool.
Words jump and dance but remain separate, do not swarm.
Sweetness and light, they say. A hard and gemlike flame. *Assisi. Provence. Languedoc, Toscana. Chartres.* Words rise up,
white and shining, images of iridescent ease, words that do
not accuse but absorb accusation. No need to fear, no need
to cringe or wait for the reproach. In the white silence
rimmed with green or gold, the dream of Europe, swallow-
ing loathsomeness and hatred, insult, terror, dread.

Until it starts again. The buzz and hiss. The torment.
"Everything you do is wrong."

VII

A Plan for Procedure

To explain this torment and its power, I remain a witness.
Then I become the police artist. Then the prosecutor. Then
the judge. And then the executioner.

I will compose a face, accuse it, try it, sentence it, and
then condemn. The outcome has never been in question.

VIII

Choosing the Features

But first: to choose the features. First: the work of the witness.

It is part of the situation of the witness to be presented
with more than she can use. To swim in the offscourings of

memory, perception, chance. To be overwhelmed by singu-
larities and the wish to cry out "I cannot possibly know. I
cannot possibly remember." Then to bask in the quick mystery of recognition. "That's the one. That mouth, those
eyes." A tone struck, of rightness. A ping, a click, then the
reverberation, waves spreading out, the YES.

I have always understood my task. I have been poring over
manifestations. Sitting at the desk of the detective, books
spread in front of me. Endless eyebrows, endless chins.
Looking for proof. Something I can point to that allows me
to press charges.

Now I am ready to present my selections to the police
artist. I have chosen four features:

the skull of Bernard Berenson
the mouth of H. L. Mencken
the hair of Ezra Pound
the eyes of Henry Roth

Rejected: the spectacles of T. S. Eliot, Kafka's outlandish
ears, the Americanized teeth of Meyer Shapiro, Bernard
Malamud's cap. They are, respectively, too Protestant, too
European, too recent in their historical sign.

I am looking for the face that stalked my father.

These choices are important, yet the reasons for my making them are, as every policeman knows, far too largely a
matter of chance.

I choose Mencken because I learn from the scholar of
American humor who had copies of *Hot Dog* that young
men like my father worshiped Mencken, modeled themselves on him. And when I read Mencken, I discover the
voice my father borrowed for his own.

I choose Berenson because I learn that, like my father, he
was born in Vilna, and that he lied on his Harvard applica-

tion, saying that his first language was not Yiddish but German; and because he stole my father's dream of Europe.

I choose Pound because one of the few books of my father's that I still have is a collection of the poems of Ezra Pound. And who can fail to think of Pound when they think of anti-Semitism?

I choose Henry Roth because in the middle of my search for my father he breaks a sixty-year silence, and I read his new books and know that I am hearing the curses, the insults, the castigations and self-castigations that my father heard. And I can hardly bear it.

Who are these men whose features prove them guilty?

They are Americans. And what they said proves they were carrying within them the poison that made my father a person I cannot easily love. A person driven to hateful speech. I accuse them of making my father what he was but might not have been. He could have been only the father who wrote me letters, the boy and then the man in love with writing. It is their fault he was not that, that he was more.

IX

THE LINEUP

The men stand side by side, facing forward.

Mencken's hair is plastered to his head. His shirt is rumpled; there are elastic braces around the sleeves. His pants are held up by suspenders. His eyes are tiny and his nose is a bulb on his fattish face. None of us dare tell him to put out his cigar.

Pound's red hair stands up like a furious brush. He will

not raise his eyes. He refuses to stand still. He paces back
and forth in the bright light, his hands behind his back.

Berenson, his beard a work of art, his skull a classic, leans
on his cane with its polished silver handle. He is tranquil,
and his eyes are calm.

Henry Roth, with the distinction of the still-living, is
dressed in a cowboy shirt, a bolo tie. He could be a very old
Indian woman. Nothing marks him as a Jew, or for that matter a man. The mouth is not kind. I have suffered, says this
mouth, and much is owed me. The two eyes give different
messages. The left, farther from the nose, is vengeful, the
right, more inturned, is full of sorrow.

My father writhes in torment. "Why are you doing this to
me?" he says.

"I wanted to know you," I tell him.

"That's impossible," he says. "At least leave me in peace."

I tell him he doesn't have to listen; I will do the listening,
and I will do the accusing. I will accuse so loudly, so co-
gently, my accusation will be so final and so damning that
none of them will dare to speak again. He has no need to
hear anything but my words to him, which will be words of
understanding, of forgiveness. I cover my father's ears with
my own hands. He has become my child, tormented by a
nightmare. I am a mother; I have borne a son with his name:
I know what to do. I will show him the light of day. I will
point out to him the lovable realities of the real world. I will
situate him in the peace of the familiar. He will see me
stronger, far stronger, than his phantoms, whom I can dis-
perse with a lift of my hand, my voice.

I signal that the men should speak.

They speak in chorus, all at once.

"Everything beautiful was Christian. . . . All that was

flawless and pure and bold and courtly and chivalric was goyish. . . . Jews lack the qualities that mark the civilized man. . . . Their character and interests are too opposed to ours to permit intelligent sympathy. . . . The kike . . . the kike . . . the kike."

"I accuse you all of murder," I tell the men under the light. "You have murdered the father I could have loved without strain."

How can it be that not one of them even begins to look abashed? They stare at me in contempt and in derision. "We didn't know your father," they say. "He was beneath our notice. He was nobody we would have thought we needed to know."

Roth separates himself from the others. "What did I do?" he says. "I suffered. I suffered more than anyone."

I am not afraid of this Olympics of suffering. "Oh, no," I say. "My father suffered more. You had something to show for your suffering. You were given greatness, you made something great of it. You have been honored. My father lived without honor. Only I can honor him. I accuse you of having been great when my father was not great, of having been honored when my father was without honor, of having told the truth so I would have to know what he buried."

"This is hardly murder," says the old, still-living man.

"And I, what did I do?" says the man with the cigar, smiling at me, the affable smile of the man-about-town. "I said what I saw to be the truth. Thousands agreed with me. He didn't have to agree with me. Thousands didn't. I forced nothing. I spoke my mind. I didn't know him; he isn't someone I would have cared about. I wasn't talking to him. He overheard, and then believed. He was nothing but an eavesdropper, a beggar with his nose to the window, ear to the wall."

The wild poet paces up and down. "He couldn't write. I would never have taken the time to speak to him. He was pathetic, rooting around the past, but without understanding. Without distinction. Do you understand that your father was a man entirely without distinction?"

The bald man leans on his elegant cane. "And I would not have allowed him in the same room with me or any of my friends. I was in rooms with Henry Adams, Edith Wharton. Can you imagine him in such a room? He would have been an embarrassment. His counter jumper's learning. All the mistakes. The name-dropping of the pitiable arriviste. He never even got to Europe. Had he come to visit me, I would have had my servant tell him, "Not at home.""

My father is writhing. My hands no longer cover his ears; he can hear everything. "Why have you done this to me? Why have you not let me rest? Why have you not taken my word, the words I left you? Why have you not been satisfied?"

"Don't worry," I say, but insecurely now. "I will condemn them, banish them."

"What does it matter?" my father says. "You keep forgetting I am dead."

"And what about you?" they cry, pointing their fingers at me. "We know about the dream."

"It was my dream," I say. "I dreamed it as my father's daughter. You cannot possibly know about the dream."

"We know about it," they say. "If you accuse us, we accuse you of your dream."

They order me behind the glass. The light shines in my eyes. I am photographed, holding a number, full face, then in profile.

"Testify," they shout, surrounding me. "Testify about the dream."

X

The Final Evidence:

The Dream

I dreamed that my father was still alive. He was living in the house we'd lived in. I phoned him; he spoke in a Yiddish accent. His voice was hoarse and cranky. Although we were speaking on the phone, I could see his face. It was the face of Henry Roth.

He was annoyed with me for calling. He said, "Don't you know I never wanted to see you." I held his death certificate in my hand. I kept saying to myself, "But who is the man buried under my father's name?"

"So you are one of us," they say, their eyes full of malignant complicity. "You are no different from what we are. You are in no position to condemn, or to accuse."

They shake one another's hands. I see they are congratulating one another. Then they turn off the lights. They leave the glass booth. I cannot raise my eyes to determine in which direction they have gone.

My father is on the other side of the glass. He is cringing. He is weeping, and I cannot break through the barrier to comfort him. I can see him but he cannot see me. In the darkness he cries out to the area of my illumination. He keeps repeating, "Why have you done this to me?"

The light affects my eyes. I can hear the men shouting at

me but I can't see them: "Tell us if you think you are a Jew,"
they say. "Start with the dream."

XI

MY TURN IN THE SPOTLIGHT

I will not let them frighten me. I will keep my voice steady.
"Listen," I say, "I can explain.

"In my dream, my father is a disagreeable old Jew with an
accent. A man I cannot recognize. A man who says he never
loved me. A man I never knew. I never knew a Jewish father.

"For most of my life, I felt I had no right to claim Jewishness for myself because I hadn't suffered for it. After my
children were born, I thought of converting. I took them to
high holiday services; in the deep mourning of Kol Nidre I
would say, 'This is where I have come from; this is where I
belong.' But I understood that I was always doing it to be
near my father; I didn't think I was a Jew: I was doing it so
he could be one again. I was doing it in atonement for his sin
of betrayal. Then I learned that I was thinking as a Christian. Jews don't believe anyone can atone for anyone else. I
spoke to a rabbi about converting. He said: 'Remain a right-
eous Gentile. We need you more there.'

"No one needed me to be a Jew. But what did I need? This
is what no one asked me, gentlemen. But that wasn't necessary: I have always known what I needed. I needed to be
with my father. But I didn't know my father as a Jew. He insisted that I not know him in that way. He buried in darkness, in silence, the images of his life as a Jew. He ensured
that I would have no pictures of it in my mind, no words, no

smells or textures. Only the muffled syllables of his blessing me every night. So that in adulthood, when I hear *'Baruch atah Adonai,'* I am jolted back to that place; it is nighttime, I am not sleepy yet, but he will stay with me, he promises, until I sleep.

"If, after his death, I had tried to think of myself as a Jew I wouldn't have known what to think of. You can, all of you, understand this. My connection with Jewishness was lodged in the hatred of the words my family insulted me with: 'That's the Jew in you.' Are they enough, those words, for me to know myself as a Jew? I knew that I was half a Jew only because my father was one. But I knew he'd turned his back on Jewishness. He said, 'I am baptized; I have taken a new name.' He said his new name: 'Francis de Sales Paul. I am a Catholic now, and not a Jew.'

"And yet, I knew he could never not be a Jew, because no one would let him forget it. I didn't know what that failure to forget might mean. I knew I was not one thing only. I was impure, unwhole. My failings were blamed on my Jewishness. My besetting sin, 'impurity,' I was told, came about because I was a Jew. But also that thing I was that they called, not lovingly, 'smart.' But whatever tone they said it in, they could never make me fail to love my mind. That was the clear place, the place where my father would live forever. And that was a Jewish place.

"You see, sirs, above all I wanted to be with my father. My father's child. His heir. So how could I dare to name myself as something he claimed he was no longer? I was his, and he insisted he had rescued me from Jewishness. In making himself a place in the arms of Mother Church, surely he made a place for me. How, as the child who loved him above all things, could I have looked elsewhere? To a place he swore he would no longer go, that he would shun as if it were the place of death.

"But perhaps you gentlemen are right to accuse me. Perhaps I am protecting myself from the evidence of the dream. Perhaps I was simply afraid. I heard what everybody said about Jews: They are interested only in money; they have no fineness, no refinement; they are filthy at heart. Perhaps I said I could be a Jew because I would not make a place for all that accusation. I would not allow myself to be set down in the place of vilification. If I shed the heavy body, I would cease to be a Jew.

"This is what the Church promised my father. Shed your filthy body. Enter with me into the place only of light. Lay your burden down. Come to me; you will be cleansed, light as air, whiter than snow.

"Now I see what he was doing in the arms of this new mother. Now I can see what an excellent strategy it was. I say this angrily, taking the part of the Jew I do not know I am. I see, gentlemen, finally I see, that in becoming a Catholic, he got his boyhood dream. And he passed it on to me. He made both of us a home in the living center of Europe, an unquestionable foothold in the heart of Rome. A place where he and I, his heir, could never be thought of as arriviste. A Jewish convert was, he must have known, a particular prize; his value was in his turning from Judaism—a convert. 'Convert,' from the Latin 'to turn from.' The Catholic Church is the one place a Jew can go, not hide his Jewishness, and at the same time be free of it. He could enter any Catholic church in the world and know himself to be at home. *Introibo ad altare Dei. Ad Deum qui laetificat juventutem meam.* I will go to the altar of God, the God who gives joy to my youth.

"And to my daughter's.

"How, in the face of this, could I say I was a Jew?"

I am standing under the light. But no one is watching or listening to me. My father has disappeared. The police artist

says, "Given this testimony, it is impossible to invent a face."
Then I am alone. I don't know whether to remain beneath
the light or leave the glassed-in room for what I can know
only as darkness.

XII

A THEORY, AND ITS RESIDUE

I am speaking to my father in the darkness. I understand that
I am not my father. There were words he heard, terrors he
had, that I cannot repeat. I can invent them, but they were
not carved into the soft, vulnerable childish flesh. He shielded
my childish body. He said, "You are entirely beloved."

Oh, yes, my father, from you I have known what it is to
be entirely beloved. But also that this love does not protect
me from the world. The world saying, "That's the Jew in
you." The hint I got of the torment that made you drown.

You lived as a man drowning. Could you drown out the
words of your father and the words of the accusers only in
the silence of the Christian God? Could you save yourself
only by climbing to a height where your father's voice and
the welter of accusation couldn't reach you? Perhaps the
bosom of Abraham was unsafe for you; you had to fall on
the breast of the risen Christ. The risen Christ looked nothing like your father. The voice of the risen Christ was not
the voice of your accusers, or your fellow victims.

I understand that I am alone in the darkness. I am without my father. I collect the evidence; I try putting things in
the proper files. But something is left over: something that
will not fit into the confines of this investigation. I must be
with you once again; I must try to understand the thing
that will not fit.

In looking for a criminal, I name you a victim. A worm and no man. And that is not enough.

There is some residue. After all the words, the accusations, the explanations. Something that grows up in silence. Something neither pathetic nor repellent. There was something that you heard and saw. Something that partook of beauty and that was your own.

I believe that in the midst of the tumult, the vilification and self-hatred, the immigrant's terror, the weak son's dread, the Eastern Jew's American abashment—or perhaps because of and including all of it—there was something else. You didn't get it from your accusers; it was neither pitiable nor the stuff of shame. Perhaps it was the voice of God. The God of singleness and silence. The font of pure, accepting love.

XIII

THE FACES THE POLICE ARTIST

CANNOT CREATE

I must try to create a face to whom I can say these things. It must be a face without features. A face of light and air. A flame. Perhaps it is the face of music. Of beauty beyond the search for beauty. A face both human and inhuman. A face of love beyond the end of love. It is a face I cannot see, but only hope for.

To this face I must say:

I cannot know my father looking on the face of God in prayer. I cannot know this silence, or this whiteness. This place where, I think but do not know, he may have gone from time to time, and been at peace. This is a place where I truly cannot join him. It would be an act partaking both of blasphemy and of taboo. Between my father and the face of God there is a curtain far more forbidding than the one I draw before my father with a woman. It would be far more permissible to watch my father having sex, even watch him spurting the very fluid that created me, than to watch him in the presence of the face of God. And who can see the face of God and live?

And was my father illumined, like Moses before the burning bush? Would I look upon my father's face and die? Or be blinded, punished for this vision by the loss of my other sight.

To this face that is a blank, a flame, I must ask the final question: "Does it matter what, if I looked at my father, I would see?"

And receive the answer: "The dead have lost their faces."

XIV

Facing the Facts

My father is dead. We cannot know the dead.

My father lied.

Records are missing.

Too much time has passed.

I have created a man in my own image, from the bereft child's yearnings and an unquenchable sense of loss.

· · ·

David Gordon is a man I cannot know.

David Gordon is a Jew who came of age before the First World War.

He is a Jew who hated Jews, condemned them, even as millions of them were condemned to death.

He is a Catholic who saw the face of God I cannot fathom and only partially believe in.

My father is dead.

The dead are lost. We can do nothing for them.

There is only one man I know.

The man I know is a man I gave birth to.

His name is not David, or Israel. It is My Father.

This man owes me his life, and he will live forever.

TELLING STORIES TO MY FATHER

I have done things to my father. I have remembered him, researched him, investigated him, exposed him, invented him. Perhaps now I can do something for, rather than to, him.

I will tell my father stories. I will tell him stories for the same reason he told them to me. I will tell you stories, my father, that will allow us to know who we are.

The title of each of these stories is the same. They are all called "This Is What It Is Like."

THIS IS WHAT IT IS LIKE

There is an archaeologist whose subject is her native city, which was devastated in her childhood. Bombed from the air, burned to the ground by a marauding army, buried underneath rubble that crushed everything beneath its weight. This archaeologist escaped with only a few objects, among which are pages of text. She has chosen not to read the text, or to read it in a hesitant, reluctant way, almost an irresponsible way, although it is the thing most dear to her: the history of her city. Each time she opens the text, there are hints she would rather not see. She decides to wait until the excavation is complete before returning to the text. She is hoping for new evidence, a context.

No one has written a history of her city; if she doesn't do it, it will not be done. She has collected the reports from some of her fellow inhabitants, but most of them are dead. Those who survive have unreliable memories. She has a few photographs, but none of them bring back to her in any fullness the life of the streets, the splash of the fountains, the smell of the harbor, the sound of the church bells, or the cursing of the merchants as they set out their wares.

When anyone asks her about herself, she says first, "I am an inhabitant of this city." And yet for many years, she hasn't had the strength to study the city. The city was corrupt. Also glorious. Also full of consoling amusements. If she doesn't look at the record, she can call up only splendor and charm. Everyone tells her this is all right to do: it was, after all, a city unusual for its splendor and its charm. And all cities are, in one measure or another, corrupt. Everyone assures her that the details of the corruption can be put aside. And so the reason for the excavation, she tells herself, is so that she can say with confidence, "You see now, you cannot help but see, that this was a remarkable city; there has never been a city more remarkable than this."

She has studied other cities. She has described their habits, their artifacts, their forms of government, their laws. She's done enough of this: it's time now. She is ready. She makes her preparations. She starts on her expedition. After a time she arrives. She puts the first spade to the red earth. Her heart is full of hope. As well as foreboding. Suppose that what she finds is that the city was, in fact, more corrupt than glorious. Or that the people who assure her that the city was glorious say so only because they have never actually seen a truly glorious city, and their standards are unreliable.

She has two simultaneous and completely conflicting desires. First, that nothing is there, that her memory is the only
source, the only witness, the only thing capable of testimony, should testimony be called for. Second, that everything is there, intact, preserved, so she has only to describe
it. Or transcribe it. In the simplest possible language. But
she tells herself that she is looking for the truth. She believes
that only in this way will she find her origins. She has that
most impossible, that most delusional of desires: the desire
of origins.

The red earth is nearly devoid of objects. Then she finds
some: the toe of a statue, the handle of a cup. Some photographs. Whole albums shot in shadow: the faces unrecog-
nizable, the food on the table a blur, the streets in darkness.
She finds bits of fabric, nearly rotten through. Then nothing. The time comes when she says, "There is nothing
more."

THIS IS WHAT IT IS LIKE

A woman knows that what she is looking for is inside a
vault. The vault is in a bank, one she went to regularly as a
child, not to do business (she was a child; she had no business), but to watch her father calmly tending to money. The
tellers knew her father by name; he even spoke to the men
at the desks in the aisles surrounding the open central area.
All their financial dealings were admirably sound. The satisfying thunk of coins, heavy coins, silver dollars falling on top
of one another, reverberated in the background.

When she was there before, as a child, the sun streamed
in through the high windows, falling prosperously on the
cream marble floors, which always seemed cool enough to
lick. The dark pens with their gold trim and blue-black ink,
the pen stands made of black marble, the stack of forms—
yellow, white, blue, pink—the sheets of glass separating the

tellers from the customers, all filled her with a fine belief in
right placement. She knew of the vault then, but she would
never have been allowed to go into it. Now she is allowed to
go into it, but never by herself. And she needs to have access, unrestricted access, to look at everything, because, although no one has said it, she has always known: Everything
in the vault belongs to her.

She passes herself off as one of the women who work upstairs. For several months she sees to it that she is there, arriving in the morning, neither the first nor the last, and
walking around the unglamorous upper area—the mortgage
department, auto loans—walking in and out of offices, carrying folders or forms. No one questions her presence. They
assume she is one of them, that she belongs. It is easy for her
to hide in a supply closet one night so that she is left behind
when everything is shut.

She has tricked the manager into revealing the combination of the vault. She thought this would be the hardest
part, but it turned out to be surprisingly easy. He is a foolish man, susceptible to flattery; she distracted him with stories; he didn't even know what he'd let slip.

It is November; night falls early. She watches the great
windows fill up with darkness, platefuls of darkness, spilling
down to the cold floors. Finally there is no light but the light
of the streetlamps, collecting in broken patches here and
there. She moves over to the vault and approaches the dial.
The sound of the combination—little scratchy clicks—
breaks into the night air. When the door gives itself over, relief falls around her shoulders. It is open. She can get
anything she wants.

On shelves, rows of boxes wait for her to open them. She
slides the boxes out, one at a time. She touches a button and
the lids spring up. At first she finds some things she has seen
before—unlovely things, chipped or broken; then she finds

pictures of a monstrosity she can only turn away from. She does turn away, thinking this is the worst.

But it isn't the worst. The worst is only about to begin to happen. Box after box turns out to be empty. She keeps pulling them out from their shelves. She presses the proper button. The lids pop up, eager, expectant, and inside there is only emptiness. She opens box after box, frantic, sure that if she looks harder, pushes deeper, there will be something there. The blackness of the vault becomes, as she grows used to it, gray-green; she is able to draw distinctions in varieties of shadow. But only that. The palpable objects she was sure of have vanished. She begins to suspect something else: that they were never deposited. The riches she'd believed in were a false rumor. Only the emptiness is true.

The light is entering through the windows. She leaves the vault door open. She walks out into the damp air of dawn, which hurts her eyes, as if she'd just been through a sickness. "Where can I go, where can I go?" she says, stretching her empty hands, knowing now what she had not even suspected: She is much poorer than she thought.

THIS IS WHAT IT IS LIKE

For many years, since the death of her father, a woman has been receiving packages. She has moved many different places and even taken different names, owing to several marriages. But the packages always reach her.

She doesn't know who they're from. The handwriting is always different, the postmarks are always illegible, and the packages arrive in a variety of conditions. Some are carefully wrapped (string, thick paper, tape). Of these she can say only that their contents are wonderfully intact. But others come packaged carelessly, sloppily. The paper is ripped; things may have fallen out in transit; she has no idea what they might be. What arrives is broken, torn, and frayed.

Each package is stamped in black letters: FROM THE ESTATE OF YOUR FATHER.

She has opened the ones that have arrived intact, has pored over the contents lovingly. Mezzotints of the old masters, with an emphasis on the Italians. Beautifully bound copies of the classics, some inscribed to her.

She never opens the battered packages. They give off a smell that fills her mouth with the taste of dust. Someday, she has always said, I'll open them all. But she has displayed the mezzotints, the copy of *El Cid* in olive-green leather, its title stamped in gold.

One day, a great number of packages begin arriving all at once.

She knows that it is time. She rents a room.

So this is who she is: a *rentier*. A legatee.

The room is very large, in a building that was once used to manufacture something, she has no idea what. There are holes in the floor where heavy machines must once have been bolted down. The windows are very high, and they are filthy; they end above her head. At the top of each window, in the center of the highest frame, there is a hole where the tip of a pole is meant to be inserted so the window can be opened, but there is no pole and she wouldn't know who to ask for one. So the windows can't be opened. The floors are filthy, covered with spattered paint.

For many months, she sits in the empty room with the packages, some opened, some unopened. Whole days she sits and grieves about the bad light coming through the windows. She can't imagine how to procure a ladder and fears the lethal fumes of the chemicals that could cut through whatever it is that obscures the light. She supposes she could paint the floor, but the prospect always exhausts her when she thinks of it, so she lies down on the bare floors and gets up covered with grime.

Then she begins opening the packages. She buys several bins and pastes large labels on them. The bins are marked OBJECTS, MEMORY, TEXTS, PHOTOGRAPHS, THE DREAM OF WHAT MIGHT HAVE BEEN OR MIGHT STILL BE. She thinks she will make something of all these things. She doesn't know what kind of thing it will be, only that its name will be THIS IS MY FATHER.

At first, she thinks of making something in the shape of a living man. Then she gives that up. She will create an image, general, abstract, but legible to everyone. Others will understand and, seeing it, remark, "So that's what he was like."

She unpacks everything. Some days her lungs constrict, because she comes up against rot. The disfigurations are not all picturesque. Holes have been created, gaps appear. When she tries to put things together to create a shape, nothing will hold.

She gives up the idea of a coherent shape. She puts things in rows, side by side on a bench a few inches above the filthy floor. She has no will to box or frame them. They must be constantly accessible, constantly interchangeable, constantly ready to be in different relations to one another. Some things she puts into a large bin marked THE FUTURE.

These are the things she leaves on the bench, in plain sight:

> a broken spring from the inside of a silver watch
> the marble finger of a god
> a skull with missing teeth
> a pot with a hole in the bottom, unable to be mended
> a luminous, rough-textured cup that cuts the lip and therefore can only be looked at, not drunk from
> a gourd that rattles in a playful way
> a blue-gray feather, motheaten to a tender shade
> a porcelain child's valentine, chipped

a pistol, misfired
a devotional weapon whose use cannot be ascertained
fragments of messages: "If only once more I could see your
    face." "Among the dead there are so many thousands
    of the beautiful."

How can she keep all these things in this huge room, for
which she must pay so much?
    How can she keep them safe?
    How could she carry them?
    And to whom?

. . .

This is what it is like. But what is the thing behind the semblance of the thing?
    Who is my father?

The origin and my source.
    My shame and my delight.

The figure behind every story.
    The stranger on the road.
    The double, feared and prized, approaching from the dis-
tance.

V
—
Transactions
Made Among
the Living

◇

My Mother Is Speaking
from the Desert

Unburying and Burying
My Father: A Journal

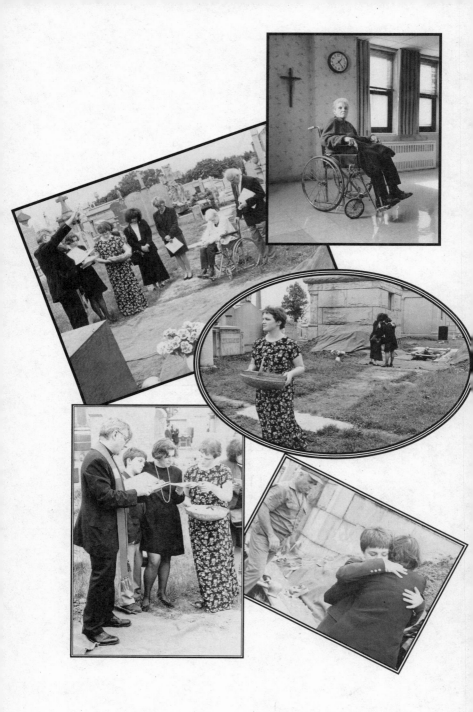

My Mother Is Speaking
from the Desert

*M*y father is dead, but I do not live among the dead. It is among the living I must move, even when they are touched by him, or the idea of him. It is their words I must respond to and to them I must speak.

There is, for example, my mother. My father's wife.

When I speak about my father, people often ask me, "But where was your mother in all this?" I don't know what to say. She was there, of course. And yet she wasn't with us. I don't know where she was.

As I don't know where she is now. She seems to be speaking from the desert. Everything she says now is spoken from the desert, a desert she has in part created. But only in part. Mostly, I suppose, the desert was created because she is eighty-six, and something has hardened, or broken, or worn out. The part she made came about through a dark will and a sense of worthlessness. Believing she deserves nothing, she surrounds herself with empty air. The sun gleams in her eyes. Her eyes can sometimes seem colorless, as if they were ruined by looking at the sun. Sometimes she looks blind. Her eyes are very beautiful. The rest of her face is gaunt now, and so you must look at her eyes: you can't look at anything else.

When she hasn't combed her hair, when she has a lost tooth she won't have attended to, when she won't cut or file her nails or change her clothes, she is distressing to look at. She used to be a very buoyant person, fleshy, with a wonderful skin that always made you think of the inner flesh of fruit: an apple or a peach. When she wore sleeveless dresses in summer, the cool thick muscles of her upper arms made you want to rest your hot cheek against them. The freshness and crispness of those dresses was a miracle. Their colors were the colors of nature: sea-green, sky-blue. It was as if she were wearing the elements themselves—the limitless sky, the refreshing sea—instead of a dress made of material whose shade was only a reminder of sea or sky.

In winter she wore hats with feathers, and tailored suits made of men's fabric, with shoulder pads and serious straight skirts. She "went to business." She was a legal secretary. She worked for one lawyer from 1937 to 1970, when he died; then she became his partner's secretary. She was proud of her business clothes, different from the clothes of mothers who had nothing at stake in what they wore; they could slop around the house wearing anything, and what would it matter? In her handbag she carried a gold compact and lipsticks that smelled like nothing else except themselves but that I knew would taste delicious if only I could taste them. I wanted to taste everything: her skin, warmed or cooled by a light dusting of freckles, her light dresses, her lipstick, her perfume.

This was the body that my father knew and loved and took in marriage. This was the body upon which he engendered me.

But underneath this freshness, this crispness, this robust, delightful not only health but healthfulness, there must always have been a secret devotion to rot. Perhaps it had to do with the polio that struck her at the age of three. Buried beneath her grief and shame about her body, and beneath the stoicism that conceals her grief and shame, like a softening tuber underneath a field.

Now the healthfulness is gone; she has burrowed down to a deeper place, a darker place, perhaps one she feels to be more truthful. Or perhaps, thought of another way, it is a place she goes to in the desert. The place of carrion. She lies down beside it, she makes her home in it: there she is at peace.

Would my father lie down beside her? And where would there be a place for me?

She has lost her memory. As I am obsessively involved with bringing back my father from the past, she is letting the past slip from her hand, a fish into dark water. She is letting it drop through a scrim of tissue paper into the night air. She is allowing it to disappear in snow.

She is in a nursing home now. If I come upon her now when she isn't expecting me, I find her sitting with her head buried in her hands. There is no need for her to do anything now but adopt this formal posture of grief. Yet I don't think she wants to die. She will not, I believe, die soon. She has, I have been told by many doctors, the heart and blood pressure of a teenager.

If I were an allegorist, if I decided to do something in the manner of Giotto, embodying the virtues in a human figure, I would paint my mother in her wheelchair, her head in her hands, wearing her magenta sweater (the only one she wears, although there are a dozen in her cupboard). I would call it "The Death of Hope."

She hopes for nothing, and because I believe that nothing can be done for her, because I have given her up, I hope for nothing on her behalf. Now everything in her life points out the futility of hope. But if I had wanted to paint Hope, the embodied virtue, I would have painted my young mother in her sea-green or sky-blue dress, her lovely arms, her white skin, and her strong and useful, perhaps rather dangerous, teeth. Because hope can be dangerous, in that it leads to the death of hope. But it does not lead in a straight path to death. There is the animal, with the animal's hope. This is not human, it is not our own. It is something, but it is not ours.

There is a link between hope and memory. Remembering nothing, one cannot hope for anything. And so time means nothing. It is a useless element. Living in time without memory or hope: a fish in air. A bird in water. Some unfortunate creature doomed to the wrong medium. Yet not, alas, to death.

I don't know what my mother does all day. She eats her meals. She sleeps.

I know that she prays. But I don't know what she's doing when she prays. What is she saying? Where is she? Is she in a blank silence, the presence of God, where there is nothing without meaning and she knows she is where she has always belonged, perhaps where she has always been? Is she silent, or is she saying words to God? Her own words or the formal words of prayer? Or is she having simple conversations, too banal to repeat, yet placing her exactly at the true, safe center of the universe? She says she prays for me. She says she prays for me and my family all the time. I believe her. But I don't know what she is thinking of us when she prays. Or even who she is thinking of, since she sometimes forgets that she has grandchildren.

I think she must be happy, praying. Or at least not suffering, in a place beyond memory. She is in a place that was the center of her marriage. What brought my parents together was their understanding that the Catholic Faith was the most important thing in their lives. Because they both believed this, and I don't, they can go somewhere that I can't follow. I'm excluded once again, as I was when they closed the bedroom door.

When my mother prays, she's once again what she often was: outstanding. I believe she sees the face of God. But who can see the face of God and live? Who can see the face of God and remember it? Perhaps that's the point. Perhaps it's the point most especially for my mother, for the way she must live now. The ways she has no choice but to live. Praying, she comes alive. Free of her body. Beautiful again: a spirit. Joyous. Not weighed down. Not even tragic. Partaking of greatness. Great. With God, outside time, so that memory is irrelevant, the anguish of its loss erased.

But when she's finished praying, her loss of memory becomes an anguish once again. I take her to a doctor at Mount Sinai to see if there's anything she can do that might reclaim her memory, return her zest for life. The doctor asks her questions.

She answers with words from the desert. "I don't have my memory anymore. I don't think about things. They were all sad."

The doctor, who is beautiful and lively and wonderfully inelligent, says gently, "What about the happy things. Do you think about your husband? You had happy times with him."

She says she doesn't remember him. But she does remember her mother. She remembers being a daughter, but not a wife.

If she doesn't remember my father as a husband, then another part of him is lost. The history of him as a husband. The history of them as a couple.

They were introduced by a priest, and then they courted,

in some way I don't understand, for several years. When she was thirty-nine and he fifty-three, they became engaged. People who knew them said they were almost embarrassingly amorous, for middle-aged lovers. They necked on the subways for everyone to see. Occasionally, they would kiss in front of me, full on the mouth, like people in the movies. I would pretend to think it was all right, but I would have to force myself not to pry them apart, not to stand between them, not to stop them. Which I'm sure I could have, if I'd only tried. But I knew it was important that they seemed to be kissing like people in the movies, because most of the time they didn't seem happy with each other. Most of the time, they fought. They fought about money.

When I heard them starting to fight, I would run upstairs to the attic. Upstairs, away from them, I felt free—what had money to do with me or I with money? I stood beneath the bare beams, in the emptiness, watching the gold light strike the bare wood floor in straight vertical shafts. I would sing loudly so I couldn't hear what they were saying. "I won't give you one red cent for carfare." "You should get your head examined." I twirled around and around, pretending my skirts were long and billowing. I thought the dust motes traveling down the shafts of light were a blessed substance, like manna. I was privileged to be in proximity to it, but I would never dream of following the light upwards to its source.

The attic was meant to be our storage place, but we had nothing to store. My mother had taken nothing from her mother's house and my father had lived nowhere: in spare rooms of other people's houses, in hotels. The people who had owned the house before our landlords were named Chamberlain. "English," my father said. Meaning: "Protestant: nothing to do with us." I associated those bare beams, that clear light, and all that space with Protestants. Cham-

berlain. The clear sound, the clipped off consonants, the relaxed polysyllable. No need to rush or argue for the Chamberlains. They'd left behind a beer stein on one of the attic
windowsills, a black background, green figures in salmon-
colored pantaloons and black tri-cornered hats. I never
touched it. I believed that if I touched it, the Chamberlains
would never come back. I longed for them to come back and
give me retroactive permission to inhabit their attic. Perhaps they would move in there with me: I could imagine the
sun striking their blond hair. Sometimes, I'd look out the
window and imagine I could see them walking up the street.
I'd never met them, but I knew I'd recognize them the first
moment they appeared.

From the attic, I could hear my father and the radio.
WQXR: The Radio Station of The New York Times. I'd
sneak up on him and tease him for conducting a phantom or-
chestra. He'd told me that music was very important, not
just the songs my mother and I sang. My mother and I loved
singing songs from musicals, and songs from the twenties.
Cheerful songs, always with upbeat, bouncy rhythms,
"When the Red, Red Robin Comes Bob, Bob, Bobbin'
Along" and "Tiptoe Through the Tulips." My father couldn't
sing. He said that one day I would play the piano, like his
mother. He ripped a picture of Beethoven out of the encyclopedia and hung it near my toy box at a level where I
could see that imposing head when I was trying to play my
games. The only other picture in the house was his print of
Holbein's *Thomas More*. No landscapes, no still lifes, no
pretty children in ornate hats. There were photographs of
ourselves, as if we were movie stars that we admired.

I think that our idea of ourselves was taken from the
movies. Certainly, my mother must have got the idea for
her marriage from the movies, or at least the courage to defy
her parents and move away from home at the age of thirty-

nine with a strange, unsuitable man. And we behaved more like people in the movies than like the people we knew. My mother and I sang; my father and I danced to the radio. We all did imitations and told jokes. We made fun of stuck-up people. We went out to eat.

Our familial ideal was from a particular kind of movie. It never included midwestern families around the dinner table; our treasured models were connected not to small towns or farmlands but to show business or crime. Our particular favorites were childless couples who lived in penthouses; food prepared and consumed inside the house was of no importance in our lives, as it wasn't for them. My parents took pride in this. "Why do you have concern for what you put in your mouth?" Jesus had said, "It goes into the belly and ends up in the drain." My parents thought they were living by these words of Jesus, but it wasn't eating that displeased them—it was cooking, and setting and clearing the table, that they didn't like. We were happy going out to eat, then going to the movies. But when we came home from the movies, my parents would begin to fight again.

No one remembers any of this now. If I ask my mother anything about my father, or our life together, she just looks confused. Not only is my father dead to her, the memory is dead. I am the only heir to a still-living memory.

The doctor whom I take her to see about her problems with her memory asks her questions on what is a standard diagnostic test for depression. But we run out of time and the doctor suggests that perhaps I could ask her the questions and simply circle the answers on the form. These are the questions:

Are you basically satisfied with your life?
Have you dropped many of your activities and interests?

Do you feel that your life is empty?

Do you often get bored?

Are you hopeful about the future?

Are you bothered by thoughts you can't get out of your
  head?

Are you in good spirits most of the time?

Are you afraid something bad is going to happen to you?

Do you feel happy most of the time?

Do you often feel helpless?

Do you often get restless and fidgety?

Do you prefer to stay at home rather than going out and
  doing new things?

Do you frequently worry about the future?

Do you feel you have more problems with memory than
  most?

Do you think it's wonderful to be alive now?

Do you often feel downhearted and blue?

Do you feel pretty worthless the way you are now?

Do you worry a lot about the past?

Do you find life very exciting?

When I first ask her the questions she answers everything
positively. She is satisfied with her life, she isn't bored, she's
hopeful, she's in good spirits, she doesn't worry. I think I understand something. I ask her if she thinks that saying
there's anything wrong with her life means that she's com-
plaining, that she's ungrateful for what she has, that she's a
weakling, a crybaby. Of course that's what I think, she says,
looking at me from the desert. I tell her that's not the way
it is; they need to know how she really feels for their work.
It's their business to get an accurate picture, I tell her. "You
have to do it for them." I never tell her who "them" is and
she never asks. "Okay, if it's their business," she says.

She answers the questions slowly. She isn't satisfied with
her life, she isn't happy, she often feels helpless, she often

feels downhearted and blue, she feels her situation is hopeless. She frequently feels like crying. On the other hand, she
doesn't feel that her life is empty, she is hopeful about the
future, she is not afraid that something bad is going to happen, she thinks it is wonderful to be alive. Her most heart-
felt response is to the question "Do you feel pretty worthless
the way you are now?" "Oh, yes," she says, "completely
worthless." She is speaking from the desert. She is looking at
me with those eyes burned by the sun. There is no softening landscape. No hidden refreshing spring. The dry land.
The harsh rock. The sky, unmediated. When I start to cry
she says, "What are you crying about? How else would I be?"
And I tell her all the wonderful things she's done, how
much she's been treasured and loved. "That was then," she
says. "I thought you were talking about now."

When I call the doctor and read her the results of the test,
she says my mother is on the border between dysphoric and
depressed. She thinks my mother might be helped with
antidepressants, but the chances are slim. She'd like to have
an M.R.I. done on my mother, because some of the neuro-
logical signs were a bit confusing.

   I don't tell my mother that we're going for a test that is
frightening, claustrophobia-inducing. I don't tell her till a
day before that she's going to have a test at all. I try to describe the procedure to her. They put you into a kind of
tube. You're a bit shut in, but if you relax it's quite bearable.
I tell her I had one myself, and that I fell asleep during it,
which was true. I decide to take her on the city bus, which
provides access for people in wheelchairs, because the first
time we went to the doctor, we waited an hour and a half
for the ambulance going, two hours coming back. "They've
got you over a barrel, and they know it and they don't care,"
the woman at the nursing home tells me. I think how

pleased I would be to firebomb the ambulance headquarters; the relief of seeing the place and the people go up in flames.

On the bus, I understand that not having a memory makes my mother ashamed. The shame of the bankrupt. She pretends she remembers things. "Oh, yes, I remember these people. I've seen them before. Their faces are familiar." On Madison Avenue in the Eighties, where she has never been in my lifetime, she says, "I remember this was where we used to get off." I can't imagine she was ever on a Madison Avenue bus. When she was young, she came to the city to go to the theater, or the rodeo at Madison Square Garden. She loved the rodeo; when it was in town she went to it every night. She had some dates with rodeo cowboys, whose names remained dear to her. Turk Greeneau and Cecil Henley. Turk married Sally Rand, the fan dancer, who was famous for causing a stir at the 1933 Chicago World's Fair. My mother always said, with real indignation at the loss to the rodeo world, "She broke his stride for good." If I laughed when she said that, she'd get angry. I wonder if my father knew about the rodeo cowboys, and was jealous. I remember that he ripped up a copy of *Photoplay* that my mother had bought for the picture of Gary Cooper.

She also regularly went to a retreat house on Twenty-ninth Street where she'd met my father. Or to Saint Patrick's Cathedral. Everything I know of her history makes me sure that she was never on the Upper East Side. And I know she's never seen her fellow passengers. I have to fight my desire to tell her, "You're wrong, you've never been here before." I wonder if she thinks she's been on these streets and seen these people before because all people and places are the same to her. Memory enables a sense of difference. The present is different from the past. The remembered event is different from the current experience, the difference is recognizable, and therefore the events can be differentiated.

Is everything for my mother in the present? Does she live like God?

Does she live like my father?

The loss of memory brings some mercy. By the time we get to the hospital for the M.R.I. my mother's forgotten it. So she's experienced no anticipatory dread.

The technician tells her to lie completely still, or the pictures will be useless. After a few minutes, I see her beginning to thrash. Through a microphone the technician tells her in an accusing voice that she is ruining everything. Instantly, I know what to do. I jump up, run over to the hole her legs are sticking out of, and thrust my head in. "We're going to say the Rosary," I tell her. And into the hole I shout, "The five sorrowful mysteries, the first mystery, the Agony in the Garden." Our Fathers. Hail Marys. The second mystery. The third. She settles down and lies quietly. The test is done. I realize that for me, who claims to live by words, there are no words that could automatically take away my terror. No poetry, no passages from great novels, could be shouted at me and cause me to lie still. She is, in this way, more fortunate than I.

When we get to the doctor's office, on the other side of the Medical Center, the doctor asks my mother if the test was difficult. What test, she asks. The doctor describes the M.R.I. I don't remember anything like that, she says.

Another piece of good fortune; without memory there is no reliving of terror. The past no longer haunts. It is finished, and for good.

But if a loss of memory spares pain, it also vexes questions of pleasure. How is pleasure judged if it cannot be relived, recalled? It seems, from a capitalist stance, a bad invest-

ment. What yields pleasure yields it at some cost. Time, effort, money. Particularly in her case, since she is immobile,
she must be brought to things or things must be brought to
her. If she is brought to something, the effort is enormous.
When I think of doing things that might please her, I often
find myself asking, "Is it worth it?" Worth what? The effort.
Also, the resentment the effort entails. The capitalist's resentment for a bad investment.

What is something worth if it doesn't lodge in memory?
Take, for instance, my son's Christmas play. I'd had a meeting with the social worker, the nurse, the doctor, who are in
charge of my mother. We all agreed that she'd been less responsive than formerly. We agreed, as a team, to be more
hopeful, more inventive, more persevering in suggesting
things that might bring her "out of herself." None of us
asked where she might be when she was in herself. As I left
the meeting, I was inspired to ask my mother if she'd like to
see her grandson as the star of the Christmas play. Usually,
she says no to everything; she hasn't been out of the nursing
home in three years. But for some reason, she said yes.

I move with extreme efficiency. No ambulette is available. An ambulette makes it possible to wheel her into a
van; she doesn't have to get out of her wheelchair. But we're
not lucky; all that's left is a regular ambulance, which, I find,
requires that she be lifted off her wheelchair onto a
stretcher. The two attendants, both very young, one a slight
Hispanic with an even slighter mustache, the other a
chunky, opulently permed Italian, are both charming, help-
ful, and kind. My mother likes them; she flirts with the
young man; she tells the young woman she's half Italian. We
go up Broadway, sirens flashing. We arrive at the school and
she's wheeled in on a stretcher. The sea of parents parts for
us. The attendants switch her from the stretcher to a wheelchair. David, my son, introduces her to his teachers, the

head of the middle school, and all his friends. When the play begins, the drama teacher says that David has asked that the play be dedicated to his grandmother. She loves everything: the Christmas carols, seeing her grandson in a major role (as Chico Marx), the dedication, all the attention. She glows with happiness as she is transferred from the wheelchair to the stretcher. We sing Christmas carols in the ambulance on the way home. I leave her at her room; she says she'll certainly sleep well tonight.

I am in love with her, with myself, with everyone involved in the evening. I tell myself that I have to do more things like this, all it takes is imagination and hopefulness and a little thought. What a difference can be made by things like this, I say, as I fall blissfully to sleep.

In the morning. I call her. I say, "Did you wake up thinking about last night?"

"What happened last night?" she asks.

"The play," I prompt her. "David's Christmas play."

"I don't remember. I don't remember anything," she says.

My first thought is that she's done this to make a fool of me. No, to make a fool of hopefulness. Then I think that it was such a wonderful experience for her, and she knew how rare it would be, so she had to forget it so as not to long for more things like it. Then I think that it doesn't matter, the experience is lost, it is worse than if it never happened. All the effort, all that expense. I vow I won't tell my son. I hope he doesn't bring it up if he sees her, or that she'll have the sense to fake it. With all my will I remind myself that she was happy at the time, that that's what matters, that it's not important that she doesn't remember it. For the moment, it was of great value; I tell myself we live for moments only. But I don't believe it for a second.

I think about this when it comes time for the spring Shakespeare play. David is playing Falstaff. I tell her I'll come and get her on the bus; the bus trip to Mount Sinai was easy enough, and it's the difference between a fare of five dollars and an ambulance fee of two hundred dollars. But when the morning comes, I am reluctant to do it. I think of what a good friend has told me, that since things mean so little to her, I shouldn't make extraordinary efforts for her. I should do what is easy for me, and pleasant for both of us. I shouldn't do anything that taxes me, anything that I'll later resent and be angry with her about. He says I have to realize the truth about the way she is: that nothing I do matters anymore.

Most of the time I don't realize it. But the day of the play is overcast and humid. I focus on how rude the bus driver was to us on the way home from Mount Sinai, how I had to fight with him to pull the bus near enough to the curb, how I lost my temper, screamed at him, filled out a complaint. Bus drivers don't like stopping for wheelchairs; they don't like getting out of their seats, moving the necessary bench, opening the lift mechanism with the special key. They don't like locking the wheel of the chair into its special clamp. This makes me hate them.

On the morning of David's play, I wake at five-thirty to write about my father. It doesn't go well. All morning I am terribly fatigued. I begin writing and reading well only at noon. I am reading Beckett's *The Unnameable*. If I take my mother to the play, I have to stop writing and reading at one-thirty. If I don't, I can work until three.

I very much want to read and write. I keep remembering the episode of the Christmas play, the episode of the M.R.I. I think how hot it is, how difficult it will be to push the wheelchair up the hill on Eighty-sixth Street, between West End Avenue and Broadway. I think of the bus driver's inevitable distaste. I read a sentence of Beckett's: "Close to me it is grey, dimly transparent, and beyond that charmed circle deepens and spreads its impenetrable veils." I remember that four days ago my mother said, when the doctor asked her, that she had no grandchildren.

I decide not to take her. I decide that what it will take out of me is greater, much greater, than what it will give her. I'm just too tired to.

I call and say I have a bad back, which I do, and that I'm afraid pushing the wheelchair up the hill might hurt my back. Which it might. It also might not. I've decided the chance isn't worth it. Which means I'm giving up on her again. Giving her up. Allowing her to fall through the sheet of tissue paper into darkness. Since it seems to be what she wants. Since I no longer have the faith to go after her. Since I would rather write about her than push her up the hill. Since I need to save my strength to find my father, who is waiting somewhere, somewhere I do not know. I know exactly where she is. I always have. There is no need to look for her. I must force myself to look at her. Force myself to resist the impulse, as strong as any in my life, to turn my face when I see her face.

My desire, my need, to punish my mother is very great. I am conscious of no need to punish my father. This is because of the totally different histories of their bodies in relation to me. If I force myself, I can call up his toothless mouth, his ripped trousers, but when I think of his body, automatically I think first of his beautiful hands with their silver ring, the buttons on the sleeves of his suit jacket. I think of the place in the center of his chest where I could rest my head, the place of comfort and safety I will yearn for till the moment of my death. I can call up the fresh young arms of my still-young mother, but only with effort. When I think of my mother's body, I think first of degradation, rot. That is my first landing; I have to push myself past that place to the place of the refreshing mother, who is wonderful to be around.

Because of her polio, my earliest vision includes the vision of a damaged female body. For many years, the only adult female body I saw unclothed was, it must be said, grotesque, lopsided, with one dwarf leg and foot and a belly with a huge scar, biting into and discoloring unfirm flesh. She'd point to it and say, "This is what happened when I had you."

For many years as a child, much longer than I should have, I imagined that all women had this slit belly, and that when I had children I would too.

I had many chances to look at my mother's body over the years, but I saw my father's only fleetingly, in stolen glimpses, in the nature of a crime. But it is a whole body: strong legs and back, dark nipples that match his maroon bathing suit, a raised mole on his chest that I finger like a talisman or toy. At the same time, a ruined mouth. I learn to take in bodies in a fragmentary way, because both my parents' bodies bear witness to a damage I would rather avert my eyes from. I must ignore my father's toothless mouth and everything about my mother except her beautiful hair, skin, eyes, fine teeth, and buoyant upper arms. But my father's damage can be corrected; all he has to do is put in his teeth. This causes me to believe that the miracle of prosthesis applies only to men. Clothed, with his teeth in, my father can become entirely desirable. My mother never can. She always limps; she is always unable to do most ordinary things. She can't walk more than a few steps. She can never carry me.

I am ashamed, as a woman, that when I say the words "my mother's body," I have feelings of revulsion, and when I say "my father's body," I have feelings of joy and peace. It's an old story. The love of the absent, of the not. The elegant beneficence of early death. An existence in memory, which has no smell. Or in photographs, where the flesh is not subject to rot.

I should feel more loyalty to the body that is more like mine. Because, if I hate my mother's body, what can I feel about my own?

But my body is not like hers. She is crippled; I am not. It shaped the way we lived, this difference between us. What was always in the front of both our minds was that she must not fall. We lived our lives in terror of her falling. It was like living on a fault line or on the top of a volcano. The anxiety that the thoughtless move, the too-forceful move, the unexpected move, would cause calamity. My mother's falling seemed like a natural disaster. The crash, the crying out. Then the immobility. I don't remember her ever rising up after she fell. She had to be brought to bed, where she would lie and weep with her eyes closed. Sometimes she would moan aloud. No sense of when she might get up again. Perhaps never.

Because she was a cripple, she felt free to give up ordinary kinds of pride and to ask help without stopping to consider where the help might come from or what the helper's response might be. I think she felt that any able-bodied person was more adult than she.

She had the, I suppose, necessary lack of physical shame that helps cripples get by. She would do things that mortified me, like going down a steep flight of stairs on her behind. She even had an expression for it: "Assing down the stairs." She would crawl up hills on her hands and knees. I would want to beg her not to, so deep was my mortification when she did something like this, even if no one could see us. But I knew that she was right: there was no alternative. It made me literally want to die, because there was too much to feel. It was easier to die than to feel all of it. There was mortification at the spectacle, pity for her, shame at my own shame, pride in her, hatred for her, perhaps a vague sense of her sadism in insisting that all this be visible. It was too much for a child. It has never stopped being too much.

But the child of a cripple was never really a child, and so has never really passed satisfactorily through childhood. You are always resentful because *you* are always in charge. You are always more able. You envy people whose parents don't need to be watched or cared for, with an envy that has the taste of hate. You want to say to the crippled parent: You have stolen my childhood, you have taken my youth. But how can you? Always, they have suffered more than you, a suffering from which there is no respite, no escape. They cannot but live with their damaged body. Should you come at them with the face of your deprivation and its rage, leaving them diminished, shaken, unsteady, adding to what they know about themselves—that they are damaged—you would still be able to walk away, able and intact. Leaving the wounded one now doubly wounded. Naming yourself a monster. In such a situation, therefore, rage is impossible. Or at least the expression of rage. It's like being angry at a starving man for depriving you of a profiterole, a cream puff, an eclair. You live always in a state of remorse for what you have not done for them and cannot do. And the fear that somehow you might weaken them, because they know what you are thinking.

And suppose one day they are thinking about it, your rage, and it takes away their hope. You know how much they need their hope. They need it because the effort of simple living is so great. Simple actions, if there are any, demand much more consideration from them. Planning, strategizing. This kind of attentiveness requires hope. And suppose they give up hope because of you. Because of you, the monster, the obscenely healthy brute. Standing above them in a wholeness that can only be called sadistic, insist-

ing on something they could never have given. Only a monster could ever have thought of saying it. The monster you
are. The monstrous, healthy animal. The monster child. The
monster child alone with the broken mother. Would I have
felt so monstrous if my father had been with me? If I hadn't
been alone?

I learned quite early that it is my fate always to be the
most able-bodied in any room. That is the way I have always
lived, alert for the scar, the concealed false limb, the tremor,
the flicker of anxiety at the prospect of uncertain terrain,
the slurred speech, the hesitant, reluctant gesture. I always
find it, and I always know that because of this I am called
upon not only to act but also to find a solution for the damage that must be accommodated to, made up for, got
around. I believe that I will always find a solution and that
it will always be right. This is the source of my worst qualities: arrogance, self-righteousness, also intense self-pity,
then resentment and contempt.

I used to believe all these could be traced to my mother's
body. I have learned they had another source: my father's
body and my understanding that it is only by my efforts that
he stays alive. The other thing I learned quite early: His
death means I have failed.

My mother will live for many years, but I have failed her,
too. I cannot keep a living spirit in her body. I cannot make
her remember. I cannot keep her from a living death, a rock-
like existence, almost without consciousness. I cannot keep
her from a life in which death would make very little difference.

I have failed them both.

When you are with my mother, it is best to have conversations that don't require a reference to the past. No interpre-

tation. Narrative is second best, far behind description. Plain description is what's called for.

Our best visits consist of my taking her to the garden in Riverside Park. I wheel her chair down the hill. I have to struggle to keep the momentum from hurtling her to disaster. I bend my legs and strain my body to keep her safe. The next day my back always hurts. But I keep my posture easily because of the horrifying vision of what would happen if I did not. My mother, hurtling forward. Her head gashed on the pavement. I see the bloody forehead, the wound with pebbles imbedded in it. Inattentiveness could bring about a tragedy: I must be hypervigilant about everything, every variation of the surface.

We wheel around the enclosed garden. We say the names of flowers or colors. Peony, we say, foxglove, lily, pansy, phlox. The words are beautiful in themselves. And we say the names of colors: red, yellow, purple, blue, deep rose. Sometimes we sing. She remembers the words to songs. Doing these things, we are both happy.

When we are doing these things, I wonder, Is it possible I still have a mother.

Of course, I say, how could it not be so.

But then, how can it be.

Having a dead father and a mother without memory of the stories of the past means that I must accept the possibility that I have never been a child.

Does she remember my childhood, my babyhood? Who am I to her? Someone she doesn't remember giving birth to, who is, somehow, fully grown. A daughter with a lost childhood. My father is gone; my mother has misplaced my childhood. So what? Why the importance of these images? To whom do they matter? The shocking insistence, the narcissism of asserting the importance of memory. Perhaps it is always only in order to be able to say: This is where I am. Magnetic north.

Where is my mother? Where does she think she is?

My mother is speaking from the desert, where she would like to disappear. But how can she disappear there, when there is no place to hide? Perhaps by the sheer force of something whose name I do not know. Perhaps it is her sorrow, creating a fog in which she will disappear. Yet she is visible to me, partly because I have ineradicable memories of her vividness. She was, above all, a vivid creature.

I'm sure that vividness was what my father loved.

She raged so, people were careful not to cross her. She kissed men right on the mouth; she'd grab the microphone at public gatherings and sing. She laughed so loudly in the movies that people she knew would meet her in the lobby afterward and say they knew just where she had been sitting. She loved foods that she could crunch and chew, particularly nuts; she would indulge in an extravagant purchase of cashews and almonds every year at the end of Lent. Just as no one alive remembers my father's body, no one remembers my mother's freshness and her vividness, because no one else now alive had a stake in it.

She was always admirable, attractive, enjoyable. Even when she was committed to a course of degradation, to her love of rot, the vivacious animal held sway.

She was the life of the party. Now she is barely alive.

For many years she used alcohol to allow herself to fall into the pit of shame, of stupor, of oblivion. Now she can enter it without chemical aid. Age provides her with a stupor from which she has no desire to escape, even if she could. My father never knew this woman. He never had an alcoholic wife, an oblivious wife. But I have had an alcoholic, oblivious mother. He left while the going was good. He left her to me.

For years I have stood at the edge of the pit, trying to keep her back, holding her back with the same muscles I use when I keep her wheelchair from hurtling down a hill. Now I realize that her desire for stupor is stronger than my ability to keep her lively. I give in to her need for darkness. I give her up. I turn my back on her. And go off, as I always did, with him.

For three weeks, at any time during the day when my mind is not taken up with the business of living—reading, writing, caring for children, shopping, cooking, speaking to friends, calling insurance companies or the super—what I am thinking about is my mother's fingernails.

She has given up attending to her nails at the very time when the head nurse on her floor has taken a three-week vacation. This woman oversees her charges with a benevolent general's intelligence and interest in the welfare of her troops. While she's away, things slip a bit. My mother's nails are not quite claws yet; they haven't begun to turn under. I know she's waiting for me to cut her nails. Everyone is waiting for me. The substitute nurse says they have no nail scissors; it's up to me to produce one. And do I? Three weeks in a row I forget. She refuses to file her nails, the nursing home says it cannot do it, and I forget to bring clippers. All of us joined in an insistence that my mother will appear more animal than she needs to.

They care for her body better than most nursing homes could. But it is up to me to keep an eye on the details. She is a difficult patient because she refuses to take a shower. I tell the nurses that she has never taken showers, because she has never been able to walk without her shoes. As I tell them that, I realize what an extraordinary thing it is: My mother has never taken a shower. Very few people in the modern West can say such a thing. Occasionally, perhaps once a year when she was younger, she would, with great difficulty and much assistance (my father's, her mother's, and then, after her mother's death, mine) take a bath. Would the nurses believe me if I told them that for most of her life she was exceptionally clean? That she reminded me of sheets hung out in the wind, of the white flesh of apples? Would they believe me, or would they say, quite properly, what does that have to do with now?

When I have to say the words, "Her hair is dirty, her teeth are falling out, she has a rash," my rage and panic literally take my breath away. I can hardly speak. I want to cry. I want to say, "She had wit and dash and beauty. She asked things of life in a world where no one dared to. You must understand that she does not deserve this. Because you don't understand it, I would like to punish and humiliate you, just as she is punished and humiliated." I am her advocate, yet I want to scream at her, "How can you allow this to go on?" It makes me want to end her life. At the same time I want to sit in her lap and say, "Don't you understand that I'm your child, and a child shouldn't have to do this?" And have a transformed mother, fragrant, buoyant, say what she was almost never able to say: "Don't worry about anything. I'll take care of everything."

Although my sense of her ability to care for me was always partial, there were times when I yearned for her presence as purely as Proust's Marcel longed for his mother's kiss in his bed in Combray. It happened only irregularly while my father was alive. I remember that one of his few moments of annoyance (he was never really angry at me) occurred when my mother was at a meeting one night and I expressed my sense of missing her. "You're never satisfied," he said. "When I'm not here you want me, when your mother's not here you want her." It didn't occur to me to defend myself on the grounds that what I really wanted was both my parents, and that that was actually rather a normal impulse.

When my mother went to work and my father went to the city, I was left with a woman from the parish whose idea of child care was to let me wander around the dark house all day, unamused, unspoken to. I was afraid of everything there: the blackout shades, the too-sharp flowers in the night-colored garden, the cat who would slink under the leaves and reappear, suddenly, her eyes baleful, with a dead bird in her jaws. For hours in good weather, I sat on the porch, waiting not for my mother but my father. And on the first miserable days of school, it was my father that I missed. He would stand on the other side of the schoolyard's chain-link fence, and I would touch him through the diamond-shaped links till the last possible second. Then the bell would carry me away to that doom-laden room, smelling so agonizingly of half-sour milk, half-eaten lunches, paste, and the spearmint leaves the nuns sold, two for a penny, during recess.

But in the summers after my father's death, when it was determined that it was good for me to get away, to get out of myself, to quit the moping, the thought of being separated from my mother's freshness, from her firm, fragrant arms and lovely clothing, was unbearable. I lived in anguish the last days of school, knowing what was to come.

The first summer after my father died, I was sent away to my mother's friend in the Bronx. She took me to museums every day. But they were the wrong ones. There was only one real museum: the Metropolitan, with its grand staircase, its madonnas, its huge statues with their smooth, high flanks. My mother's friend took me to the displays in the

Museum of the American Indian and the collection of antique dolls in the Museum of the City of New York. She took me to the Museum of Natural History, where I was frightened of the huge skeletons I thought at any moment would come to life. There was only one successful outing, to the Hayden Planetarium, where I lay back and looked at the model of the heavens, convinced that once again my father and I were seeing the same thing.

Although I knew that on principle I was too old to be missing my mother—the appropriate time for that having passed with my first communion, when I achieved the age of reason—I didn't dread what would happen to me if I cried in front of my mother's friend. I knew she would understand. The shame would emanate from a standard held only by me: my helplessness at keeping intact the thin skin that contained my tears like an overstretched balloon. But when I was with my aunts and uncles, my mother's family, it was their response, not something coming from myself, that was the thing most to be feared.

They had an ideal called "toughness," whose dark opposite was "sensitivity." "She's so goddamn sensitive," I always heard them say about me. "You have to watch every word you say." One day, when I'd been caught crying, my aunt and uncle decided they were going to try an experiment to toughen me up. They told me to stand at the opposite end of the room. They shouted insults at me, mostly about how big my stomach was. If I cried, I had to go into the bathroom and compose myself, then come out and start again. I never won, or they never lost. I don't know what made them stop. Probably, it was time for a meal, or for something they wanted to watch on television.

I cried again during the last half hour of that visit. My endurance was simply at an end; like an exhausted runner, I couldn't go the last steps. "Are you crying because you're remorseful?" my uncle asked. "Yes," I said. I was sure I had something to be remorseful about, or he wouldn't have used such a serious word. They didn't like "big words." Finally, I assumed that what I had to be remorseful about was the fact of my crying.

Once, during the summer after my father's death, when I was at my uncle's camp, my aunt reprimanded me for crying. My grandmother, who was usually anything but sympathetic to me, banged down a pot and said to her, "Leave her alone, for God's sake. Can't you see her little heart is broken?" My grandmother never defended me like that again, but her remark made clearer than ever to me how my mother failed to protect me. She would never stand up to her brothers and sisters. When I complained about her siblings' insulting me from across the room, she said, "They're just doing it for your own good. Let's not make waves."

But however partial her protection was, I missed her terribly. I knew she loved me. More, I knew she admired me. I knew that from the moment of my birth.

I think her admiration for me combined with her sense of her own unworthiness to make her feel always that she ought to be giving me up. She perceived, at a very early stage, that I was more like my father than like her. So she stood back and let him take me.

On one of our walks to the garden she says, "I don't remember your father's face but I remember he was crazy about you. Sometimes I felt I could hardly get near you." "That must have been difficult for you," I say. "No," she says, "because I realized how important that made me. I was the mother of the person who was so important to him. I was the stupid one. But I was the one that brought you forth." When she uses words like "brought you forth," I realize all she was deprived of because of having to work so early. She wanted to be a teacher but was rejected by the normal school because of her handicap—rejected in a particularly cruel way. She'd been accepted on the basis of her test score, but when the people at the school saw her, they were surprised. They put her through a series of humiliating physical tests. Then they told her she had to understand that in case of a fire she wouldn't be able to get the children out of the building fast enough. She said she understood. With the same stoicism, she understood that I belonged to my father.

When I think about these things, I am filled with love for her, and I remember how lovable she was, and how intensely I missed her in the times we were apart. What I missed most was the sense of rightness, of right choices, that she represented, her crispness, her business acumen, the fact that up and down the street and all around the parish, people asked her advice about "letters from the government" or tax returns, or wills. She would put on her blue-framed glasses and, within minutes, solve their problem. Or she would get on the phone. She was brilliant on the phone. She prided herself on having "a good telephone voice." How irresistible she was on the telephone, of course no one could resist her. And she was delightful in any situation having to do with money: at the bank, where she was immediately given pride of place because her boss was the bank's attorney (she never had to stand on line; she could get any check approved), or even in the butcher shop, or the vegetable market. As long as she was touching coins or bills, or something representing them, she was at ease and powerful and, most of all, effective. Yet she didn't care about money, in the sense of accumulating it for herself. She just liked being involved in its movement.

I understood very well that my father's death had only enhanced her social position, and therefore mine. She had been the unfortunate wife of an unfortunate husband; now she was the noble widow and I the gallant orphan. Everyplace we went this was immediately legible. But never more so than when we entered our pew in the front of the church, always getting there early so my mother wouldn't be jostled by crowds and thrown off balance. There was a terrible crush at Sunday Mass in those days. The whole congregation had an admiring eye on us. We were consistently admired.

And she would occasionally, though sparingly, use her status as a noble and competent cripple for my good. There was the memorable incident that occurred when I was thirteen, the only one in the class with a working mother. I invited some boys and girls over one afternoon to dance. It was a disaster. The boys stood on one side of the room and smoked. The girls danced with each other. One boy, trying to be cool and light his cigarette from the gas stove, set his hair on fire. Another burned a hole in the rug. A third opened the storm door with such force that it broke off its hinges. One of our neighbors reported all this to the Rosary Society; it spread through the parish. The principal threatened me with not being allowed to take part in the graduation ceremony. My mother went up to the school. She made a point of how difficult it was for her to walk down the long corridors, and to take time off from work. She said to the principal, "What do you think those kids were doing? I don't think they were doing anything. It shows the difference in our minds." She never blamed me, which was unusual for her. I was tremendously proud of her—none of the other parents stood up to the nuns—but it made me feel unworthy. And I was aware I had been spared punishment because she was a cripple and a widow.

But that was only part of it. I was also spared because she was daring and articulate. When she knew she was right, she was fearless. Part of the pride she felt she had to give up as a cripple transformed itself into something morally positive: she didn't care what people thought about her. She took pride in appearing outrageous, vulgar even, in saying "hell" and "goddamn" freely and in all company. When I went through a squeamish phase, at about the age of ten, she said that she'd never trust anyone who was afraid of the word "shit." And when, in early adolescence, I dreaded changing clothes in front of other girls, she said, "If you see anyone with anything you don't have, throw a shoe at it."

But it was this same lack of regard for public opinion that allowed her to stop grooming herself, to give in to her love of rot. Looked at in this way, a regard for the opinion of the world, a consciousness of and concern for how one is seen, seems infinitely precious and humanizing. But my mother's dashing lack of regard for public opinion gave her, when she was younger, a richer and fuller humanity, more fun, more scope for self-expression and satisfaction of her strong nature. And it was a great gift to me: I never had to endure what many girls did, the blunt hoof of propriety crushing my chest, the beast mother, with her blood-red eyes, enforcing the implacable rules of the household gods. She was not afraid of being in the world, as the mothers of many of my friends were. She took me into it.

She took me into it as her escort. The companion of a widow and a cripple, taking my father's place. But pleasing her more than he had done. At weddings I was often the only child invited. We were a couple.

We even went on dates. We went to restaurants—only two of them, but they were important ones in the place we lived—she was always given the best table, and was always waited on by someone she knew. After my father died, she made a little home for us in restaurants. No, not a little home. A vacation spot. A resort.

I understood that all the food I was eating on these occasions came to us because of my mother's relationship to money. She made it; she could spend it; she was willing to spend it on fun. I don't know if it was because of this that all the food on these occasions seemed extraordinarily delicious. Bright colors, good textures, satisfying, clear, unclouded tastes. Many foods frightened me to the point of panic in those years. Mayonnaise, cocoa, fat and gristle on meat, the smallest spot on the skin of a tomato. I thought they would poison me or choke me, would be, in some way, the cause of my death. My mother seemed magically able to avoid all these disturbing aspects of food on our outings together. She assured, by her assurance in ordering, that we would come near none of these things. She made them seem not to exist, or to be a distant memory from a deprived past. Everything she suggested we eat was festive, modern, possibly unnourishing, but full of the electric joy of the life I knew when she and my father and I lived alone. None of her family knew anything about things like that, and I hugged our superior skill to myself, as I folded my menu, unfolded my napkin, took the paper off my straw.

In the local luncheonette, we were waited on by her friend Tess, an iron-haired, thin-lipped woman, who seemed to come to life around my mother. She always said, "God bless her," to me, always brought us our orders without our having to ask for them. She knew what we wanted: "the regular." Grilled cheese sandwiches, and chocolate milk for me, coffee for my mother. For my dessert the specialty of the house: lemon ice cream.

Every time I got a good report card (and I always did), she would drive to the next town to a bar and grill called the Brick Café. It was owned by a man named Charlie, a former prize fighter who had briefly been one of my mother's beaux. It is rather odd that my mother, a cripple, though a beautiful one, had one beau who was a prize fighter and an-

other who was a rodeo cowboy. These are the only two she
ever spoke of, and I think they were the only ones. Except
for John Gallagher, a widower, an undertaker. John wanted
to marry her. The cowboy and the prize fighter, I think, did
not. My father must have had the slightly illicit appeal that
the prize fighter and the cowboy did, but he was sanctioned
by the priests she worshiped. And he did, remarkably, want
to marry her. And he wrote her poetry. He would buy her
greeting cards, then cut or rip out the printed verse on the
inside and substitute one of his own. In 1945, her birthday
message included the words: "Never in all the annals of
recorded time / existed such sweet pretext for a rhyme."

I'm sure Charlie, the boxer, didn't write her poetry. By
the time I was born, he'd long been retired. He tended bar
at the Brick Café; his brother Paul, a morose, dark, heavy
German, cooked in the back. He was never visible except
when he came out to say hello to my mother in a filthy
white T-shirt and grease-spattered pants. Here also we
never had to ask for what we wanted. My mother had Welsh
rarebit, which Paul made miraculous by generous lashings
of beer and luxurious slatherings of butter on the toast
points. I was brought a shrimp cocktail with Russian dressing. The coral stripes of the shrimp beautifully matched the
orange-pink of the dressing, and the polite green under-
statement of the lettuce cut what would otherwise have
been too rich for a young palate. I drank a Shirley Temple
and my mother a Manhattan. We were the only unescorted
females in the place. Charlie would whisk us to our car, to
see that we got home safely. We were on top of the world,
far exalted above her brothers and sisters. On those nights I
always wished we were living by ourselves, in our own
apartment, but I know she felt she needed her family's help.
I know they didn't understand our exalted position: they
thought we were somehow pathetic, somehow beneath

them, needy dependents. I knew we weren't. But as it turned out, they were right—my mother and her family—and I was wrong.

Because, as it turned out, my mother needed her family's support. She wasn't very good at being a mother. It wasn't her widowhood—being without my father, no longer being a wife—that diminished her capacity; I don't believe she minded being without my father at all. But when her mother died and she was no longer a daughter, she couldn't be a very good mother to me.

My grandmother died, without a will, after a long illness during which my mother and I took care of her virtually by ourselves. After my grandmother's death, the family split in half, some taking my mother's side in her claim to deserve the house, on the grounds that she had paid the mortgage entirely from 1929, the beginning of the Depression, to 1947, the year of her marriage. I don't know what my aunt's claim to the house was: perhaps that she had always lived there. She left—ran out—to get married at the time my grandmother was dying and came home only after the deed was done to tell my mother and me. My mother was un- done; she blamed my aunt for abandoning her and her mother; she called her a goddamn sneak. My aunt, with- holding, silent, won the day. Half my mother's brothers and sisters—there were nine of them—no longer spoke to her after this time. So all at once my mother was both orphaned and bereft of the idea of herself as a person protected by the inviolable carapace of family life. This dipped her nature in a bath of acid. She began to disintegrate. She began to drink.

This coincided with the ascendancy of polyester, which I tie to her physical decline. She drank every night, she no longer ironed. The breadlike smell of the iron on the damp cloth was no longer part of the evening air. The smell of al- cohol took its place.

The fragrant mother, the dappled mother, turned into a horror. And I was left alone with her: what I had dreamed of, what I had wanted since my father's death. At twelve, I had to clean up after her, pick her up when she fell, listen to her lament about her hardships at the hands of her brothers and sisters.

But she wasn't like this all the time. She wasn't like this before dark. She got up fresh and ready to work each morning. How could she be an alcoholic, she would say, when she got up every day and worked like a horse? And she did. But at night, she took her work clothes off, put on pajamas, and by nine was a blubbing, slobbering mess. A mess I had to clean up.

Having won the house, she let it go to ruin. It was never possible to be proud of our house. I was glad when it was sold, twenty-one years after we began living there alone. I will never go near it again.

The details of the house's disintegration are almost unbearable for me to recall. First, she let things pile up. Books, newspapers, mail. She didn't replace what broke or faded. She allowed her dog to sleep on the furniture, so every piece was stained and covered with hair. Unable to walk him, she tied the dog to the side porch railing, giving him only a foot or two of leeway, so that he had to piss and shit in the same spot for fifteen years. She picked up his shit but did nothing about the urine smell by the staircase against which he lifted his leg many thousands of times. I wonder now why I didn't walk the dog. I don't know the answer, only that I did not.

For five years I lived alone with her, ashamed of her, proud of her, thinking I had no other choice. Then I went to college, a non-Catholic college, an Ivy League college, somewhere no one we had ever known had gone, although it was only twenty miles from where we lived. Barnard. Columbia. Morningside Heights. I had to live at home for the first two years; it was considered unthinkable that I should leave her alone. But then, after two years, I earned the money to live in a dorm, promising to come home every weekend. A month before I was to leave, my mother fell and was confined to a wheelchair for six months. Heartlessly, I kept to my original plan, leaving her to the care of her cousin's wife, a plain and dour German woman who despised me and adored my mother. Throughout her life, my mother was always able to draw to her dark-hearted, intensely practical, yet secretly yearning women who saw in her immense vitality the font of life from which they had been kept.

After I left for the dorm, my mother closed off the upstairs part of the house, separating it from the rest by many plastic cleaning bags, which she stapled together. They hung from the ceiling and flapped horribly. They were as unsightly as eczema, but she claimed they cut the heating bill way down. They also made it necessary that I sleep with her in her bed when I was home. I know we both enjoyed that; watching late movies and eating junk food like roommates, then curling into each other's bodies. "Sleeping like spoons," we called it, "the big spoon, the little spoon," perfectly suited for repose. She didn't drink so much those nights.

I left New York to go to graduate school in Syracuse, and for three years I came home as little as I could—only on holidays, if there was no other choice. Then I got married to a man she didn't like. She wouldn't pay for the reception, although she allowed me to have it in the house. Three years later, when I came home to tell her I was leaving my husband, I decided, for some reason, to thoroughly clean her house. Neatness had been an issue in my marriage; at one point, my husband declared that I didn't deserve to live in a house. I ripped down the plastic bags, weeping in fury. "These are horrible, horrible, horrible," I kept saying. My mother said, "Why didn't you just tell me you didn't like them? I would have taken them down." I called in a man to make a set of heavy curtains to close off the upstairs. I paid for it, but then I gave up on the house. My mother was sympathetic to my divorce and defended me to all her family. I was the first in the family to be divorced. When I told her that my husband's tidiness drove me mad—I didn't tell her that the real reason for the divorce was that I had fallen in love with someone else—she said, quite casually, "All I ever wanted was a man to clean up after me."

Who are "you," my mother? How could I find a "you," as I tried to find one for my father? What is your humanity? Are you still human?

The attempt to find a "you" is, perhaps, now even more crucial than the search for my father was. I knew that in his case I would be involved in a process of search, remembrance, and invention. I didn't know that I would have to do the same for you. I didn't know that in the year when I was taken up with finding my father, you would be slipping away. That some surface, some responsive, vibrant material, would turn to stone. And the past would become something I alone had access to, like a power of attorney, a legacy in your name that you were prohibited from spending. A legacy suddenly taken from you and sent—where? Where has your memory gone, my mother? It was not an object; it was spirit, and the spirit, like the flesh, it seems, can be entirely consumed.

I don't know what it means to you to use language. When you speak, you sound like a machine—a computer voice or a tape recorder. You reproduce the words you somehow sense are called for in a situation whose defining marks are no longer legible. So when you say how much you love me, what, exactly, does that mean? I always knew what my father meant each time he said it. Or wrote it. I have nothing that you wrote.

I don't know if you suffer.

I imagine you in the desert, but a desert covered in fog. The landscape has been laid bare, you don't know by what. You know only that this bareness is final, and is all.

I keep trying to bring you to life. I think that if I bring you to the garden and we can use words to describe flowers, or if we sing songs, you are alive again. But it isn't very much, and some days, if I'm tired or overworked, I ask myself if it's worth it. And some days I say no. I sometimes go more than a week without seeing you.

On the days I decide not to see you, I think I would prefer that you were dead.

I have never lived a day not wishing my father was alive.

This is, I know, entirely due to the difference between the ideal (dead) body and the actual (living) one.

I think regularly about the desirability of your death. Yet if anyone did anything to cause you even the slightest discomfort, did anything to show you even the smallest disrespect, I would raise my voice and strike that person to the heart.

At the very same moment when I find the sight of you unbearable, the same moment when the sound of my voice, the tone of it, which you very well understand, may be striking you to the heart.

The social worker in charge of my mother's case has written to tell me that I must sign a D.N.R. form. Do Not Resuscitate. Do not use unusual means. Don't keep her alive. Let her die.

I sign a piece of paper that authorizes that someone will look on while my mother dies.

It is possible to say that from my father I learned the sovereignty of the mind and the imagination; from my mother that there is nothing so important as piss and shit and flesh that can rot or be kept from rot. It would be possible, therefore, to say that my father taught me the greater lesson. But there is something so indomitable about my mother's insistence on the body's finality, its determination to exist, that it seems to have a stoic and tragic grandeur that my father's vision—vague and watery—does not possess. She is older than the rock she has become. My mother has become one of the ancients. She is out of our time, this time, and because she has no memory, out of time as a whole. This gives her a harsh, unloving beauty before which one has the impulse to bend the knee. Simultaneously, the impulse to take one's own life. If this is it, this is life, I want no part of it. My father's vision, less truthful, is far more full of hope.

My friend says to me, "She's not there anymore. You have to give her up." I have to give up hope, but her body continues to be there. The hopeless body at the center of the world.

My father's body, which no longer exists, is the hopeful body at the center of what I call my imagination.

We walk down to the garden. Or rather, we don't walk, I push her, making sure not to let her momentum drag us down. We get to the level part, where it is no longer difficult to walk. I point out daylilies, a pair of infant twins, a pigeon pecking at mulberries. I name colors. I insist that she look. I insist that she tell me which of the flowers is her favorite. "I like them all," she says. "No, you have to pick one." "The purple one," she says. "Hibiscus," I tell her.

I say that it's my favorite one too.

"I know that," she says. "That's why I said it."

I would like to believe that she is still capable of liking one color more than another but it's probably too much to ask. Does she still remember that I like purple? Or is she faking again?

I believe that somehow, unfocused, but in a white light she sees all the time, is her love for me. Which may be the only thing that she still knows.

And once again I understand that despite the wreckage of my parents' lives, I have been, I still am, greatly beloved.

She keeps telling me it's too hard for me to push her so far. She keeps telling me the time. It's eleven-thirty. Lunch is at noon. She keeps saying we'd better get back, that if we're late to lunch they won't keep anything for her.

I can tell that she wants nothing more than to get back. I have no way of knowing whether it's a good thing to take her to the garden, whether she's still capable of being pleased, or whether she would prefer, above all, not to be bothered, to be left alone. Whether I am taking her to the garden because I think it is pleasant for her or because I can tell people about it and they will think I'm doing something pleasant for her, think how good I am. Such a good daughter. She takes her mother to the garden. But perhaps my mother would prefer to be left alone.

I leave her in the dining room. She asks when she'll see me again. I tell her in a week. "What are you doing with yourself between now and then?" she asks, with a hint of her old bite.

"Gallivanting," I say.

"Just as I thought," she says, opening the cellophane that holds her plastic fork, knife, and spoon.

I leave the dining room and, standing a little to one side of the doorway, watch my mother as she eats. She doesn't talk to her neighbors at the table. Her face shows no enjoyment in her food. She stares ahead of her, her glance vacant as a blind woman's, chewing as if it were a mildly difficult task she knows she must perform. She is staring ahead at an infinite present which holds no savor for her. I don't know what it holds.

I can imagine a life for my father. I can think thoughts

that I believe might be his. In death, he is more vibrant for me than she is in what is called her life. A life I cannot understand or recognize. She will go on and on. I will have to see her as she is and not as I have made her. I cannot make her any different. This, of course, is the problem.

The problem of the living. It's not a problem with my father. My father is entirely up to me.

Unburying and Burying

My Father: A Journal

Sitting on a bank,
Weeping again the King my father's rack,
The music crept by me upon the waters,
Allaying both their fury and my passion . . .

Full fathom five thy father lies,
    Of his bones are corals made,
Those are pearls that were his eyes;
    Nothing of him that doth fade
But doth suffer a sea-change
    Into something rich and strange.
                                            —*The Tempest*

When I tell my mother that I want to move my father's body to a new grave, she fixes me with a look I know very well. "That's the thing about you," she says, "you always had wacky ideas."

My father lies in a grave under a stone that bears not his name but that of my mother's family: Gagliano. He lies among people who at best tolerated or patronized him, at worst despised him. He lies with his father-in-law, my mother's father, who refused to appear at my parents' wedding. As my mother walked out the door to go to the church, her father handed her a card upon which he had written, "You will work till the day you die." In the cemetery plot with my father, along with my grandfather and grandmother, are my grandfather's mother, Anna Gagliano, and one of my uncles, Santo Giuseppe Gagliano, known as Joe. Perhaps to seem more American, he changed his name legally to Samuel Joseph. Also his wife, Edna, who converted from Presbyterianism in her last illness (she was nursed by my grandmother). There are also stillborn twins, children of my uncle Anthony's. Reading the names on the stone, you would think it was the grave of any Italian family. No one could guess there is a Jew there. No one, passing, would know he had passed the remains of my father.

The remains. "Those are pearls that were his eyes; / Nothing of him that doth fade / But doth suffer a sea-change / Into something rich and strange."

But into what? He is not under the sea. What is left of my father's body?

During a panel on art and ethics in which I participate, a slide of a photograph of Andres Serrano's is shown. It is a picture, called "Jane Doe killed by police," taken in a morgue. The face is blackening with rot. There are holes instead of eyes.

Holes, not pearls, that were his eyes. I have to consider the fact that what I want to move was once an object in the state of the image in the photograph. It frightens me to look at Serrano's picture, and frightens me to make the connection with my father. I think it is my father I am horrified for, not myself. But how can I be sure? I have to reckon with thoughts of worms and grinning skulls. But I don't have to dwell on them for long. I can concentrate on a headstone.

With his name. Which I do. Which I allow myself to do. I don't allow myself to think that under the ground my father will be still alive, and that, wiping the earth from his eyes, he will say, "Thank you, thank you, you have rescued me from all these years of burial." Of course I have imagined it. But I don't allow myself to think it might be true.

The last time I saw my father, he was in his coffin, still and stiff, surrounded by flowers—gladiolus and chrysanthemums, I think—and to me (had I feared the sight of him?) he was surprisingly beautiful, considering what he'd been through. He was still recognizably himself.

The night after he died, my mother's two best friends and five of her brothers and sisters who lived nearby were collected around my grandmother's dining-room table. I felt an itching on my side, then a little pimple. I knew that chicken pox was spreading through my class. I tried to believe the sore would go away. There were some transitional moments when it still seemed possible. You know that moment, like the moment after the flash of lightning when a person afraid of storms believes or hopes thunder won't follow. But the moment I mean is always connected with a physical breakdown: a sore throat, an abscessed tooth. Desperately, the ailing one tells herself that it is possible the suffering will not develop. That it will never be the case. And then it is the case.

I went from being a child shocked by her loss to being a sick child, overcome by fever and miserable itching sores. Overcome by a disease with a trivial, jokey-sounding name.

In the Metropolitan Museum, there is a thirteenth-century seated figure from an area in Africa called the Niger. It is a figure of mourning. His back is bent, his legs are crossed, the side of his face rests on top of his knee, one arm cradles the top leg. His eyes are closed. His mouth is open. Covering his

back are bumps in a regular pattern; the accompanying explanation says the bumps could indicate either disease or ritual scarification.

It is possible for him to do nothing but mourn. Nothing
can be expected of him. His only work: to represent grief.

After my father's death, I should have done nothing but
grieve, but my fever stole the consciousness of grief from
me. And since no one looked at me, I could represent nothing. I was exiled to a dark room upstairs in my grandmother's house. I could hear the wall of voices, roaring like
the sea, the clink of a knife against a plate. I was incapable
of witnessing anything. I was entirely absorbed in my body's
occupation by disease. I was given over to sickness, perhaps
like the seated mourner from the Niger, who experienced
his body's defilement either, like me, because of disease, or
by the loving act of his own hand.

Did I make myself sick so that I could enact, on my own
skin, my sense of defilement? I was abandoned, cut off, like
a limb that grows gangrenous because the heart's work is
not being done. Did I believe that my loathesomeness without my father should be marked?

The defilement of the dead. The defilement of those attached to the dead.

Why does losing the beloved to death make one feel polluted? I touched my father's dead hand; I was glad to touch
it. That wasn't the thing that made me feel polluted; I was
sorry to give it up.

What is the source of the pollution? Touching the dead
hand, or letting go of it?

The seated figure from the Niger has no choice. He takes
his place: the mourner's.

It was impossible for me to take my place.

I don't know who cared for me while I lived in that room.
The events of my father's death and burial seemed like sub-

atomic particles, far from the orbit I inhabited, the orbit of fever, where my head spun and my mouth was parched and my skin itched. ("Don't touch it. You'll make permanent scars.") I was given a pair of my grandmother's white cotton gloves so that I wouldn't hurt myself if I scratched in my sleep. There I lay in my red-and-white-striped pajamas— they had, I remember, a high, split collar, a style called "mandarin."

The last day of my father's "laying out," my uncle carried me into the funeral parlor so I could get a last glimpse. I know I wasn't wearing my white gloves because I remember the cold feeling of my father's hand, which I tried to hold. I wanted to climb up to embrace him, but I was prevented. I had the sense that everyone wanted me taken away. I seem to have knelt before my father's coffin only a few seconds. It was all very fleeting, very fast. For a few minutes, I was near him. Perhaps people were made nervous by my visibly infected state. Very quickly I was carried out, carried home. Back to the dark room, to a deep sleep I think must have lasted many days. I know there were guests in the house outside the room where I was sleeping. In my spinning fever I could hear them. No one came for me, no one told me the progress of these important events. My father was being brought from above the ground to a life below it. I believed it was possible no one would come for me ever. I knew my father was dead, buried, no longer a possibility of rescue, no longer any help.

What did I see in that coffin? I remember the fixity of the face, the calmness of the mouth. And then what?

I cannot say. A gate closed, and I have not allowed it to be opened. This is the gate between the girl who saw her father and the person who did not.

. . .

I am looking at the plates in a book about Caspar David Friedrich, pictures that wound me by their lucidity, so that I can't look at them for long. I see that he often paints death as a gate through which one must walk to get to an unclear, though more beautiful, world.

When my uncle carried me out of the funeral home, the film snapped. The broken tape flapped forever in the air.

Can I repair the break? Restart the film?

Time lapse: thirty-eight years. The child in the dark room in a lost sleep, brought on by fever.

Cut.

Mourners, in fifties costume, at an open grave.

Cut.

Time: the present.

Scene: another open grave.

I have had for many years, at least since my adolescence, a desire to disinter my father's body.

I have not been willing or able to imagine the practical details. Now, I can.

Before it can happen, there are transactions that need to be made among the living. There is the law, which, in relation to the moving of the dead, is complicated and must be obeyed.

Moving a body to a new grave is a practical issue, and one day I took practical steps. One of my closest friends, Gary, is a Jesuit, now connected to a parish on the Upper East Side. He puts me in touch with an undertaker he's worked with, Harry Finnan, of Charles Peter Nagel, Inc. Harry is cooperative, intelligent, efficient. I can see this from the moment we walk into the funeral parlor and he comes to the door, apologizing for being engaged with "a family," people in mourning, in shock. Gary and I head for a bench at the back of a corridor, passing workmen, ladders, sawdust, plastic sheets. Restoration, Harry explains, is going on.

He shows me into the office. He looks at all my papers. He asks me some questions.

"How many are with him?"

"How many what?"

"Bodies."

"Oh, I don't know."

"Well, the important thing is, who's on his level."

"Oh, none of them is on his level," I want to say. "He's above all of them. That's why I want to move him out of there."

But I remember who I'm talking to. And that it's important to stay quite literal.

Harry makes a call—one call—and finds out that it's possible for me to move the body. I need affidavits from every living member of my mother's generation. And a new plot for my father and my family. Do I want the same cemetery? Not necessarily, I say. As a matter of fact, I'd prefer somewhere else. He suggests Calvary, in Queens. It's a cemetery I've always liked, because a lot of immigrant Irish women paid for their own graves there. I'm glad of this choice. Also, my father will officially be buried in the City of New York. Our Town.

But I will have to ask permission of my two uncles and the aunt who has been my nemesis. Who has always frightened me. Who has always disliked me. Whose actions in relation to my grandmother's house badly hurt my mother. Who could always make my mother and me feel in the wrong with her coldness, her fanatic law-abidingness. When a priest in her parish quoted approvingly from *Final Payments*, she wrote to the bishop, demanding the priest's dismissal. When my uncle, her brother, showed her a write-up of an interview with me, she threw the newspaper across the room with the words "I don't read trash."

I have always known myself as the person who has had to defend myself against her.

As her enemy.

If she goes along with my request, will she no longer be my enemy?

Then who will I be?

My beloved cousin agrees to speak to her for me. My cousin Joseph, whose name in our childhood was Peppy, whom I continue to call Peppy, although he has dropped the name. I've given up my childhood name: Mary Kate. Peppy never calls me that. I never call him anything but Peppy. Peppy, whom I have no memory of life without, who has always, for all my life, provided me with joy, solace, and tremendous laughter. We used to have to be separated at family dinners because we laughed so much we couldn't eat. The adults would always say, "This laughter will end in tears." It never did. This year, at my birthday, Peppy said, "What kind of people would separate children because they were laughing? Wouldn't you want children to laugh?" Oh, my darling Peppy, from you I have learned to be a sister, to be a female, easily, among males. I can never give you what you have given me. You were the easy child; I was the difficult one; you the smoother-over; I the pointer-out. How did I ever have the good luck to be loved by you? It would have been impossible for me not to love you, but your love for me is a miracle, a gift. I like to feel that I understand you: understand your great imagination and the depth of your knowing heart. At least I can give you that.

I am worried that Peppy's goodness won't be strong enough to overcome my aunt's resistance. The day after I. talk to him, I am sitting in the living room with the children. I begin crying because of my father. Anna takes my hand. I tell her how much I want to move his grave, how afraid I am that my aunt will stop me. She says, "Don't worry, Mom, you'll eventually have your wish. You'll probably outlive her, and even if you don't, I will. And I promise that I'll move your father's grave so you'll be buried together."

Suddenly, I am filled with pity for my aunt. She is old and I am young. She is childless and I've borne children. She was crippled and I've been healthy. I want to stop thinking of her as my enemy.

She says she won't stand in my way. My cousin tells me she says, "What do I care what she does?" My aunt is much more interested in a boycott of Disney, started by Mother Angelica, a TV evangelist based in South Carolina, who has an audience of millions. A former cloistered nun, Mother Angelica once saw a television studio and said to herself, "I have to get me one of these." And God provided. Mother Angelica is spearheading a boycott of Disney because it is the parent company of Miramax, which produced the movie *Priest*, portraying a homosexual priest and a priest who is the common-law husband of his beautiful black housekeeper. I loved the movie; I thought the Church should give Miramax a nice stipend for producing it. If all priests were like those two—committed, and utterly with their people—the Church would be flooded, I think, with members.

My aunt tells Peppy that another cousin of ours will be visiting her with his children on the way to Disneyland, and when he arrives, she'll make sure he doesn't get there. Peppy asks what she'll do to stop him. "Never mind," she says.

I feel bad about writing this because I'm grateful to my aunt and I don't want to do anything to offend her at this moment of possible reconciliation. But the fanaticism that seems to be part of my heritage on both sides of the family terrifies me, and I have to see the humor of it or be overwhelmed.

The question: In an age of television nuns, would my father stand closer to me, laughing at them, or to the people sending donations via MasterCard?

I think my father wouldn't stop children from having fun.

But perhaps his sense of outrage at the things I stand for would overcome his love of jokes and children.

I'll never know.

And I'm no longer interested in that kind of speculation.

He is the father who loved me.

He is the father whom I love.

He is the father whose bones I am about to move.

I call one of my uncles, who has just gotten out of the hospital. He was someone who was, at best, of no help to me when I needed help as a child and a teenager. At his worst, he made things harder for me by reproaching me for crying. By insisting that I be "tough."

Seven years ago, when we traveled back to New York from Florida after Peppy's mother's funeral, he expressed regret that the family had fallen apart. He'd like to be back in touch with me, he said. Then I became the tough person he wanted thirty-five years earlier. I told him it was too late. I told him there was a time when I needed him quite badly, but I didn't anymore. I told him everything I had had to endure that all of them made worse.

He began to cry. I saw that he was an old man. He said I had to understand that he was always sickly as a child, that he always felt he was the weakest of them all. That he went along with the others. That he wanted to be a priest. That he hadn't lived up to his potential. He kept saying over and over again, "None of us lived up to our potential."

I cried with him, because I could understand how he suffered from his position as the weakest, the youngest boy. But I didn't get in touch with him again. It seemed impossible. Too much had come before.

His son called my house when his mother, my uncle's wife died. They said I had the deed to the Gagliano plot. But I was in Rome for two weeks, unreachable. When I got home, it was too late. She had been buried somewhere else.

At first, I felt guilty, then angry. They knew she was ill; why didn't they get in touch with me before she died? Then I spoke to my uncle, and he was so obviously shattered, and so quick to reassure me that none of it was my fault, he was so old, so weak, that I could only promise to straighten everything out that had to do with the grave.

Which I am doing.

When I call about his signing the affidavit, he says he'll be happy to sign. He asks for my mother. When I tell him she doesn't recognize anyone, he weeps again. "Poor Anne," he says. "Poor, poor Anne."

He says he'd love to see my children. I say I'll bring them to him. And this time, it seems right. After my father's out of the Gagliano plot, I'll give my uncle a certified copy of the deed. I don't seem to have the original, although everyone, including the cemetery, thinks I do. It must have been among my mother's papers; now it's lost, with many of her other things. When my father is out of their grave, I'll give over all connection, all responsibility, to that family. The idea makes me feel light and full of joy.

I have another uncle, whom I've never known very well. He was trained as an osteopath and practiced osteopathy for thirty years; now he's a psychiatrist. He and his family lived in Philadelphia, so he wasn't part of the web of family gatherings that were so constant a feature of my childhood. When *Final Payments* was published, he wrote me a letter saying he wanted to collaborate on a book with me. At that time, everyone I'd ever met seemed to want to collaborate on a book with me, or want something from me, some contact, some favor, some remembrance. I was turned off by his getting in touch with me after so long a silence, so I never responded to his request. Now I ask my lawyer, who is also my friend, to take care of the correspondence for me. She writes to him at his office, requesting that he sign the affidavit. He phones her back and insists upon speaking to me.

With real dread, I phone him at his home in Tulsa, Oklahoma. He says, "I'm your uncle, why would you contact me through a lawyer?" I tell him that it seemed appropriate since we hadn't spoken in thirty-three years, since my grandmother's funeral. "Oh, yes, we have," he says, and I hear the frightening cadences of my mother's family's accusation: the monotone, slow and staccato, that feels like needles being pushed into my eyes. "I phoned you when your book came out. I wanted you to collaborate on a book about a patient of mine. It would have been kind of a mystery. You gave me the name of another girl who was successful that year too."

I realize that he's correct; he did phone, rather than write a letter, although I'd blotted that conversation out. I understand that he has something I want, that if he chooses, he can stymie the project of my father's reburial. I make myself abject. I think I use the word "stress" several times. This is a period of stress. I was under great stress when I published *Final Payments:* all that sudden attention, in the midst of my getting a divorce. He says that he's read all my work, all of it, and he hopes I have a good therapist, because I sound like a very depressed person.

I tell him I think of myself as more hysterical than depressed. He says, "Are you very withholding with everyone, or do you just come across like that to me?" I tell him I don't think I'm particularly withholding, but that I don't know him very well. I tell him I don't have good feelings about the family, and that I hope he'll forgive me for lumping him in with them and fearing that he would be censorious and rejecting of me, as they have been.

He says he's the one who got away: he's different.

He tells me about his children. His oldest daughter, whom I knew slightly and was in awe of, was the perfect teenager; she even looked like Sandra Dee. She had, I remember, a friend named Bubbles, and she wore Yardley lip gloss before anyone I knew thought of it. Now she has cancer. He is estranged from his son. One of his daughters has been married somewhere between five and eight times. Another is the vice president of the Oklahoma Bar. Another is married to a Cherokee, and they are professional bowlers. "Perhaps you've seen her on *Wide World of Sports*," he says. I say that unfortunately I have not. His wife gets on the phone. She doesn't have the family voice; she's warm and friendly. She tells me she's a Jew, and wouldn't my uncle's mother die to think that her little boy, the one she wanted to be a priest, was divorced and married to a Jewish woman. She tells me that my uncle is a brilliant man and that his daughters adore him. She says I have a wonderful family in Oklahoma, and they are there for me if I want them. I am well disposed toward her, but I want to say, "What I want isn't family. I have Peppy. Peppy has me: that's enough. I have more than enough people in my life—I'm drowning in people. What I want is for your husband to sign the affidavit." He talks about the family's misunderstanding of him. He says, "You and I have been on the same path all these years without knowing it." He doesn't ask for my mother. He agrees to sign the affidavit. He says, "Be gentle opening that grave, because my twin babies are there."

· · ·

I take my mother's affidavit to her in the nursing home and we go upstairs to the business office, where there's a notary. He's eighty-two years old himself. My mother praises him for being a notary and tells him she was a notary herself. "It was very important in my work," she says. "In the old days not just anyone could be a notary; you had to be someone." He perks up. He tells her that he's been a notary for fifty years, and in all that time he's never taken a cent in fee. My mother says she did the same thing, although I know that's a lie; she often took me out for a treat on her notary fees. But she told him what he wants to hear. He likes her very much; he's much more interested in her than in me. And she wants to talk to him about interesting signatures she's had to witness. He tells her to bring herself up sometime for a chat. I can tell that, like many of the people who knew her professionally, he thinks she's hot stuff. As I wheel her into the elevator she says, "What was this paper I just signed?" I tell her it was an affidavit allowing my father to be reburied. "Oh, that crazy idea of yours," she says. I tell her she has a choice now: She can be buried with me and my father, or with her parents. She says, "You're the only one that matters to me. I don't care about anyone else."

I bring Harry all the affidavits. "Everything's shipshape," he says. "You know, Miss Gordon, when I saw all the complications involved, I wasn't sure you could do it. But I have to say one thing for you. You're an extremely persistent person."

I'm very pleased by this compliment. Harry and I are colleagues. We understand each other.

We talk about the headstone. He offers me a book of samples. Some people have their signatures carved into the stone; it is possible to have a likeness of your face: one man has his face next to Jesus in the Garden. Harry says, "Just this week, one of our clients had a nature scene, I wish you could have seen it. Beautiful work. The man was a hunter, so it's a deer, running in the woods. But the cemetery insisted on a religious symbol, so the deer is running past a cross." He tells me that a couple had a Mercedes-Benz carved into their son's stone; he died at nineteen, and what he had most wanted in life was a Mercedes. Harry says, "Two things you need for this job. One: a sense of humor. Two: you have to like people." He says that he's fallen into several graves. Once he was covered by AstroTurf and no one could see where he was.

People seem to be telling me stories about burials and graves. Or perhaps I am hearing them now, perhaps people have always been telling them. My friend Phil tells me that his mother regularly moved her family's remains around whenever there was a family feud, which there often was. Her excuse was that a large cemetery was moved when the Interborough Parkway was created, so it couldn't be a very big deal. She used to go to court and get the city to pay for the disinterments. It never cost her anything. Phil doesn't know how she did it, but he said there was a period in her life in which it took up a great deal of her time.

My friend Elena Levin tells me that her father, a Russian, was buried in Harbin, China. Many years later she got a letter from the Chinese government saying they were going to build an airport on the land now occupied by the Russian cemetery. For a great sum of money she could have her father's body moved. She and her sisters decided not to do it, since it was very unlikely that anyone in her family would get to China to see it. Then she indeed went to China and was asked if she wanted to go back to Harbin. She said no, because there would be no grave to visit.

What she doesn't say: If there had been a grave, she would have gone.

If she flew to Harbin, would she be afraid that the wheels of the plane were crushing her father's bones?

An old priest tells me this story. He is a little drunk when he tells it.

He was traveling on a train from Chicago to New York. There was a terrible smell on the train, a smell of garbage or maybe shit. An Arab family, in traditional costume, was sitting straight ahead. The father was holding a baby in his arms. The baby was tightly swaddled. After a while, the priest and the Arab family were the only ones in the car. Wanting to make conversation, the old priest said, "Your baby's very well behaved. It hasn't cried all this time."

The father looked at him. "It's dead, the baby's dead," he said. "We're taking it to the place where it needs to be buried."

Thinking of moving my father's "remains," I have to think about and talk about this kind of story.

The story raises questions. Could they have carried the baby some other way? In some sort of bag? Or wrapped in plastic? How does one transport the dead? How will my father be transported?

And where is the place the parents were carrying the dead baby to be buried? What made it the right place? What about it was so important?

Because of what I'm doing with my father's body, I understand these people. I think of us as the same.

Some of my friends think what I'm doing is crazy. They say it worries them. It smacks of the fanatical, the fetishistic.

I fall back on Shakespeare. I tell them that what I want for my father is simply this: "A local habitation and a name."

Then I look up the whole quote. It's from the last act of *A Midsummer Night's Dream.*

> The lunatic, the lover, and the poet
> Are of imagination all compact.
> One sees more devils than vast hell can hold;
> That is, the madman. The lover, all as frantic,
> Sees Helen's beauty in a brow of Egypt.
> The poet's eye, in a fine frenzy rolling,
> Doth glance from heaven to earth, from earth to heaven;
> And as imagination bodies forth
> The forms of things unknown, the poet's pen
> Turns them to shapes and gives to airy nothing
> A local habitation and a name.

The lunatic, the lover, and the poet. In relation to moving my father's bones, I am all three. There is madness in what I want to do: a confusion of the symbolic and the actual. It's obsessive: I won't give up; no obstacle stops me. And like a lover, I wish to lie with my beloved for all eternity. Then there is the problem of the writing, the bodying-forth of the form. What is the unknown thing, the airy nothing? My father? My love for him? Do I believe that if I get him into words properly, he can live again? Or is it that by getting him properly into words, I can finally allow him to be dead.

"A local habitation and a name." He has a local habitation: he is in a grave in Long Island; he has been there for the whole career of his death. His bones are in a place, have always been. But the name under which he lies is not his. Or mine. I will bring him to a piece of earth purchased by me. By my money, earned by writing. Also by my lunacy. And this unseemly love. This love that doesn't fear being called grotesque. This love that fears nothing.

"And a name." I will make my father legible. The conjunction of location and identity will finally be inscribed. I will make visible, record the fact that, in Auden's words, "one more series of accidents came to its end." I will be able to point to something and say, "My father's bones are here.

And here is his name." He will cease to be anonymous. He will no longer be one of the unmarked dead.

My friend Helen understands exactly what I'm doing. She said people were repelled when she told them she wanted to prepare her mother's body for burial. She loved her mother very much; she knew it was the right thing. She said she knew it was the right thing because you always know something's right if primitive people do it, or animals.

I ask Harry what he thinks is left of my father's body. He says, "Hard to tell. So much depends on the moisture. We buried one woman, twenty-five years ago, and when we dug her up, you could recognize her. Dress and everything. But we buried a baby six months ago, and last week . . . nothing."

Later he tells Gary that since my father was buried in a wooden casket, there will be nothing left but dust and bones. He says Gary should tell me that sometime. Gary, my Jesuit friend, tells me one morning when we're drinking coffee, looking out the window at First Avenue, watching people in raincoats going to work. For the rest of the day, whenever I'm not engaged in an utterly absorbing task, I find myself weeping.

Bones and dust.

What did I think there would be?

I wish I hadn't put Gary in the position of having to tell me this kind of thing. But without him, his clerical authority, none of this would have been possible.

I have to earn money to pay for my father's grave. I will write an introduction to a book by a neglected Irish woman author. And an article about being the daughter of a handicapped mother, and how this creates difficulties for female embodiment.

I don't want to do either of them. They are drudgery, sheer labor. But the idea of earning money for my father delights me. A labor for my father! I can work while he rests. I can toil for his monument.

Part of the money, at least half, will come from the article I am writing as my mother's daughter. Writing—which I do as *his* daughter, about *her*.

The cemetery where the new grave will be, Calvary, is the one we used to pass every time we drove into the city, every time we took the Long Island Expressway to the Midtown Tunnel. I was scared of that cemetery because it seemed too crowded. The dead seemed massed and teeming, unprosperous slum dwellers. And I always resented having to think about death before I got into the city.

Now I live in Manhattan and to examine the potential gravesite must cross the river the other way to get to Calvary. I take the Fifty-ninth Street Bridge to Queens Boulevard, then turn on to Van Dam Street, then to Greenpoint Avenue. An unlovely strip of factories, graffitied walls. The occasional house sided with fake-brick shingles, empty, hopelessly for sale. We pass La Guardia Community College. Students, mostly black and Hispanic, their books in their arms, Walkmans in their ears. I realize that my father wouldn't know what a Walkman was, wouldn't be able to identify what these students were doing, walking with these things in their ears. I wonder what gestures and habits of the future, begun after my death, will be commonplace for the inhabitants of the future, incomprehensible to me.

We turn into the cemetery. It is not the tenement city of the dead I saw from the highway as a child. It seems luxurious, elegant: the Central Park West of the no-longer-alive.

A statue of the Crucified Jesus, the Mourning Mother, and the Apostle John is just inside the gates. I know this would please my father.

It is exactly the cemetery I would have chosen for myself, had I had the choice of many. The section where graves are available, Section IX, is in the old part of the cemetery. It is a work of Victoriana. Art nouveau angels and obelisks. The ornate cult of melancholy, indulged in unapologetically. Invested in. Its artifacts procured, engraved, tended, visited. I think of Victorian melancholia and envy it. It is one of the ways I would like to live: shut up in a dark house, thinking only of my father. Of course this requires money; if you don't have money, you have to leave the house to work. These words are my mother's, and it is because of my mother, perhaps, that shut up in a dark house, mourning, is only one of the ways I would like to live, and not the most dominant among them.

Among the old stones and monuments there is a wooden cross tied with a red bow. Inscribed in Magic Marker: *Isabella Ruiz*. Born the year of my birth, dead this year. I know how much even the cheapest headstone costs, and I understand not being able to afford it. In front of the wooden cross there is a blue vase without flowers. On the way out, we pass a Hispanic couple by a new, raw-looking grave. They have with them—are they turning it into a monument?—a baby's car seat with a teddy bear strapped into it. I wonder if they lost their baby in a car accident, and I can say nothing to them as I pass by.

Walking up the path is a woman holding an empty plastic bag and a dog's lead. Following her is an exuberant, yapping mutt. I pet him; he runs in circles around me. She walks with the dog to a water spout, runs the water, and cools his fur. I say her dog is nice. She answers, in a Spanish accent, that she can't speak English.

Most of the ornate monuments in this section, our section, were built by the Irish between 1890 and 1935. Many of the new stones will have Spanish names. I note, with sadness, that my father and I will not be buried among Jews.

I wish I had the money to buy my father a really lugubrious nineteenth-century monument. Weeping angels. Cherubs with their chins in their hands.

But it might cost as much as sending my children to college for a year.

This is the kind of thing I have to think about: the aspect of it that involves money. How much is too much? What figure would I balk at—$10,000, $20,000, $50,000, $100,000? What is it worth? And what is the *it*? This last is a question I can't answer. I only know that it is something of value. But of what value? Comparable to what? Children's education? A down payment on a house? I know that there is a point at which I'd say, "It's not worth that." And the clarity of that refusal would be a relief. "It's out of my hands," I would have to say. "I have to think of my children's future."

If only I were someone who could ruin herself for a gesture. A gesture in the direction of the past. A useless gesture, merely symbolic. *Merely symbolic.* If only I were someone who believed that the word "merely" should never be placed in front of the word "symbolic." Alas for me, one foot in the practical world, the other somewhere else. Some people find it excessive that I'm doing it, but I am not capable of the excess that would entail financial ruin, although the word "ruin" is thrilling. I am in love with it and the idea of it, it's an idea to which I could give my whole heart, but which I could not begin to live, even for one day. My children's future—as incorporeal as my father's past—takes precedence. Also the sparing of myself from financial terror.

My father lived without margin. He never had to face ruin

because he never had anything to lose. He felt not financial terror but financial dread.

How did he live?

In a way I could not.

I am my mother's daughter.

I go to a store on Madison Avenue (which I usually patronize only when they are having sales) to buy the perfect black dress. The "little black dress" I have never shopped for. I consider buying a mantilla, so I can look like Jackie Kennedy at America's most famous burial, but I don't know where to buy one and there's no one I know whom I could ask. When I tell one of my friends I'm considering a mantilla, he says, "I guess it's the closest you can come to a bridal veil."

I read a book by Erwin Panofsky called *Tomb Sculpture*. I learn many interesting things, among which is that in many cultures, the dead were thought of as extremely thirsty. And I find the word "necropole," the city of the dead. A city, I am learning, that had its own government, its taxes, its civic rules. I learn that the Etruscans began any settlement by building two separate cities, one for the living and one for the dead. I would, if I could, build my father a beautiful city.

Harry goes on vacation for a week, and when he comes back he calls to say, "All systems are go."

It will happen now. It will happen in two days. And suddenly it seems a bad idea. I no longer remember why I am doing it, and all the voices, expressed or politely silenced, who say it is ghoulish or mad seem to be the right ones now. My son, David, is upset. He says he can't put his finger on why, but it disturbs him, and this worries me. Suppose it rains. I'm worried that my mother will want to go to the bathroom, or will refuse to go because she's afraid of having to go to the bathroom. I wonder if I should ask her if she wants to go or simply tell her that she has to. She is living, unlike him. I cannot move her at my will. And yet, since I am mobile and articulate and she is not, it is possible, in the short run, to bend her to my will. In the long run, her will, for oblivion, the state of carrion or stone, is stronger than anything I have or can do.

I feel that Harry's efficiency has bulldozed me: I haven't had enough time to prepare. My husband says, "Do it soon, get it over with." And what is it I would prepare for? What is it I think I won't have time to do?

I'm moving the dead. Is this sacrilegious? Suddenly I'm frightened. Am I trifling with something awful?

What I tell Harry is that I'm surprised everything's happening so fast. I ask if we could postpone it for a week, and he says, "But I've done it. You wouldn't want me to undo it." The way he says "it" makes it sound unthinkable, and I haven't the force to resist him. He's made it happen: a vague yearning turned into reality.

But our perfect relationship has clouded.

He says, "You're very lucky. I just went to a conference upstate and I found out about a new stainless steel disinterment box. It'll save you six hundred dollars. Usually, we have to go for the pine, and then pay a solderer. Of course, after this length of time, thirty years, there's no question of odor."

I tell him it's forty years.

"I guess I'm showing my age," Harry says.

I bring the last affidavit to his office. He asks me about my son's upcoming tonsillectomy and reminds me that I'd told him about it, which was one reason for "the narrow window of time I had to work with."

I tell him about my concern that because of our insurance, David won't be allowed to spend the night in the hospital. We agree on the villainy of insurance companies.

Harry says, "But it'll be worse after socialized medicine. And AIDS is going to completely overburden the system. Then there are those bleeding-heart liberals that think we should let immigrants in and pay for their medical care."

"Harry," I say. "I'm one of those bleeding-heart liberals. After all, our people were immigrants."

"Yeah, but *we're* here now," he says. His face is very red. I think he's angry.

I go to Gary's to work on creating a service. Gary is wearing running shorts and a T-shirt. We sit in his room, with its view of the roofs of Eighty-seventh Street, under the print of Bronzino's arrogant young man I gave him as a moving-in gift. Sitting on this couch, I have listened to music, talked for many hours, been part of an election night party, an Oscars party. Now we have spread between us the *Modern Order of Ritual* and the old Latin one. I'm starting to be dazed by an overabundance of texts and choices. Gary takes my hand. I understand that he has said these prayers hundreds of times. He is a priest, and I am comforted by his priestliness. He is able to provide the consolation of the priesthood but refuse its aura of privilege and immunity. Also, to allow enormous latitude in his definition of acceptable human behavior. He's always thought this reburial was a crazy idea, but he will be with me, beside me all the way. In running shorts, he intones, "*Miserere mei, Deus, secundum magnam misericordiam tuam.*" Have mercy on me, Lord, according to thy great mercy.

These are formal words, emptied of particularity. It is from this emptiness their solace comes. I choose to say the psalms in Latin because I know my father would have liked that. And because the very opacity of the language gives it power.

"*In paradisum deducant te angeli.*" May the angels take you into paradise. May the martyrs come to welcome you on your way and lead you into the Holy City, Jerusalem. May the choirs of angels welcome you, and with Lazarus, who was once poor *("quondam paupere")*, may you have eternal rest.

This is the best of the Church: the splendor of angelic choirs, the reminder of Lazarus, one of the poor. I think they're conflating two Lazaruses: the brother of Mary and Martha, and the beggar, covered with sores, who is taken to heaven, whereas Dives, the rich man, is punished in hell; Dives begs Father Abraham to send Lazarus to dip his finger in water and reach down to cool his parched tongue. His request is refused. "If you didn't listen to the words of the prophets, it's too late now."

The beautiful words: *eternal rest . . . perpetual light . . . ashes to ashes, dust to dust . . . the peace that passes understanding.* We choose some passages from the new order, because they are superior to the old: "He will see you face to face and in your light will see light." This is much better than the sin-ridden prayers of the old lectionary.

We decide to include the *Dies Irae*, the Day of Wrath of the sequence of the Requiem Mass. Because terror is a part of death, and I think we need to make a place for that.

There is no way that the words I have chosen can be of use without the structure or the semblance of belief.

I don't know what I believe about the fate of the life these bones represent. But the form of belief seems deeply precious, irreplaceable. The form can contain more than most forms and is therefore conducive to more beauty, more truthfulness.

Is this a hateful, a cowardly, hedging of the bets?

Whatever it is, I will not give up these forms, these words.

I phone the cemetery for directions. One of the people I speak to says, "What's the name of the deceased?"

I say, "David Gordon."

"Oh, yeah, we have him," he says.

In what sense, I want to ask, do you mean "have"? And where are the bones right now? And do they mean my father?

In preparation for the event I bathe, shave my legs and underarms. When my father died, this would not have been necessary. I had the body of a child. What has happened to that body?

It is the day. I've told everyone to meet at my mother's nursing home. I have lent her my favorite black silk blouse and she looks beautiful, except for her teeth, which are now blackened stumps. No one is disturbed by this but me; when I look at them, it's the only thing I can think of.

Yesterday, when I came by to tell her what was going to happen, I found her at a sing-along. I looked at her through the door. She was smiling and singing, "After the ball is over / After the break of dawn / After the dancers' leaving / After the stars are gone."

I sat next to her and we sang, "Peg O' My Heart." She looked at me with an absolutely loving look. I started crying.

"What's the matter?" she says. "Are you upset that you can't sing as well as you could? None of us can."

It occurs to me that our deepest and most truthful conversations have happened in these songs.

I remind her of my father's reburial. I tell her what time we're going to pick her up, and that I've arranged to have her hair done first. She complains that it's too early, and that she'll miss Mass. I tell her that my friend Father Gary will bring her Communion.

"Well, that'll be a privilege," she says.

She tells me that she's going to get dressed right now and stay in her clothes all night.

I don't bother trying to argue. This is the nurses' problem.

I go to Zabar's to buy food for the guests after the ceremony. Orzo-and-crayfish salad. Assorted grilled vegetables: eggplant, yellow peppers, zucchini, carrots. Marinated string beans. I will buy the bread tomorrow so it will be fresh. I buy four dozen roses. My husband has the idea of taking the heads off the roses and throwing them on the coffin as blossoms. When I make a schedule for the morning I write, "7:45–8:15: behead roses."

I take a stone from Cape Cod and one from Rome—the places I have most loved and where I've been most happy—and put them in my purse to throw into the grave.

Everyone arrives at the nursing home. My husband, Arthur, gets in the ambulance with my mother because if she becomes agitated, I'll go into a panic, and I want to be calm. Gary drives me through horrible traffic on the East Side, over the Fifty-ninth Street Bridge. I look at nothing on the way. We arrive at the cemetery, this urban necropole, and we can't find our way to Section IX, where my father is going to be buried. We ask a grave digger, who answers in a Polish accent and gives directions that are incomprehensible. I can imagine driving around the cemetery for the rest of the day while my father is buried once again without me, because of my habit of lostness.

Then Harry finds us. He leads us to Section IX, and to the open grave, where there is a gray wooden box on a platform above a raw, gaping hole. Everyone leaves me. They leave me with my father. I touch the box. And this makes me very happy. Then I weep because I understand fully for the first time how much of my life I've lived without him. How little of our lives we've shared. The weeping is comforting. Anna and David come over and they touch the box. I introduce them to their grandfather. Then I ask them to leave me alone. With what? The box? The bones? The dust? The remains?

What remains?

I don't want to ask Harry what the grave diggers found.

The ambulette with my mother and Arthur arrives. Two of my friends are late, and I keep trying to stall, but Harry says, "There's another one going in right next to him at eleven forty-five. We can't wait."

I agree to start.

Gary intones, *"In paradisum,"* and it begins. My friends arrive. I keep my composure until the words, "May the Lord shine his face upon you," and I break down completely when I try to read the prayer "For consolation at the death of my father, David."

We throw blossoms on top of the coffin. I'm terrified that my mother's wheelchair will hurtle over the edge, but she wants to be brought closer so she can throw petals herself.

Then the coffin is lowered. It is a long way down. I see it travel, covered with petals, with the stones I put on it to stand for earthly delight.

Then it's over. It's time to go. Another "party" is collecting. I feel their impatience to bury their own dead.

Everyone embraces. There is tremendous exhilaration in the air. My mother says to me, "I'm so proud of you. My one and only."

Harry calls me aside. He gives me the deed and the bill for his services. I sign twice, under my father's name. Once next to the word "Owner," and then next to the word "Daughter."

We drop Anna off at school and drive home, to the West Side. I put food on platters. My friends and I eat and laugh and talk about books and movies.

I realize that if I make my friends leave, I can still get to the farewell party of a writing class I taught for elders at a local community center. We've been meeting for a year. It was an experience of great mutual love and nourishment, and I was distressed that I wouldn't be able to say good-bye properly.

I ask my friends to leave, and they get up and clear plates. One of them drives me to the party. She says, "Somehow this makes me feel better about dying." The mood of the day has been elation.

After I come home from the party I take David to the doctor for the checkup before his tonsillectomy. He's pronounced healthy.

For supper I make the children an omelet of onions, peppers, and tomatoes, tomato-and-cucumber salad, French bread.

After supper I go swimming because I want to do something physical. But water is an element that has so much of the spirit in it that the distinction between the spiritual and the physical melts. All distinctions seem false under the blue water, despite the wavy black lines, meant to demarcate lanes, indicating separation. In this element, the borders between the living and the dead, the absent and the present, seem indistinct, and I feel happy and at peace. As I swim, I thank my father and my mother for the gift of their extreme, excessive, passionate, exclusive love.

I fall asleep before the children do. I wake up at six-thirty the next morning. Anna has slept badly; she found a bug in her room and it scared her. She doesn't like the way the pleats fall on her skirt. She can't find her sandals. Before she leaves, she tells me not to be sad today, that she loves me, that she'll be home late. "Don't wait dinner," she says. "I don't know when I'll be back." The door closes behind her, and I wake David up.

As I eat breakfast with David, I realize that I'm not sad at all. That I'm very happy. There was something to touch, to be lowered, to put flowers on, and dirt, and a few stones. A thing to which it was possible to bid a farewell. This has made a great difference. What I have taken from the cemetery is a sentence that keeps running through my mind like music: Love is stronger than death. I say this to David as we eat our eggs and toast. He says, "You should write that down before you forget."

PERMISSIONS ACKNOWLEDGMENTS

Grateful acknowledgment is made to the following for permission to reprint previously published material:

America magazine: "Prayer for My Mother" (first published in *America* magazine, July 9, 1938) and "Conscientious Objector" (first published in *America* magazine, October 14, 1939). Reprinted by permission of *America* magazine.

Pantheon Books, a division of Random House, Inc.: "Introducing My Father" (originally published as "David") by Mary Gordon, from *Fathers: Reflections by Daughters*, edited by Ursula Owen. Copyright © 1985 by Mary Gordon. Reprinted by permission of Pantheon Books, a division of Random House, Inc.

Rogers, Coleridge & White Ltd.: Twelve lines from "Poem of the Mountain," from *Selected Poems of Marina Tsvetaeva*, translated by Elaine Feinstein (Oxford University Press, 1993). Copyright © 1993 by Elaine Feinstein. Reproduced by permission of the author c/o Rogers, Coleridge & White Ltd., 20 Powis Mews, London, WII IJN, England.

Photos: Pages iv, 2, 42, 108, family photos and memorabilia courtesy of Mary Gordon. Page 166, Ezra Pound, courtesy of The Bettmann Archive; Henry Roth, photo © 1993 by Becky Clark; H. L. Mencken, courtesy of UPI/Bettmann; Bernard Berenson, courtesy of The Bettmann Archive. Page 204, Anna Gordon (top), photo by Mary Ellen Mark; family photos, courtesy of Nola Tully.

BLACK ICE
by Lorene Cary

The story of a bright, ambitious black teenager from Philadelphia, who, when transplanted to an elite school in New Hampshire, becomes a scholarship student determined to succeed without selling out. In recounting her journey into selfhood, Lorene Cary creates a universally recognizable document of a woman's adolescence.

"Probably the most beautifully written and the most moving African-American autobiographical narrative since Maya Angelou's *I Know Why the Caged Bird Sings*."   —Arnold Rampersad

Autobiography/African-American Studies/0-679-73745-6

THE ROAD FROM COORAIN
by Jill Ker Conway

A remarkable woman's clear-sighted memoir of growing up Australian: from the vastness of a sheep station in the outback to the stifling propriety of postwar Sidney; from an untutored childhood to a life in academia; and from the shelter of a protective family to the lessons of independence.

"A small masterpiece of scene, memory and very stylish English. I've been several times to Australia; this book was the most rewarding journey of all."   —John Kenneth Galbraith

Autobiography/0-679-72436-2

TRUE NORTH
by Jill Ker Conway

In this second volume of her memoirs, Jill Ker Conway leaves Australia for America, where she becomes a renowned historian and, later, the first woman president of Smith College. She enters a lively community of women scholars and examines the challenges that confront all women who seek to establish public selves and reconcile them with their private passions.

"A thinking woman's memoir . . . it resounds with ideas about nature, culture, and education. . . . *True North* shines with the lasting luster of hard marble."   —*Philadelphia Inquirer*

Memoir/Women's Studies/0-679-74461-4

AN UNQUIET MIND
A Memoir of Moods and Madness
by Kay Redfield Jamison

Kay Redfield Jamison is one of the world's renowned authorities on manic-depressive illness; she is also one of its survivors. It is this dual perspective—as healer and healed—that makes her bestselling memoir so lucid, learned and profoundly affecting.

"Written with poetic and moving sensitivity...a rare and insightful view of mental illness from inside the mind of a trained specialist."
—*Time*

Psychology/Memoir/0-679-76330-9

RIDING THE WHITE HORSE HOME
A Western Family Album
by Teresa Jordan

A haunting memoir about the generations of women who learned to cope with physical hardship and loneliness in the beautiful yet grim landscape of the West. *Riding the White Horse Home* is at once Teresa Jordan's family chronicle and a eulogy for the West her people helped shape.

"Spellbinding. . . . the emotional scope of Jordan's prose is as vast as the ranch she grew up on—succoring one moment, shattering the next."
—*Seattle Times*

Memoir/Travel/0-679-75135-1

GIRL, INTERRUPTED
by Susanna Kaysen

Set on the exclusive grounds of McLean Hospital, Kaysen's memoir encompasses horror and razor-edged perception while providing vivid portraits of her fellow patients and their keepers. In this brilliant evocation of a "parallel universe," Kaysen gives a clear-sighted depiction of various definitions of sane and insane, mental illness and recovery.

"Poignant, honest and triumphantly funny . . . [a] compelling and heartbreaking story."
—Susan Cheever, *The New York Times Book Review*

Autobiography/Psychology/0-679-74604-8

REFUGE

An Unnatural History of Family and Place

by Terry Tempest Williams

Through tragedies both personal and environmental, Utah-born naturalist Terry Tempest Williams creates a document of renewal and spiritual grace that is a moving meditation on nature, women, and grieving.

"Moving and loving . . . both a natural history of an ecological phenomenon, along with a Mormon family saga . . . a heroic book."
—*Washington Post Book World*

Women's Studies/Nature/0-679-74024-4

FIRST COMES LOVE

by Marion Winik

Amid the wild festivities of Mardi Gras, Marion Winik fell madly in love with Tony Heubach. This is the sometimes hilarious, sometimes heartbreaking but always fearlessly honest memoir of that love between a straight woman and a gay man, an extraordinary passion whose (seemingly) impossible beginnings produced a marriage and two beautiful children, despite a life of drug addiction, sexual betrayal, and the AIDS that would eventually kill Tony.

"Gritty, funny, moving, horrific, outrageous—and above all, fearlessly honest . . . Ultimately a joyous story."   —*Newsday*

Memoir/0-679-76555-7